Table of Contents
See back cover for alphabetical index of lakes

MAPS IN THIS GUIDE ARE NOT FOR NAVIGATION

The lakes selected for this guide were confined to those that are accessible to the public. Some of the terminology used by the DNR in its reports that may not be self-explanatory: Centrarchid refers to panfish, Bass. Proportional Stock Density (PSD) is the proportion of fish of quality size in the sample. Also note that larger fish and Largemouth Bass often don't show up in the test nets. Pay particular attention to the dates of the test netting and stocking history. Also, some lakes test with more reliability than others and weather and other factors can skew results.

Lake Symbols:

E.V. = Emergent Vegetation
S.V. = Submerged Vegetation
F.L. = Floating Leaf Vegetation
L.P. = Lily Pads

Length to weight conversion scale

Northern Pike

Inches	24	25	26	27	28	29	30	31	32	33	34	35	36	37	38	39	40	41	42
Pounds	3.9	4.4	5.0	5.6	6.2	7.0	7.7	8.5	9.3	10.2	11.2	12.2	13.3	14.5	15.7	16.9	18.3	19.6	21.2

Walleye

Inches	14	15	16	17	18	19	20	21	22	23	24	25	26	27	28	29
Pounds	1.0	1.2	1.5	1.8	2.2	2.5	3.0	3.4	3.9	4.5	5.1	5.7	6.5	7.2	8.1	9.0

Largemouth Bass

Inches	12	13	14	15	16	17	18	19	20	21	22	23
Pounds	1.0	1.3	1.7	2.1	2.5	3.0	3.6	4.2	5.0	5.7	6.6	7.6

Crappie

Inches	8	9	10	11	12	13	14	15	16	17
Pounds	0.4	0.6	0.8	1.1	1.4	1.8	2.2	2.8	3.4	4.1

Grand Rapids-Winnibigoshish Area Fishing Map Guide
by Sportsman's Connection

Editor: James F. Billig
Editorial/Research: Steve Meyer, Jon Wisniewski, Jack Tyllia
Cartography: Thomas Communications
Typesetting: Shelly Wisniewski

Sportsman's Connection
3947 East Calvary Road
P.O. Box 3496
Duluth, Minnesota 55803

Lake Winnibigoshish

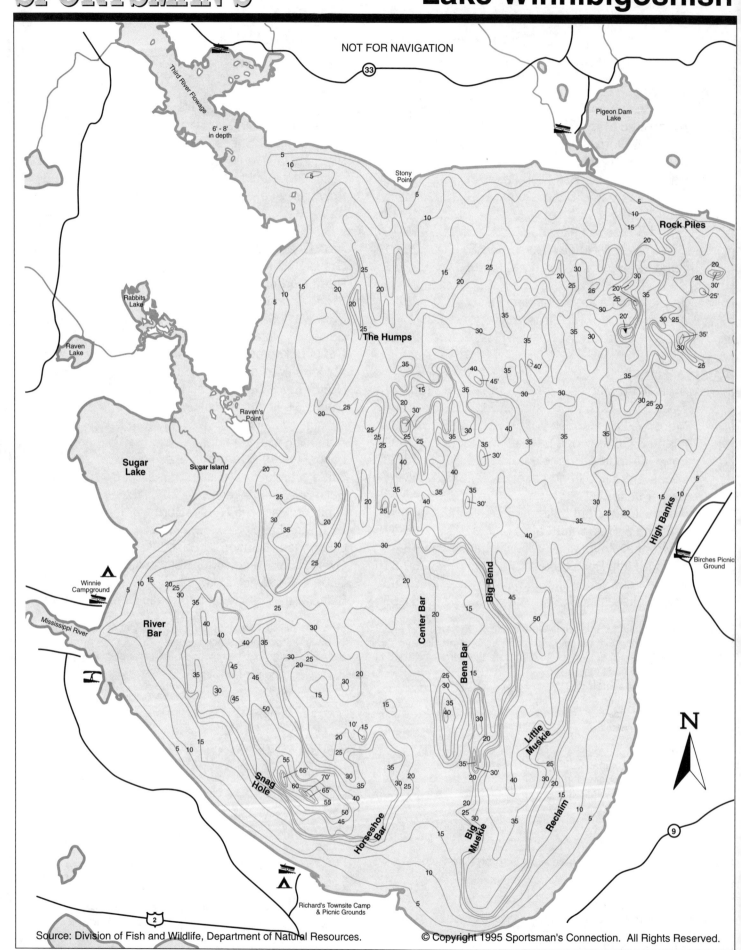

NOT FOR NAVIGATION

Third River Flowage

6' - 8' in depth

Pigeon Dam Lake

Stony Point

Rock Piles

Rabbits Lake

Raven Lake

The Humps

Sugar Lake

Sugar Island

Raven's Point

High Banks

Birches Picnic Ground

Center Bar

Big Bend

Bena Bar

Winnie Campground

Mississippi River

River Bar

Little Muskie

Snag Hole

Horseshoe Bar

Big Muskie

Reclaim

N

Richard's Townsite Camp & Picnic Grounds

Source: Division of Fish and Wildlife, Department of Natural Resources.

© Copyright 1995 Sportsman's Connection. All Rights Reserved.

Lake Winnibigoshish

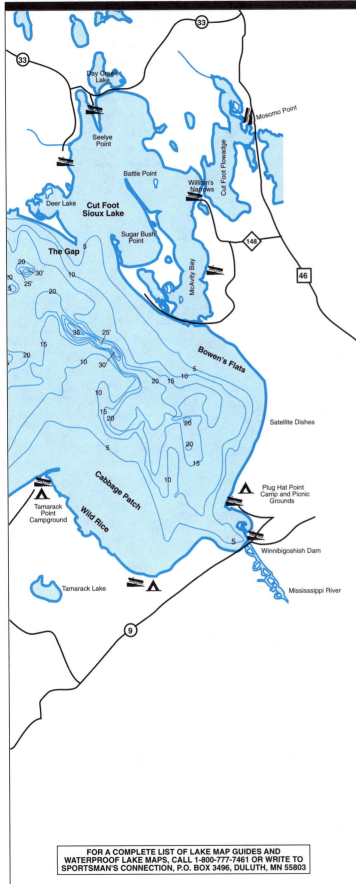

Mike Auger, Blue Horizon Guide Service out of Pokegama Sports in Grand Rapids, has logged many hours on this famous Walleye factory. Following is an excerpt from our interview with Mike:

Sportsman's Connection: Where do you fish around opening weekend on the big lake?

Auger: On opening weekend from Bowen's Flats through The Gap is real good. The whole north shore is also real good the first couple weeks of the season in seven to twelve feet of water. The Pigeon River Flowage area is good on up to Stony Point. At this time of year twelve to fifteen feet is the deepest water you'll want to fish on a calm, sunny day. Most of the fish are caught along here early in the season. Do you know about the migration of Winnie?

Sportsman's Connection: No, not really.

Auger: About 90% of the Walleyes migrate from the area around Cut Foot Sioux called The Gap and along the north shore, down around the east side and on up onto Bena Bar which is a huge area that includes the Center Bar, Big Muskie, Big Bend and the Little Muskie areas. The top of Bena Bar averages around 13 feet. Fish right at the breakline in about 17 feet.

Sportsman's Connection: So this whole area is the Bena Bar?

Auger: Yeah. A good spot in early June is Big Bend, almost straight out from the access to the middle of the lake (actually about a third of the way across). Follow the schools along the High Banks area a couple of weeks after opener into the first week of June. Then follow the migration right down the shore, moving 300-400 yards each day.

Sportsman's Connection: Just follow them as spring progresses?

Auger: Right. Then move out onto the Bena Bar, usually around the second or third week of June and also up into the area called The Humps which drops down and comes back up. The top of the break actually tops out at about 15 feet of water (the two twenty foot circles just above the name "The Humps" on the map are what he is referring to).

(Continued on page 6)

Source: Division of Fish and Wildlife, Department of Natural Resources.

LAKE WINNIBIGOSHISH

(Continued from page 5)

Fish the breaklines right at the top of the break in about 17 to 18 feet of water.

Sportsman's Connection: What's the best fishing method: jigging, drifting?

Auger: Drift, jig, troll, cast, everybody seems to be doing a little bit of each. Jig and minnows and lindy rigs with leeches are the most common. We hit 'em real good over at Raven's Point the third week of June. We worked the south side of the point where its real rocky and we nailed them. It's probably also good earlier than then because you can catch the fish that spawn up in Raven Lake and Sugar. Horseshoe Bar is real good in a northwest wind all along the breakline. It's a good area from early June all the way through summer. Late summer can be real good.

Sportsman's Connection: What about Big Muskie down here?

Auger: Bena Bar is the whole flat area down there. Fish the east side of the breakline all the way down. A sunken island not shown on the map off of Big Muskie is good when you get a hard northwest wind. Everything including bait fish gets pushed off the bar up onto the east side of the sunken island. You can line up straight north with the Bena radio tower and follow the Bena bar.

Sportsman's Connection: What's in Sugar Lake?

Auger: Sugar Lake has some good Northern and Bass.

Sportsman's Connection: What about the area around Cut Foot?

Auger: Cut Foot Sioux has three or four sunken islands straight out from The Gap toward Battle Point which come up to 13 feet. Early in the season, they're all good. Just fish the edges again, 13-17 feet. A breakline runs right behind Sugarbush Point which is real good at 17 feet. The weedline runs right around there, from about 13-17 feet.

Sportsman's Connection: What's the average Walleye caught out of Winnie?

(Continued on page 30)

Location: Township 145 - 147 Range 26 - 29
Watershed: Mississippi Headwaters
Size of lake: 69,821 acres
Shorelength: 35.0 miles
Secchi disk (water clarity): 6.9 Ft.
Water color: NA
Cause of water color: NA
Maximum depth: 65.0 Ft.
Median depth: 15.0 Ft.
Accessibility: Plug Hat Point, Tamarack Point, Birches, W. Winnie Campgrd, Third River, Winnie Dam
Boat Ramps: All concrete
Parking: Ample
Accommodations: Campground, Resorts, Picnic Areas

Shoreland zoning classification: General Development
Dominant forest/soil type: No Tree/Wet
Management class: Walleye
Ecological type: Hard-water Walleye

FISH STOCKING DATA

year	species	size	# released
83	Walleye	Fry	6,000,000
85	Walleye	Fry	3,000,000
86	Walleye	Fry	8,000,000
89	Walleye	Fry	8,500,000
91	Walleye	Fry	3,000,000
92	Walleye	Fry	3,400,000
93	Walleye	Fry	5,236,400

NET CATCH DATA
survey date: 07/06/92

species	Gill Nets # per net	avg fish wt. (lbs.)	Trap Nets # per set	avg fish wt. (lbs.)
Yellow Perch	102.4	0.22	-	-
White Sucker	1.1	2.45	-	-
Walleye	1.0	6.64	-	-
Tullibee (incl. Cisco)	16.8	0.37	-	-
Shorthead Redhorse	0.4	3.38	-	-
Rock Bass	0.2	0.64	-	-
Northern Pike	5.3	2.62	-	-
Burbot	0.1	2.60	-	-
Brown Bullhead	0.1	1.45	-	-

LENGTH OF SELECTED SPECIES SAMPLED FROM ALL GEAR
Number of fish caught for the following length categories (inches):

species	0-5	6-8	9-11	12-14	15-19	20-24	25-29	>30	Total
Yellow Perch	-	1,592	843	22	-	-	-	-	2,457
Walleye	-	10	3	14	27	28	1	-	83
Tullibee (Cisco)	-	204	115	66	15	-	-	-	400
Rock Bass	-	2	6	-	-	-	-	-	8
Northern Pike	-	-	-	-	15	79	33	1	128
Brown Bullhead	-	-	-	2	-	-	-	-	2

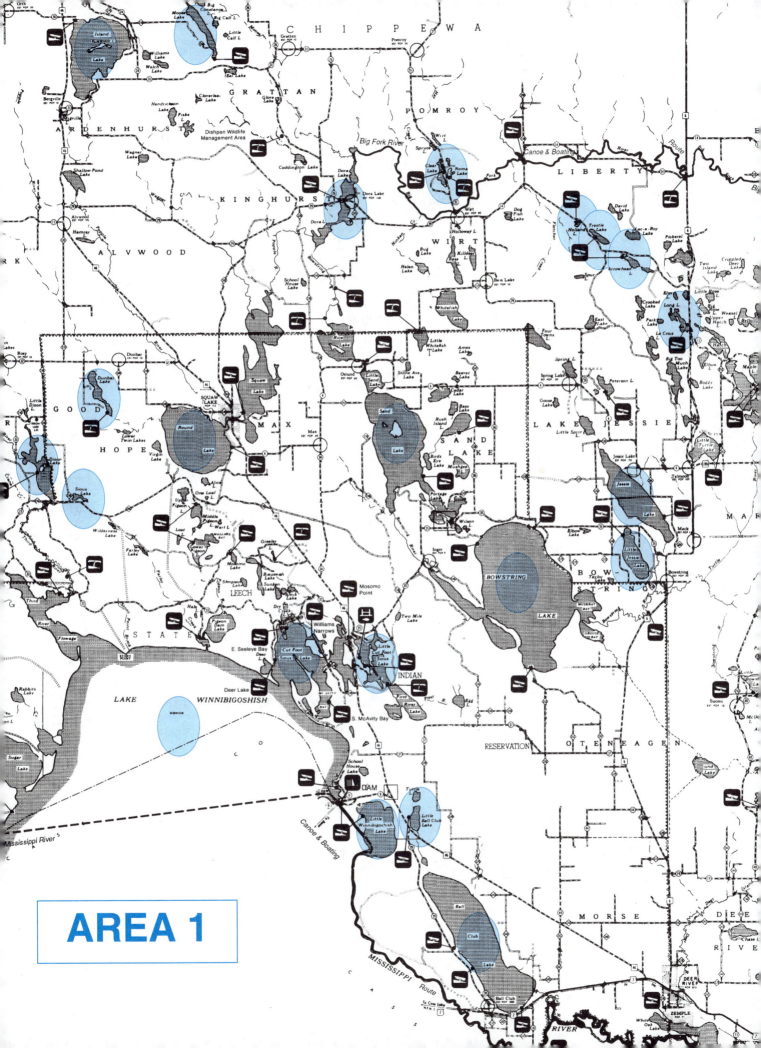

AREA 1

CUT FOOT SIOUX LAKE   LITTLE CUT FOOT SIOUX LAKE

Location: Township 146, 147   Range 26, 27
Watershed: Mississippi Headwaters

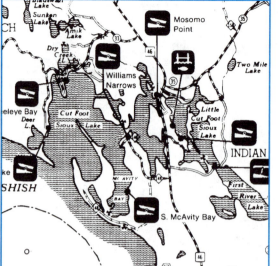

Size of lake: 3,222 Acres
Shorelength: 18.2 Miles
Secchi disk (water clarity): 3.8 Ft.
Water color: NA
Maximum depth: 78.0 Ft.
Median depth: 23.6 Ft.
Accessibility: Close to Hwy; five public accesses: Section 35; Section 25 (2); Section 22; and Section 11
Boat Ramp: Concrete
Parking: Ample
Accommodations: Campground, Resorts
Shoreland zoning classif.: Rec. Dev.
Dominant forest/soil type: NA
Cause of water color: NA
Management class: Walleye
Ecological type: Hard-water Walleye

Size of lake: 1,357 Acres
Shorelength: 2.9 Miles
Secchi disk (water clarity): NA
Water color: Brown
Maximum depth: 20.0 Ft.
Median depth: 9.4 Ft.
Accessibility: USFS earth ramp at Onegume campground; USFS carry-in access at first river campground
Boat Ramp: Earth
Parking: Ample
Accommodations: Campground, Resorts, Fishing Pier
Shoreland zoning classif.: Rec. Dev.
Dominant forest/soil type: Decid/Sand
Cause of water color: Bog stain and slight algae bloom
Management class: Walleye
Ecological type: Hard-water Walleye

DNR COMMENTS:
Walleye and Northern Pike populations are above local medians. Perch and Cisco populations are also quite high. Bullhead population is fairly high but periodic commercial removal is being done. Other fish populations are within normal limits for this type of lake. Evidence suggests that Walleye fry stocking in Little Cut Foot Sioux Lake may benefit the Walleye population in Big Cut Foot Sioux Lake. Direct fry stocking to Big Cut Foot Sioux had little effect on Walleye population.

FISH STOCKING DATA

year	species	size	# released
89	Walleye	Fry	NA
89	Walleye	Fry	14,555,000
92	Walleye	Fry	10,000,000
93	Walleye	Fry	11,824,800
94	Walleye	Fry	9,955,000

NET CATCH DATA NOT AVAILABLE

LENGTH OF SELECTED SPECIES SAMPLED FROM ALL GEAR
Number of fish caught for the following length categories (inches):

species	0-5	6-8	9-11	12-14	15-19	20-24	25-29	>30	Total
Bullhead	-	-	23	4	-	-	-	-	27
Crappie	-	-	2	1	-	-	-	-	3
Northern Pike	-	-	-	9	28	27	12	4	80
Rock Bass	-	1	2	1	-	-	-	-	4
Tullibee (Cisco)	-	29	21	31	8	-	-	-	89
Walleye	-	2	47	30	22	4	-	-	105
Yellow Perch	-	31	34	1	-	-	-	-	66

FISH STOCKING DATA

year	species	size	# released
89	Walleye	Fry	13,000,000
90	Walleye	Fry	11,190,000
91	Walleye	Fry	14,100,000
92	Walleye	Fry	12,015,364
93	Walleye	Fry	13,197,600
94	Walleye	Fry	14,936,000

survey date: 06/25/90

NET CATCH DATA

species	Gill Nets # per net	Gill Nets avg fish wt. (lbs)	Trap Nets # per set	Trap Nets avg fish wt. (lbs)
Yellow Perch	36.9	0.13	7.0	0.32
Yellow Bullhead	0.4	0.45	14.3	0.41
White Sucker	1.3	3.04	0.3	2.00
Walleye	2.7	1.24	-	-
Tullibee (incl. Cisco)	3.0	1.98	-	-
Rock Bass	0.1	1.00	0.3	0.70
Pumpkin. Sunfish	0.2	0.25	4.8	0.38
Northern Pike	2.8	3.71	0.5	0.23
Brown Bullhead	13.8	0.45	5.0	0.51
Black Bullhead	48.2	0.39	33.7	0.41
Largemouth Bass	-	-	0.2	2.50
Bluegill	-	-	2.5	0.42
Black Crappie	-	-	3.2	0.49

LENGTH OF SELECTED SPECIES SAMPLED FROM ALL GEAR
Number of fish caught for the following length categories (inches):

species	0-5	6-8	9-11	12-14	15-19	20-24	25-29	>30	Total
Yellow Perch	1	54	52	2	-	-	-	-	109
Walleye	-	-	-	11	13	-	-	-	24
Tullibee (Cisco)	-	-	1	6	19	-	-	-	26
Rock Bass	-	-	1	-	-	-	-	-	1
Pumpkin. Sunfish	1	1	-	-	-	-	-	-	2
Northern Pike	-	-	-	2	8	4	6	3	23
Brown Bullhead	-	7	97	20	-	-	-	-	124
Black Bullhead	-	69	34	3	-	-	-	-	106

DNR COMMENTS:
Walleye pop. appears to be within normal limits for this lake. It is, however, subject to seasonal fluctuation, as fish move between this lake and others of the Lake Winnibigoshish flowage to spawn and then return. Gillnet samplings of 2.7/set are similar to those for other river-type lakes in this class within the area.

FISHING INFORMATION: Cut Foot is probably the most popular fishing spot in the entire region on opening weekend as well as at other times. A classic spawning area for Big Winnie's Walleyes, the heavy concentrations are fished relentlessly boat to boat at times, especially around William's Narrows. 1 to 1-1/2 pound males are usually the most active early in the year with some 8-10 pound females becoming more responsive after the post-spawn period. Many of the spawners are resident to the Cut Foot Lakes and simply move out to deeper water as the season progresses. The Gap, Battleship Point and the island of the east of Battleship point give up some good fish later in the year around autumn. Like most Walleye lakes, plan on some Northern line bite offs. Slab Crappies are also found throughout the Cut Foot Lakes with 3/4 pound-plus fish the norm. (See Lake Winnibigoshish pages for more information on Cut Foot).

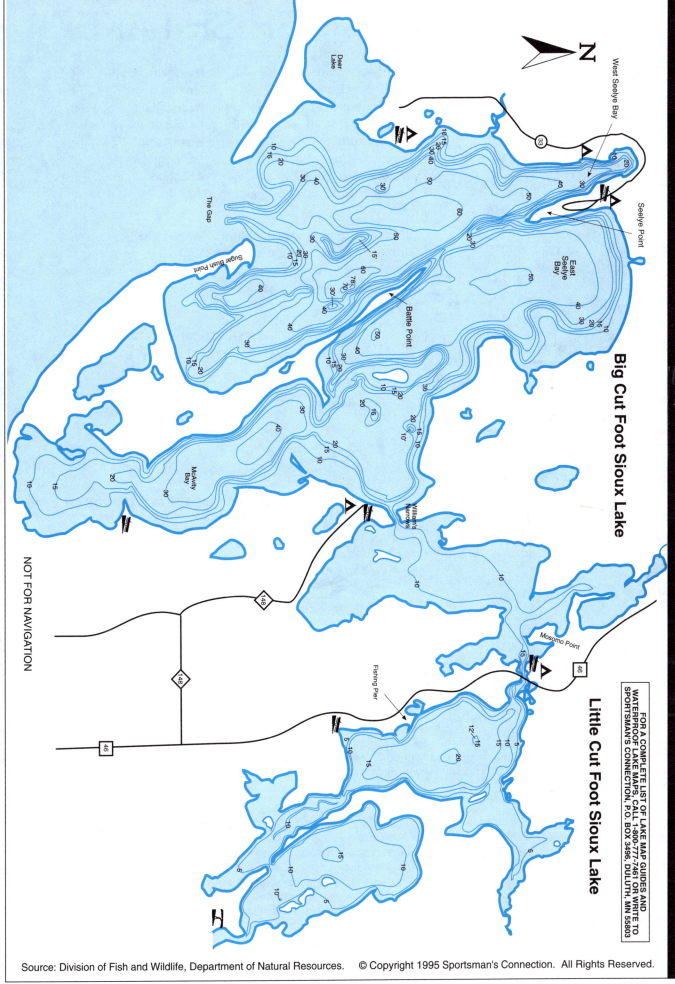

Big Cut Foot Sioux Lake

Little Cut Foot Sioux Lake

NOT FOR NAVIGATION

FOR A COMPLETE LIST OF LAKE MAP GUIDES AND WATERPROOF LAKE MAPS, CALL 1-800-777-7461 OR WRITE TO SPORTSMAN'S CONNECTION, P.O. BOX 3496, DULUTH, MN 55803

LITTLE WINNIBIGOSHISH LAKE

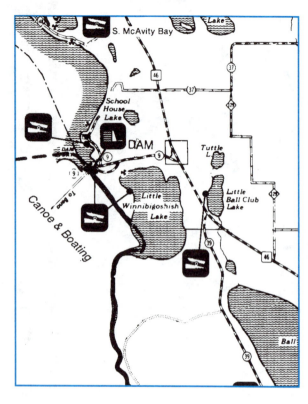

Location: Township 145, 146 Range 26, 27
Watershed: Mississippi Headwaters
Size of lake: 1,287 Acres
Shorelength: 5.0 Miles
Secchi disk (water clarity): 4.9 Ft.
Water color: Green
Cause of water color: Algae

Maximum depth: 26.0 Ft.
Median depth: 17.5 Ft.
Accessibility: USFS-owned access on the NW shore
Boat Ramp: Earth
Parking: Limited
Accommodations: Resort

Shoreland zoning classification: Recreational Development
Dominant forest/soil type: No tree/Wet
Management class: Walleye
Ecological type: Hard-water Walleye

FISH STOCKING DATA

year	species	size	# released
90	Walleye	Fry	1,300,000
92	Walleye	Fry	1,300,000
94	Walleye	Fry	1,300,000

NET CATCH DATA

survey date: 07/31/89

	Gill Nets		Trap Nets	
	avg fish		avg fish	
species	# per net	wt. (lbs.)	# per set	wt. (lbs.)
Yellow Perch	52.1	0.25	2.0	0.11
Yellow Bullhead	0.5	1.07	0.1	1.30
White Sucker	6.4	2.48	0.5	2.28
Walleye	4.0	1.51	0.1	5.30
Tullibee (incl. Cisco)	1.3	0.64	-	-
Shorthead Red.	0.9	2.09	0.1	2.80
Rock Bass	0.6	0.93	0.5	0.90
Pumpkin. Sunfish	0.3	0.10	8.0	0.90
Northern Pike	17.3	1.31	1.3	1.20
Brown Bullhead	16.3	1.10	-	-
Black Crappie	0.1	0.40	1.3	0.75
Black Bullhead	5.4	0.58	-	-
Bowfin (Dogfish)	-	-	0.1	4.20
Bluegill	-	-	2.1	0.10

LENGTH OF SELECTED SPECIES SAMPLED FROM ALL GEAR

Number of fish caught for the following length categories (inches):

species	0-5	6-8	9-11	12-14	15-19	20-24	25-29	>30	Total
Yellow Perch	9	51	63	1	-	-	-	-	124
Yellow Bullhead	-	-	1	5	-	-	-	-	6
Walleye	-	-	-	18	30	-	-	-	48
Tullibee (Cisco)	-	2	1	13	-	-	-	-	16
Rock Bass	-	-	7	-	-	-	-	-	7
Pumpkin. Sunfish	3	1	-	-	-	-	-	-	4
Northern Pike	-	-	1	-	83	13	2	2	101
Brown Bullhead	-	2	29	76	3	-	-	-	110
Black Crappie	-	1	-	-	-	-	-	-	1
Black Bullhead	-	24	23	18	-	-	-	-	65

DNR COMMENTS: Walleye abundance at statewide median with many year classes represented. Northern Pike are very abundant at 17.3/gillnet. Age III fish dominate the sample. The number of Tullibee continues to decline and presently is at 1.3/gillnet. Bullheads are abundant and large in size. Yellow Perch are within historical range at 52.1/gillnet.

FISHING INFORMATION: Little Winnibigoshish or "Little Winnie" is less famous and receives considerably less fishing pressure than its larger namesake. The Mississippi River flows in and out of Little Winnie providing excellent spawning grounds for Northern and Walleye which reach trophy size. According to Joe, at the River Rat Trading Post on Hwy. 2 near Cohasset, a good population of 20 pound-class Northerns roam the lake and the Walleye fishing can be very good. Trolling the weedline produces good Northern action - especially early in the season after ice out. Little Winnie also holds some big Muskies. George, at The Bait Shop in Deer River, told us of a 50 inch Muskie caught from shore by a Walleye fisherman last year. If you locate a school of Crappie, count on some nice average sizes, typically 3/4 pound-plus, with an occasional 2 pounder. Little Winnie is a fairly dark, relatively shallow lake, and warms up earlier than many of the clear, deep lakes in the area. Try the north end and river inlet and outlet for early Crappie. Sam, of Fred's Live Bait and Tackle in Deer River, said that anglers get good Walleye catches up river toward the Big Winnie dam early in the year. Move out to the deep side of the weedline of the lake later in the season.

NOT FOR NAVIGATION

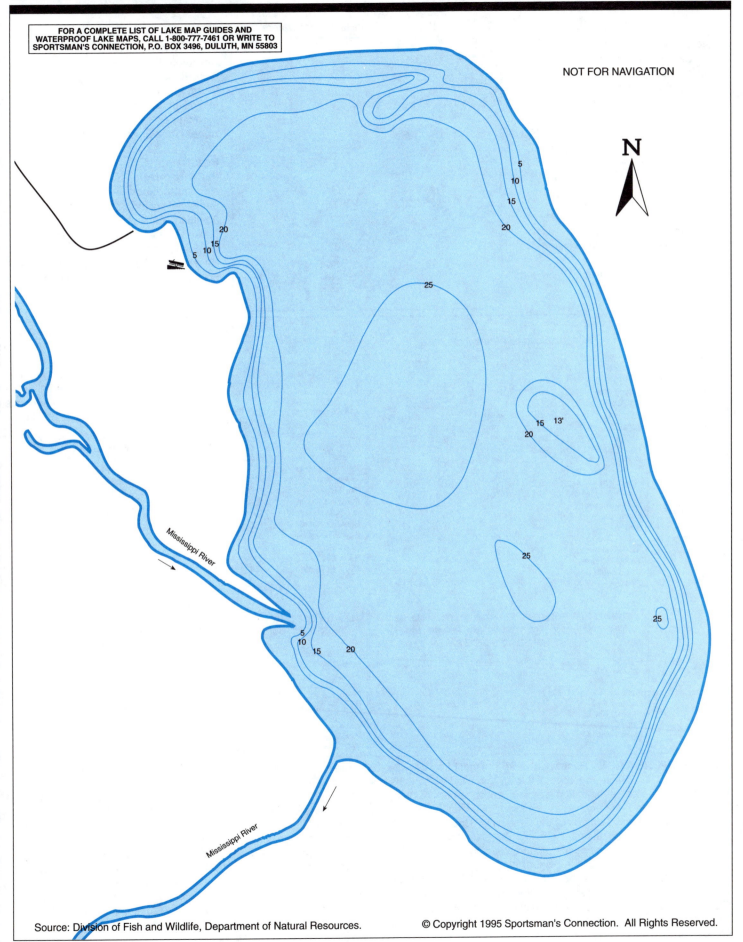

Source: Division of Fish and Wildlife, Department of Natural Resources.

BALL CLUB LAKE   LITTLE BALL CLUB LAKE

Location: Township 145 Range 25, 26
Watershed: Mississippi Headwaters

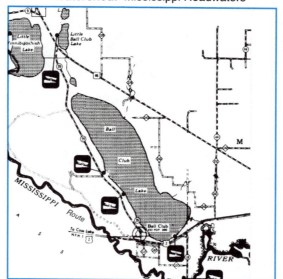

Size of lake: 4,951 Acres
Shorelength: 15.0 Miles
Secchi disk (water clarity): 9.8 Ft.
Water color: Light green
Maximum depth: 85.0 Ft.
Median depth: 45.0 Ft.
Accessibility: County access 1.5 miles
E of Ball Club, MN, on Hwy. 2; DNR
access off Hwy. 39
Boat Ramp: (2) Concrete, Earth
Parking: Ample
Accommodations: Resorts
Shoreland zoning classif.: Rec. Dev.
Dominant forest/soil type: NA
Cause of water color: Algae bloom
Management class: Walleye
Ecological type: Hard-water Walleye

Size of lake: 184 Acres
Shorelength: 3.3 Miles
Secchi disk (water clarity): NA
Water color: Brown
Maximum depth: 29.0 Ft.
Median depth: 20.0 Ft.
Accessibility: State-owned access on
W side
Boat Ramp: Earth
Parking: Ample
Accommodations: Resorts
Shoreland zoning classif.: Rec. Dev.
Dominant forest/soil type: Decid./Wet
Cause of water color: Bog stain and
suspended silt
Management class: Walleye-Centrarchid
Ecological type: Centrarchid-Walleye

DNR COMMENTS:
Northern Pike and Perch populations are well above state and local medians. Walleye abundance at state median. Larger size Walleyes are most abundant. Large size Black Crappies common.

FISH STOCKING DATA NOT AVAILABLE

NET CATCH DATA
survey date: 08/08/88

	Gill Nets		Trap Nets	
		avg fish		avg fish
species	# per net	wt. (lbs)	# per set	wt. (lbs)
Yellow Perch	25.2	0.25	15.0	0.20
White Sucker	0.6	1.83	0.1	1.20
Walleye	3.7	1.47	0.1	0.80
Tullibee (incl. Cisco)	0.5	0.41	-	-
Rock Bass	0.2	1.17	1.1	0.77
Pumpkin. Sunfish	0.1	0.60	2.8	0.28
Northern Pike	6.5	2.50	0.3	1.33
Brown Bullhead	0.3	1.56	-	-
Bowfin (Dogfish)	0.1	6.50	0.3	6.17
Black Crappie	0.2	0.27	0.6	1.03
Black Bullhead	1.3	0.86	0.1	0.50
Yellow Bullhead	-	-	0.1	1.00
Largemouth Bass	-	-	0.3	3.00
Bluegill	-	-	0.1	0.10

LENGTH OF SELECTED SPECIES SAMPLED FROM ALL GEAR
Number of fish caught for the following length categories (inches):

species	0-5	6-8	9-11	12-14	15-19	20-24	25-29	>30	Total
Yellow Perch	1	76	61	3	-	-	-	-	141
Walleye	14	-	5	13	20	4	-	-	56
Tullibee (Cisco)	-	3	1	4	-	-	-	-	8
Rock Bass	-	-	3	-	-	-	-	-	3
Pumpkin. Sunfish	-	1	-	-	-	-	-	-	1
Northern Pike	-	-	-	-	38	48	10	1	97
Brown Bullhead	-	-	-	5	-	-	-	-	5
Black Crappie	2	-	-	1	-	-	-	-	3
Black Bullhead	-	1	15	3	-	-	-	-	19

FISH STOCKING DATA

year	species	size	# released
89	Walleye	Fingerling	30
89	Walleye	Yearling	333
91	Walleye	Yearling	81

NET CATCH DATA
survey date: 06/25/84

	Gill Nets		Trap Nets	
		avg fish		avg fish
species	# per net	wt. (lbs)	# per set	wt. (lbs)
Yellow Perch	55.2	0.15	2.3	0.07
Yellow Bullhead	0.8	0.48	0.8	0.23
Walleye	1.2	3.13	0.3	3.00
Rock Bass	0.2	0.50	0.3	0.30
Pumpkin. Sunfish	1.0	0.08	1.0	0.08
Northern Pike	9.8	2.57	0.5	3.00
Brown Bullhead	6.8	0.66	-	-
Bowfin (Dogfish)	1.2	3.67	1.0	4.50
Bluegill	0.8	0.50	0.3	0.30
Black Crappie	7.4	0.21	2.5	0.17
Black Bullhead	9.4	0.55	1.0	0.13

LENGTH OF SELECTED SPECIES SAMPLED FROM ALL GEAR
Number of fish caught for the following length categories (inches):

species	0-5	6-8	9-11	12-14	15-19	20-24	25-29	>30	Total
Black Bullhead	3	-	47	1	-	-	-	-	51
Black Crappie	-	35	10	2	-	-	-	-	47
Bluegill	1	3	2	-	-	-	-	-	6
Brown Bullhead	-	-	18	16	-	-	-	-	34
Northern Pike	-	-	-	-	6	25	18	2	51
Pumpkin. Sunfish	2	7	-	-	-	-	-	-	9
Rock Bass	-	1	1	-	-	-	-	-	2
Walleye	-	-	-	1	3	1	2	-	7
Yellow Bullhead	-	1	5	1	-	-	-	-	7
Yellow Perch	-	108	12	-	-	-	-	-	120

DNR COMMENTS:
Perch numbers are at a high level. All other fish within limits for this type of lake.

FISHING INFORMATION: Renowned as an excellent Panfish lake, Ball Club also provides some nice Northern Pike, hefty Walleye and big Largemouth Bass. Steve Prescher of the Ball Club Lake Lodge has been fishing the lake for years, since even before he bought the resort. He confirmed the lake's reputation as a top Panfish Lake with Crappies in the 1-1/2 to 2 pound range and 1 to 1-1/2 pound Bluegills. Walleye averaging 2-1/2 to 3-1/2 pounds are caught by working the various points and other Walleye structure, including the sandbars on the south end of the lake. Try working off of the large point (Cook's Point); the underwater island just south of the point near the Ball Club River outlet; and the creek on the southeast shoreline. Ball Club's deep, light colored waters warm up slowly, making it a late Walleye lake. Action heats up in June with minnows being the preferred bait earlier and leeches later in the summer. Steve said that an afternoon of Northern fishing can yield some 3-1/2 to 8 pound fish. Shoreline dropoffs along the lake's cattails are productive as are the weedbeds near the sandbars on the south end. Ball Club's sandy bottom and deep, cold water provide excellent-tasting fish year round. Little Ball Club is small (lakes on map page are not in scale) and has little in common with Big Ball Club. The little lake does have a history of producing some nice Crappies and Bluegills, however. It also gives up some decent Walleyes, including some up to ten pounds. Casting or trolling the shoreline can produce some larger Northern Pike mixed in with a lot of smaller ones. You can also pick up some Largemouth Bass by working the bulrushes and weedbeds.

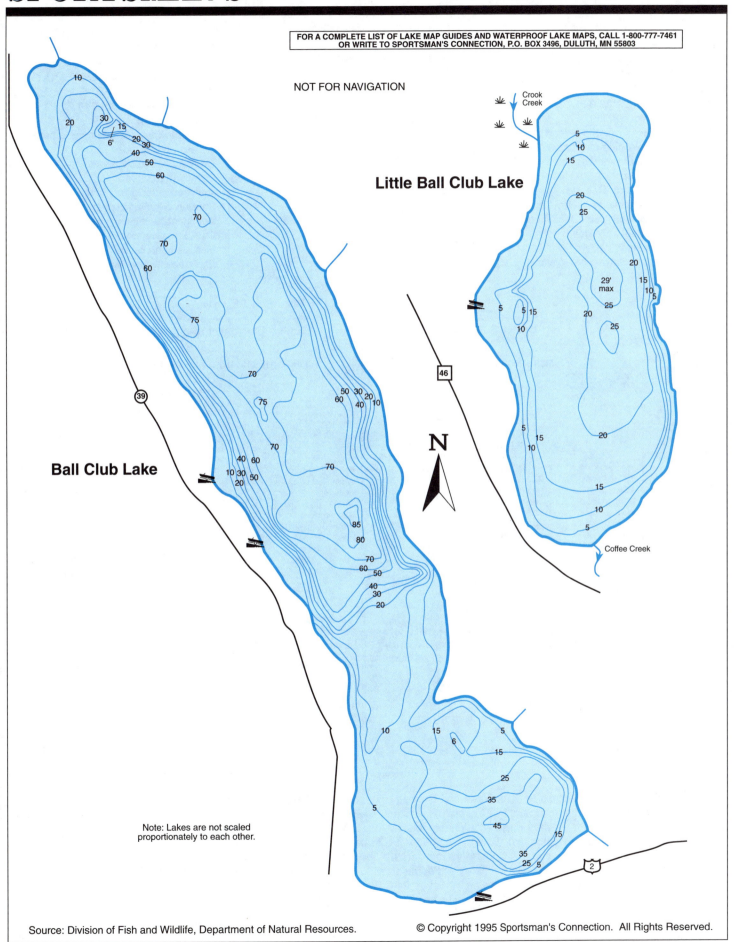

NOT FOR NAVIGATION

Crook Creek

Little Ball Club Lake

29' max

46

N

Ball Club Lake

Coffee Creek

39

Note: Lakes are not scaled proportionately to each other.

2

Source: Division of Fish and Wildlife, Department of Natural Resources.

DIXON LAKE   DUNBAR LAKE

Location: Township 148   Range 28, 29
Watershed: Mississippi Headwaters

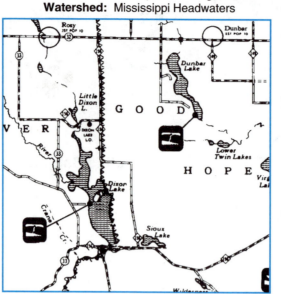

Size of lake: 666 Acres
Shorelength: 9.3 Miles
Secchi disk (water clarity): 3.3 Ft.
Water color: Green
Maximum depth: 29.0 Ft.
Median depth: 12.0 Ft.
Accessibility: Township-owned carry-in access on NW side of S basin
Boat Ramp: Carry-down
Parking: Limited
Accommodations: Resorts
Shoreland zoning classif.: Rec. Dev.
Dominant forest/soil type: Decid/Loam
Cause of water color: Algae bloom
Management class: Walleye
Ecological type: Hard-water Walleye

Size of lake: 273 Acres
Shorelength: 4.5 Miles
Secchi disk (water clarity): NA
Water color: Brown
Maximum depth: 30. 0 Ft.
Median depth: 15.0 Ft.
Accessibility: County-owned public access on NW side
Boat Ramp: Carry-down
Parking: Limited
Accommodations: Resort
Shoreland zoning classif.: Rec. Dev.
Dominant forest/soil type: Decid/Loam
Cause of water color: Bog stain
Management class: Walleye-Centrarchid
Ecological type: Centrarchid

Dixon Lake

DNR COMMENTS:
Northern Pike pop. moderate; growth good at 110-120% of statewide avg. for lake class. Walleye pop. within 1st-3rd quartile range for lake class; growth is good, with size ranging from 13-30". Black Crappie relatively scarce; growth very good. Yellow Perch abundant, as are Brown and Black Bullheads.

FISH STOCKING DATA

year	species	size	# released
90	Walleye	Fry	700,000
92	Walleye	Fry	700,000

NET CATCH DATA
survey date: 07/27/92

	Gill Nets		Trap Nets	
species	# per net	avg fish wt. (lbs)	# per set	avg fish wt. (lbs)
Yellow Perch	33.8	0.20	2.6	0.18
Yellow Bullhead	0.3	0.48	0.6	0.36
White Sucker	5.2	2.00	-	-
Walleye	2.1	1.64	0.1	2.20
Rock Bass	0.2	1.05	0.4	0.58
Pumpkin. Sunfish	1.4	0.35	0.3	0.20
Northern Pike	5.8	1.80	0.8	1.47
Brown Bullhead	13.9	0.52	1.0	0.63
Black Crappie	2.4	0.31	0.4	0.13
Black Bullhead	34.1	0.39	0.4	0.30
Largemouth Bass	-	-	0.1	1.20

LENGTH OF SELECTED SPECIES SAMPLED FROM ALL GEAR
Number of fish caught for the following length categories (inches):

species	0-5	6-8	9-11	12-14	15-19	20-24	25-29	>30	Total
Yellow Perch	-	96	44	-	-	-	-	-	140
Yellow Bullhead	-	-	4	1	-	-	-	-	5
Walleye	-	1	1	5	10	7	1	-	25
Rock Bass	-	-	1	1	-	-	-	-	2
Pumpkin. Sunfish	0	15	2	-	-	-	-	-	17
Northern Pike	-	-	-	2	24	32	10	1	69
Brown Bullhead	-	1	101	31	-	-	-	-	133
Black Crappie	9	13	1	6	-	-	-	-	29
Black Bullhead	-	23	99	1	-	-	-	-	123

Dunbar Lake

DNR COMMENTS:
Northern Pike scarce; sample dominated by ages 2-3; avg. weight 2.3 lb.; growth 15% faster than avg. statewide. Walleyes few; growth rates avg.; all fish sampled were naturally occurring. Black Crappie and Bluegill pop.s dominated by quality-size fish; growth for Crappies avg., for Bluegills, 26% above avg. Yellow Perch small. Black Bullheads over-abundant and may be adversely affecting Panfish pop.

FISH STOCKING DATA NOT AVAILABLE

NET CATCH DATA
survey date: 07/15/91

	Gill Nets		Trap Nets	
species	# per net	avg fish wt. (lbs)	# per set	avg fish wt. (lbs)
Yellow Perch	4.6	0.16	0.3	0.30
Yellow Bullhead	0.2	0.40	0.2	0.40
White Sucker	1.4	2.13	-	-
Walleye	1.6	1.16	0.3	1.35
Tullibee (incl. Cisco)	0.2	3.50	-	-
Northern Pike	1.4	2.29	0.5	1.93
Brown Bullhead	0.2	1.30	1.3	0.50
Black Crappie	0.2	0.30	4.2	0.43
Black Bullhead	82.0	0.43	5.3	0.39
Pumpkin. Sunfish	-	-	0.5	0.33
Bluegill	-	-	3.2	0.48

LENGTH OF SELECTED SPECIES SAMPLED FROM ALL GEAR
Number of fish caught for the following length categories (inches):

species	0-5	6-8	9-11	12-14	15-19	20-24	25-29	>30	Total
Yellow Perch	-	21	2	-	-	-	-	-	23
Yellow Bullhead	-	-	1	-	-	-	-	-	1
Walleye	-	2	2	-	3	-	1	-	8
Tullibee (Cisco)	-	-	-	-	1	-	-	-	1
Northern Pike	-	-	-	1	4	2	-	-	7
Brown Bullhead	-	-	-	1	-	-	-	-	1
Black Crappie	-	-	1	-	-	-	-	-	1
Black Bullhead	-	16	88	-	-	-	-	-	104

FISHING INFORMATION: Access to Dixon Lake and Dunbar Lake can be difficult which helps ease fishing pressure. Jack, at Squaw Lake Sports Center, warns that the roads into the public launches (classified as "carry-down" by the DNR) are very poor. Fishermen with four-wheel drive vehicles and winches which enable them to slosh through the mud, or those who gain access at the resorts, are rewarded with good Crappie fishing on both lakes. Dixon is notorious for its slab sized Crappies in the 1 pound to 2 pound-class. Plate-sized Bluegills are also present with some 1-1/2 pounders registered in the Blue Book each year. Dunbar receives much less pressure than Dixon and produces some 3/4 pound-plus Crappies and some decent Walleyes. There are also some decent Bluegills and Pumpkinseeds in Dunbar. When Third River is open, spawning Walleyes from Big Winnie that make their way into Dixon, get hammered by anglers crowded boat-to-boat. Dixon also gives up five pound-class Northerns with some frequency.

NOT FOR NAVIGATION

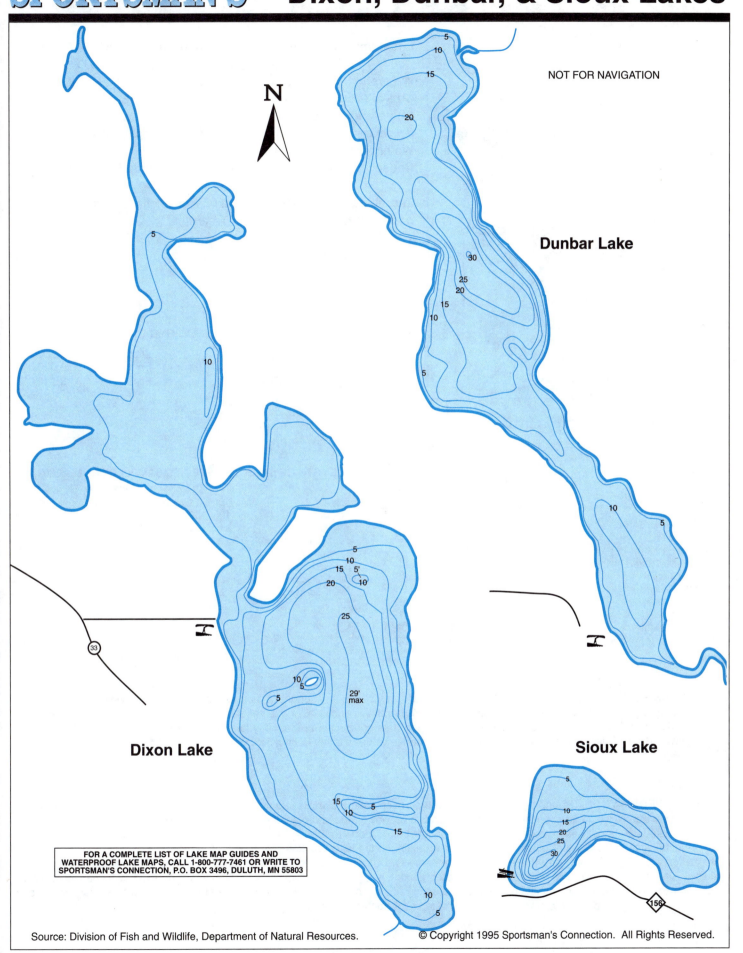

Dunbar Lake

Dixon Lake

Sioux Lake

N

29' max

FOR A COMPLETE LIST OF LAKE MAP GUIDES AND WATERPROOF LAKE MAPS, CALL 1-800-777-7461 OR WRITE TO SPORTSMAN'S CONNECTION, P.O. BOX 3496, DULUTH, MN 55803

Source: Division of Fish and Wildlife, Department of Natural Resources.

ROUND LAKE

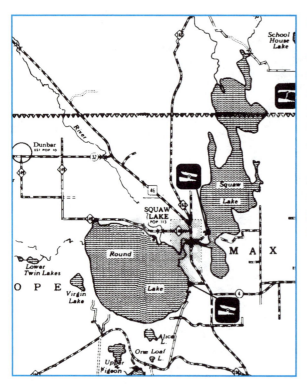

Location: Township 148 Range 27, 28
Watershed: Big Fork
Size of lake: 2,959 Acres
Shorelength: 8.2 Miles
Secchi disk (water clarity): 2.3 Ft.
Water color: Light brown
Cause of water color: Bog stain

Maximum depth: 24.0 Ft.
Median depth: 12.0 Ft.
Accessibility: (2) State-owned access on S.E. end of lake; also behind Squaw Lake Coop
Boat Ramp: (2) Earth
Parking: Limited
Accommodations: Resorts

Shoreland zoning classification: Recreational Development
Dominant forest/soil type: No Tree/Wet
Management class: Walleye
Ecological type: Hard-water Walleye

FISH STOCKING DATA

year	species	size	# released
90	Walleye	Fry	3,000,000
92	Walleye	Fry	3,000,000

NET CATCH DATA

survey date: 06/22/92

species	Gill Nets # per net	Gill Nets avg fish wt. (lbs.)	Trap Nets # per set	Trap Nets avg fish wt. (lbs.)
Yellow Perch	47.6	0.34	4.2	0.18
White Sucker	4.3	2.76	-	-
Walleye	5.3	2.55	0.2	3.40
Tullibee (incl. Cisco)	0.7	0.41	-	-
Northern Pike	13.1	2.18	0.4	2.32
Burbot	0.1	2.25	-	-
Brown Bullhead	17.3	0.88	4.1	0.89
Black Crappie	0.9	0.23	0.4	0.65
Black Bullhead	3.4	0.91	2.7	0.54
Yellow Bullhead	-	-	0.1	0.40
Rock Bass	-	-	0.3	0.70
Pumpkin. Sunfish	-	-	1.7	0.09
Bluegill	-	-	0.3	0.08

LENGTH OF SELECTED SPECIES SAMPLED FROM ALL GEAR
Number of fish caught for the following length categories (inches):

species	0-5	6-8	9-11	12-14	15-19	20-24	25-29	>30	Total
Yellow Perch	-	110	152	28	-	-	-	-	290
Walleye	-	1	4	1	42	25	6	-	79
Tullibee (incl. Cisco)	-	9	1	-	-	-	-	-	10
Northern Pike	-	-	-	2	28	134	29	1	194
Brown Bullhead	-	2	99	126	7	-	-	-	234
Black Crappie	11	2	-	3	-	-	-	-	16
Black Bullhead	-	2	18	28	1	-	-	-	49

DNR COMMENTS: Northern Pike pop. down a bit, but still well above 3rd quartile values for lake class; mean weight 2.2 lb.; growth rates mixed; excellent spawning areas contribute to good reproductive success for this species. Walleyes present in roughly avg. numbers for this lake class; mean weight is 2.6 lb., and the pop. has good number of quality-length fish; growth rates good. Yellow Perch pop. down. Brown Bullheads numerous and above 3rd quartile values. Black Bullheads present in avg. numbers for lake class. Only 2 Yellow Bullheads sampled.

FISHING INFORMATION: Round Lake, located within the Leech Lake Indian Reservation and Chippewa National Forest, is well known for its jumbo Perch, which attract fishermen from Wisconsin as well as the rest of Minnesota. Winter fishing can be fast and furious with hundred-fish catches not uncommon. Both Jack at Squaw Lake Sports Center and George of The Bait Shop in Deer River told us that 10-12 inch Perch in the 3/4 to 1 pound range have been hitting in the lake. Jack also told us that the Walleyes in Round are nice when they're on the bite with fish up to 9 pounds being landed. The Crappies are few but nice sized. Round's 3,000 acres warm up fairly quickly after ice out due to dark, relatively shallow water, making it a good opener lake. Round Lake is connected by a channel to Squaw Lake which provides spawning habitat and takes on a spring migration of Walleyes. Anglers do get some good catches early in the season. Squaw Lake's wild rice attracts some good duck flights for hunters in the fall.

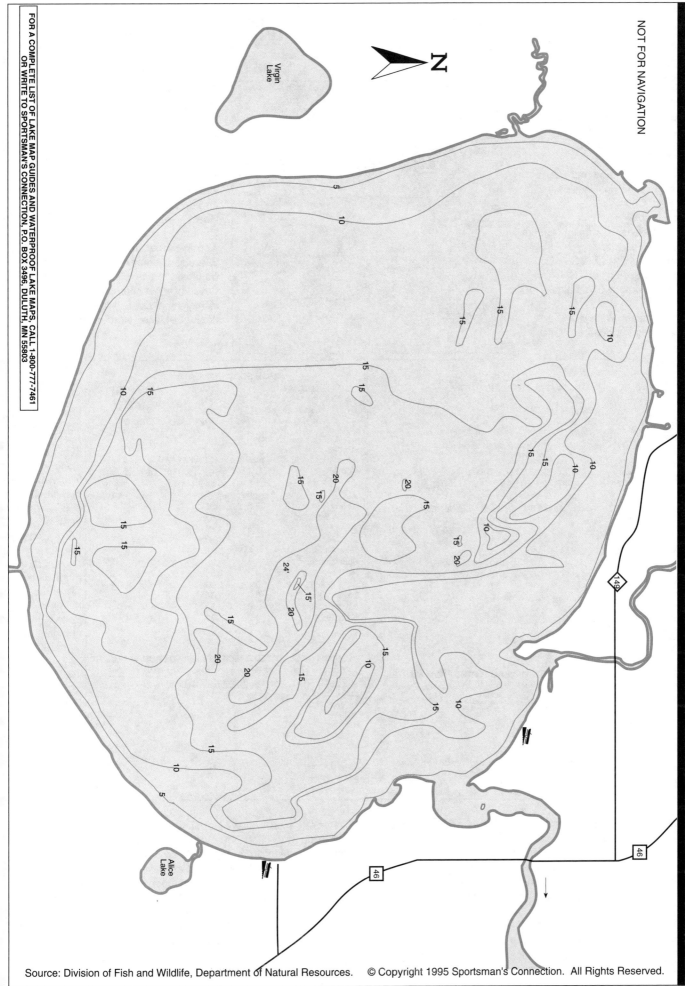

SPORTSMAN'S
connection

NOT FOR NAVIGATION

N

Virgin
Lake

Alice
Lake

Source: Division of Fish and Wildlife, Department of Natural Resources.   © Copyright 1995 Sportsman's Connection. All Rights Reserved.

ISLAND LAKE

MOOSE LAKE

Location: Township 150 Range 28
Watershed: Big Fork

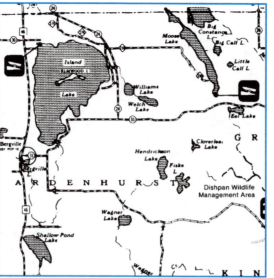

Island Lake

Size of lake: 2,920 Acres
Shorelength: 11.3 Miles
Secchi disk (water clarity): NA
Water color: Light green
Maximum depth: 35.0 Ft.
Median depth: 17.0 Ft.
Accessibility: State-owned public access off Hwy. 46 on NW side
Boat Ramp: Concrete
Parking: Ample
Accommodations: Camping (on Elmwood Island); Resorts
Shoreland zoning classif.: Gen. Dev.
Dominant forest/soil type: NA
Cause of water color: Slight algae bloom
Management class: Walleye
Ecological type: Hard-water Walleye

Moose Lake

Size of lake: 373 Acres
Shorelength: 6.2 Miles
Secchi disk (water clarity): NA
Water color: Clear
Maximum depth: 52.0 Ft.
Median depth: 26.0 Ft.
Accessibility: Federal access on S side; from Hwy. 46, E on Co. Rd. 31, N on Forest Road 3335
Boat Ramp: Metal
Parking: Limited
Accommodations: None
Shoreland zoning classif.: Rec. Dev.
Dominant forest/soil type: Decid./Loam
Cause of water color: NA
Management class: Walleye
Ecological type: Hard-water Walleye

DNR COMMENTS: Northern Pike about avg. in numbers; sample aged 2-4 years; growth about avg. Walleyes present in avg. numbers; sample corresponds to stocked years; normal-good growth for most year classes. Rock Bass pop. high, about twice quartile value. Tullibees below 1st quartile. Other species present in about avg. numbers.

FISH STOCKING DATA

year	species	size	# released
90	Walleye	Fry	3,000,000
92	Walleye	Fry	3,000,000

NET CATCH DATA
survey date: 06/24/91

species	Gill Nets # per net	Gill Nets avg fish wt. (lbs)	Trap Nets # per set	Trap Nets avg fish wt. (lbs)
Yellow Perch	38.5	0.20	3.1	0.13
White Sucker	2.2	2.25	0.1	0.10
Walleye	5.0	1.63	0.1	0.50
Tullibee (incl. Cisco)	0.8	1.08	-	-
Rock Bass	9.3	0.40	0.9	0.32
Pumpkin. Sunfish	0.8	0.16	3.0	0.10
Northern Pike	5.6	1.91	0.4	1.45
Burbot	0.1	3.00	-	-
Brown Bullhead	0.3	1.43	0.1	1.60
Black Crappie	-	-	0.2	1.00

LENGTH OF SELECTED SPECIES SAMPLED FROM ALL GEAR
Number of fish caught for the following length categories (inches):

species	0-5	6-8	9-11	12-14	15-19	20-24	25-29	>30	Total
Yellow Perch	3	89	26	2	-	-	-	-	120
Walleye	-	7	1	5	24	19	4	-	60
Tullibee (incl. Cisco)	-	2	-	5	2	-	-	-	9
Rock Bass	3	58	49	1	-	-	-	-	111
Pumpkin. Sunfish	4	5	-	-	-	-	-	-	9
Northern Pike	-	-	-	1	16	40	9	-	66
Brown Bullhead	-	-	-	4	-	-	-	-	4

FISH STOCKING DATA

year	species	size	# released
89	Walleye	Fry	700,000
91	Walleye	Fry	375,000
94	Walleye	Fry	375,000

NET CATCH DATA
survey date: 08/24/92

species	Gill Nets # per net	Gill Nets avg fish wt. (lbs)	Trap Nets # per set	Trap Nets avg fish wt. (lbs)
Yellow Perch	102.6	0.31	1.6	0.3
Yellow Bullhead	0.3	0.63	0.1	1.00
White Sucker	1.3	1.86	-	-
Walleye	10.7	1.86	0.1	8.60
Rock Bass	1.4	0.36	-	-
Pumpkin. Sunfish	1.4	0.32	2.6	0.25
Northern Pike	4.3	2.58	0.7	1.27
Largemouth Bass	0.7	0.83	1.0	0.11
Bowfin (Dogfish)	0.2	2.30	-	-
Black Crappie	2.9	0.63	0.3	0.30
Black Bullhead	0.2	0.70	-	-

LENGTH OF SELECTED SPECIES SAMPLED FROM ALL GEAR
Number of fish caught for the following length categories (inches):

species	0-5	6-8	9-11	12-14	15-19	20-24	25-29	>30	Total
Yellow Perch	1	31	89	1	-	-	-	-	122
Yellow Bullhead	-	-	3	1	-	-	-	-	4
Walleye	-	-	4	7	72	9	5	-	97
Rock Bass	-	11	3	-	-	-	-	-	14
Pumpkin. Sunfish	-	13	2	-	-	-	-	-	15
Northern Pike	-	-	-	-	8	21	7	1	37
Largemouth Bass	-	2	1	3	-	-	-	-	6
Black Crappie	-	4	18	5	-	-	-	-	27
Black Bullhead	-	-	2	1	-	-	-	-	3

DNR COMMENTS: Northern Pike pop. down sharply from last sampling, but still nearly avg. for lake class. Walleyes very numerous, with pop. above 3rd quartile values. Black Crappie gillnet sampling above 3rd quartile values. Rock Bass numerous. Yellow Perch numbers very high, with sampling at 102.5/set. Bullhead pop. low. Other species present in about avg. numbers.

FISHING INFORMATION: Island Lake's structure provides excellent habitat for its high Walleye population. It is normally a late starter, according to Jim at Cedar Hill Resort on the lake. From Memorial weekend through the first three weeks in June it produces some nice fish. At this time of year, Walleyes are found near the rocky points and other spawning areas in 5 to 10 feet of water. The underwater islands and deeper water points produce better during the summer months. Jim said that he knows of at least 25 good structure areas that usually hold Walleye - some in the 5 to 8 pound-class. The lake also holds its fair share of "cigars," but you can usually count on some 2 pound fish. Average Perch size has also been increasing in recent years with some 1 pounders being taken. When you can find the Crappie, they run 3/4 pound-plus. Northerns are plentiful but count on more hammer handles than large ones. To the east of Island Lake on County Road 159 lies Moose Lake. Unlike Island, Moose's structure is fairly simple with relatively steep shoreline dropoffs. Jim told us to work the secondary breakline for the Walleyes which average in the 2 pound range. Largemouth Bass up to 3 and 4 pounds are caught by anglers willing to learn the lake. Walleye fishermen have reported catching some pound Crappies along the breaklines.

Island & Moose Lakes

NOT FOR NAVIGATION

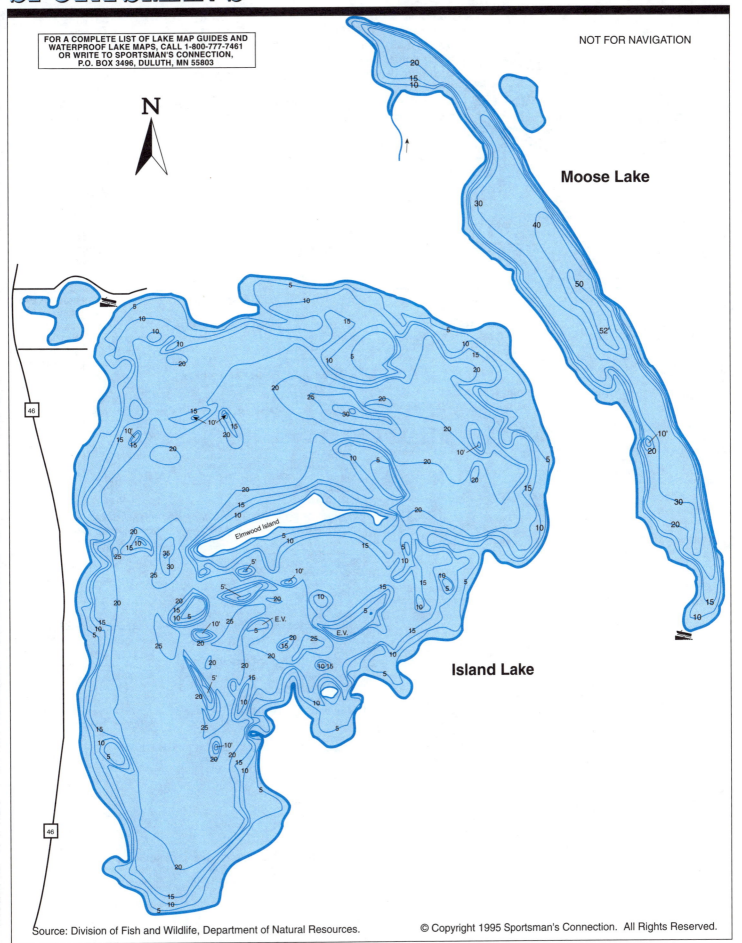

Moose Lake

Island Lake

Elmwood Island

Location: Township 149, 150   Range 26, 27
Watershed: Big Fork

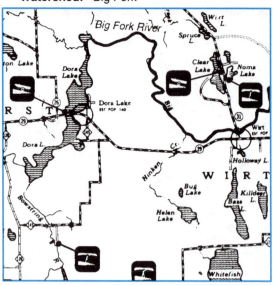

	DORA LAKE	CLEAR LAKE	NOMA LAKE
Size of lake:	477 Acres	137 Acres	59 Acres
Shorelength:	10.3 Miles	3.3 Miles	1.3 Miles
Secchi disk (water clarity):	6.6 Ft.	NA	8.9 Ft.
Water color:	Brown	Clear	Clear
Maximum depth:	18.0 Ft.	29.0 Ft.	47.0 Ft.
Median depth:	12.0 Ft.	17.0 Ft.	14.5 Ft.
Accessibility:	USFS-owned picnic grounds just N of W end of Cty. Rd. 29 bridge	County-owned on East Shore	Federal-owned access on S side
Boat Ramp:	Concrete	Earth	Carry-down
Parking:	Limited	Limited	Ample
Accommodations:	Resort	Resort	Campground
Shoreland zoning classif.:	Rec. Dev.	Rec. Dev.	Nat. Envt.
Dominant forest/soil type:	No tree/Wet	NA	NA
Cause of water color:	Bog stain	NA	NA
Management class:	Walleye	Walleye-Centrarchid	Centrarchid
Ecological type:	Hard-water Walleye	Centrarchid	Centrarchid

DNR COMMENTS:
Walleye numbers are lower than expected although the gill netting information could be biased because of weed growth that caused inability to net effectively. All other species are within normal limits for this type of lake.

Dora Lake

FISH STOCKING DATA

year	species	size	# released
89	Walleye	Fry	4,000,000
90	Walleye	Fry	750,000
93	Walleye	Fry	750,000

survey date: 06/10/91

NET CATCH DATA

	Gill Nets		Trap Nets	
		avg fish		avg fish
species	# per net	wt. (lbs)	# per set	wt. (lbs)
Yellow Perch	45.9	0.25	2.9	0.27
White Sucker	9.0	1.93	0.6	1.68
Walleye	1.9	1.38	0.3	4.10
Silver Redhorse	2.1	3.47	0.1	2.50
Shorthead Red.	1.1	1.48	1.1	2.00
Pumpkin. Sunfish	0.3	0.45	0.1	0.60
Northern Pike	3.4	2.63	0.6	0.78
Hybrid Sunfish	0.1	0.80	0.1	0.80
Brown Bullhead	8.1	0.54	0.8	0.67
Black Crappie	0.1	0.90	0.8	0.80
Black Bullhead	4.3	0.38	1.3	0.25
Yellow Bullhead	-	-	1.0	0.46

LENGTH OF SELECTED SPECIES SAMPLED FROM ALL GEAR
Number of fish caught for the following length categories (inches):

species	0-5	6-8	9-11	12-14	15-19	20-24	25-29	>30	Total
Yellow Perch	-	71	27	-	-	-	-	-	98
Walleye	-	-	1	7	7	1	-	-	16
Pumpkin. Sunfish	-	2	-	-	-	-	-	-	2
Northern Pike	-	-	-	1	8	10	2	3	24
Hybrid Sunfish	-	-	1	-	-	-	-	-	1
Brown Bullhead	-	-	49	8	-	-	-	-	57
Black Crappie	-	-	-	1	-	-	-	-	1
Black Bullhead	-	12	18	-	-	-	-	-	30

Clear Lake

FISH STOCKING DATA

year	species	size	# released
89	Walleye	Fingerling	1,404
91	Walleye	Fingerling	459

survey date: 08/22/83

NET CATCH DATA

	Gill Nets		Trap Nets	
		avg fish		avg fish
species	# per net	wt. (lbs)	# per set	wt. (lbs)
Yellow Perch	39.3	0.16	2.3	0.17
White Sucker	3.5	1.20	1.0	1.95
Walleye	3.8	1.57	-	-
Northern Pike	5.3	1.90	0.5	1.00
Brown Bullhead	0.3	0.80	-	-
Bluegill	2.0	0.13	6.5	0.11
Pumpkin. Sunfish	-	-	1.5	0.20
Black Crappie	-	-	1.0	0.38

LENGTH OF SELECTED SPECIES SAMPLED FROM ALL GEAR
Number of fish caught for the following length categories (inches):

species	0-5	6-8	9-11	12-14	15-19	20-24	25-29	>30	Total
Black Crappie	-	1	3	-	-	-	-	-	4
Bluegill	4	30	-	-	-	-	-	-	34
Brown Bullhead	-	-	-	1	-	-	-	-	1
Northern Pike	-	-	1	2	4	16	1	-	23
Pumpkin. Sunfish	2	4	-	-	-	-	-	-	6
Walleye	-	-	-	3	6	5	1	-	15
Yellow Perch	-	79	27	3	-	-	-	-	109

DNR COMMENTS:
Northern Pike have declined slightly but are still quite abundant. There has been a substantial decline in Perch abundance but numbers are still higher than local medians. Walleye numbers have increased substantially since the last survey. Bluegill numbers have declined while Pumpkinseed and Crappie abundance remains low.

Noma Lake

FISH STOCKING DATA

year	species	size	# released
90	Walleye	Yearling	54

survey date: 07/10/85

NET CATCH DATA

	Gill Nets		Trap Nets	
		avg fish		avg fish
species	# per net	wt. (lbs)	# per set	wt. (lbs)
Yellow Perch	7.3	0.10	-	-
White Sucker	0.7	2.75	-	-
Northern Pike	1.3	4.88	-	-
Bluegill	1.0	0.60	40.5	0.15
Pumpkin. Sunfish	-	-	2.0	0.15
Brown Bullhead	-	-	0.3	1.00

LENGTH OF SELECTED SPECIES SAMPLED FROM ALL GEAR
Number of fish caught for the following length categories (inches):

species	0-5	6-8	9-11	12-14	15-19	20-24	25-29	>30	Total
Bluegill	73	85	7	-	-	-	-	-	165
Brown Bullhead	-	-	-	1	-	-	-	-	1
Northern Pike	-	-	-	-	-	4	-	-	4
Pumpkin. Sunfish	4	4	-	-	-	-	-	-	8
Yellow Perch	-	22	-	-	-	-	-	-	22

DNR COMMENTS:
Bluegill populations three times greater than the averages. All other species below the averages.

FISHING INFORMATION: Dora Lake is a part of the Big Fork flowage that provides some excellent early season Walleye fishing in the narrows, according to Joe at the River Rat Trading Post in Cohasset. Some Northerns are also pulled from Dora but it is basically known for its Walleye. Clear Lake gives up some nice 2 to 3 pound Walleyes, along with a few larger ones, every season. Twenty pound-class Northern Pike also lurk in its waters, feeding on the heavy Perch population. Noma Lake has a good Bluegill population and some decent Northerns. The DNR has been stocking Walleye over the last several years which should be taking hold. Noma Lake also has a nice campground.

NOT FOR NAVIGATION

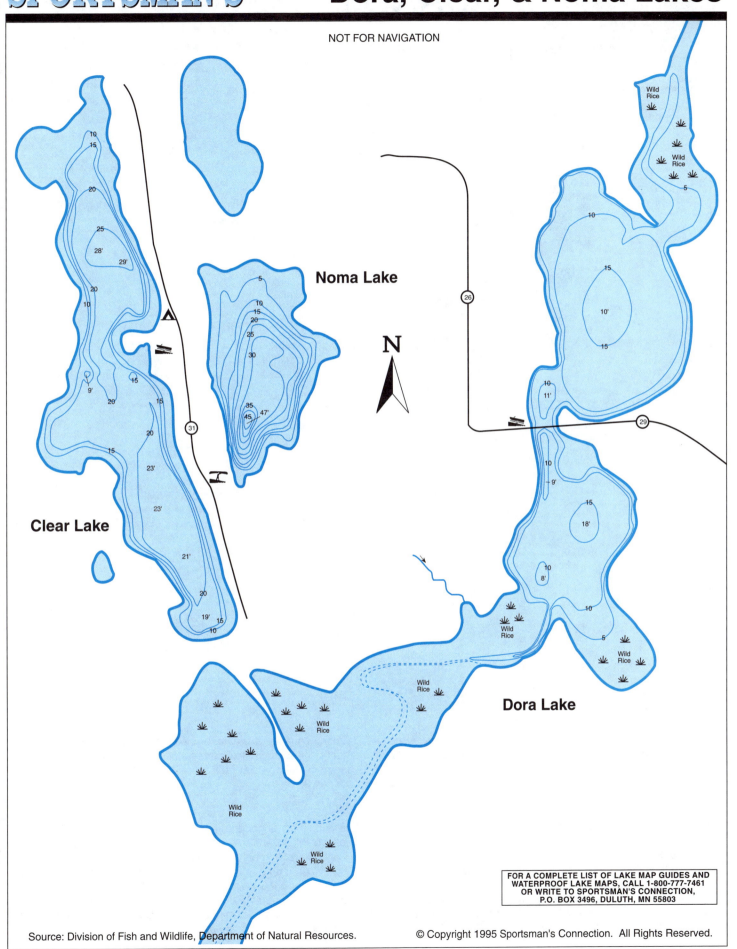

Noma Lake

N

Clear Lake

Dora Lake

Wild Rice

Source: Division of Fish and Wildlife, Department of Natural Resources.

SAND LAKE

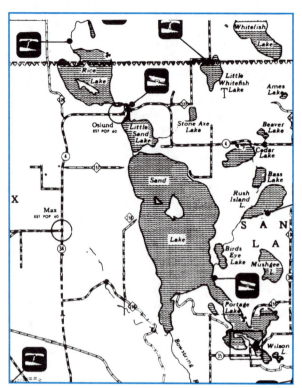

Location: Township 147, 148 Range 26
Watershed: Big Fork
Size of lake: 3,785 Acres
Shorelength: 19.9 Miles
Secchi disk (water clarity): 6.1 Ft.
Water color: Light brown
Cause of water color: Bog stain

Maximum depth: 70.0 Ft.
Median depth: 17.0 Ft.
Accessibility: State-owned access on the SE shore of the SE bay of lake
Boat Ramp: Concrete
Parking: Ample
Accommodations: Resorts

Shoreland zoning classification: Recreational Development
Dominant forest/soil type: Decid/Loam
Management class: Walleye
Ecological type: Hard-water Walleye

FISH STOCKING DATA

year	species	size	# released
90	Walleye	Fry	3,800,000
92	Walleye	Fry	3,800,000

NET CATCH DATA

survey date: 07/13/92

species	Gill Nets # per net	Gill Nets avg fish wt. (lbs.)	Trap Nets # per set	Trap Nets avg fish wt. (lbs.)
Yellow Perch	14.5	0.25	1.8	0.14
White Sucker	2.2	2.43	2.1	3.95
Walleye	5.3	1.09	0.1	2.05
Tullibee (incl. Cisco)	0.3	1.23	-	-
Smallmouth Bass	0.2	2.57	-	-
Silver Redhorse	0.3	4.00	-	-
Shorthead Red.	1.8	2.13	1.3	2.08
Rock Bass	1.1	0.66	0.4	0.53
Northern Pike	5.4	1.27	0.8	0.90
Burbot	0.1	0.70	-	-
Brown Bullhead	0.5	1.04	0.5	0.51
Bluegill	0.1	0.50	2.1	0.24
Black Crappie	0.4	0.85	0.2	0.37
Black Bullhead	0.2	0.47	-	-
Pumpkin. Sunfish	-	-	1.9	0.34
Largemouth Bass	-	-	0.1	0.20
Bowfin (Dogfish)	-	-	1.6	4.31

LENGTH OF SELECTED SPECIES SAMPLED FROM ALL GEAR

Number of fish caught for the following length categories (inches):

species	0-5	6-8	9-11	12-14	15-19	20-24	25-29	>30	Total
Yellow Perch	1	54	37	3	-	-	-	-	95
Walleye	-	3	9	27	31	9	1	-	80
Tullibee (incl. Cisco)	-	-	2	1	1	-	-	-	4
Smallmouth Bass	-	-	-	-	3	-	-	-	3
Rock Bass	-	6	7	3	-	-	-	-	16
Northern Pike	-	-	-	-	53	27	1	-	81
Brown Bullhead	-	-	-	5	-	-	-	-	5
Bluegill	-	-	2	-	-	-	-	-	2
Black Crappie	-	-	-	5	-	-	-	-	5
Black Bullhead	-	-	3	-	-	-	-	-	3

DNR COMMENTS: Northern Pike mostly aged 1-3 years; sizes small, although growth above statewide mean for this age group. Walleye sample consisted of all age groups, with age 4 being most prominent; about 65% of sample corresponds to years in which stockings occurred; growth slower than avg. for all age groups. Black Crappie sample small; growth fast; mean length of 9.8" at last annulus. Bluegills mostly aged 2,3; growth avg. for age 2 and slightly above avg. for age 3.

FISHING INFORMATION: Sand Lake's rolling structure provides anglers with plenty of good areas to fish for its good numbers of Walleye, Crappie, Jumbo Perch and Largemouth Bass. Brian Krecklau, of the Pole Bender Guide Service, said that you can expect Walleyes to average in the 1-1/2 to 2-pound range; Crappies around 3/4 pound and some 10-inch-plus jumbo Perch. Hammer handle-sized Northerns also infest the lake. Brian likes Sand because he can usually count on a mixed bag of fish. Crappies are taken consistently throughout the year with an occasional 2-pounder mixed in with the more typical 3/4 pound average catches. If the Walleye fishing is slow, Perch are almost always active with a good percentage of them being keepers. Largemouth Bass numbers are good, but be prepared to catch several small fish for every decent-sized one. Most Bass caught are released, and more and more anglers are now releasing the larger female Walleyes, which will help the natural reproduction of this important species.

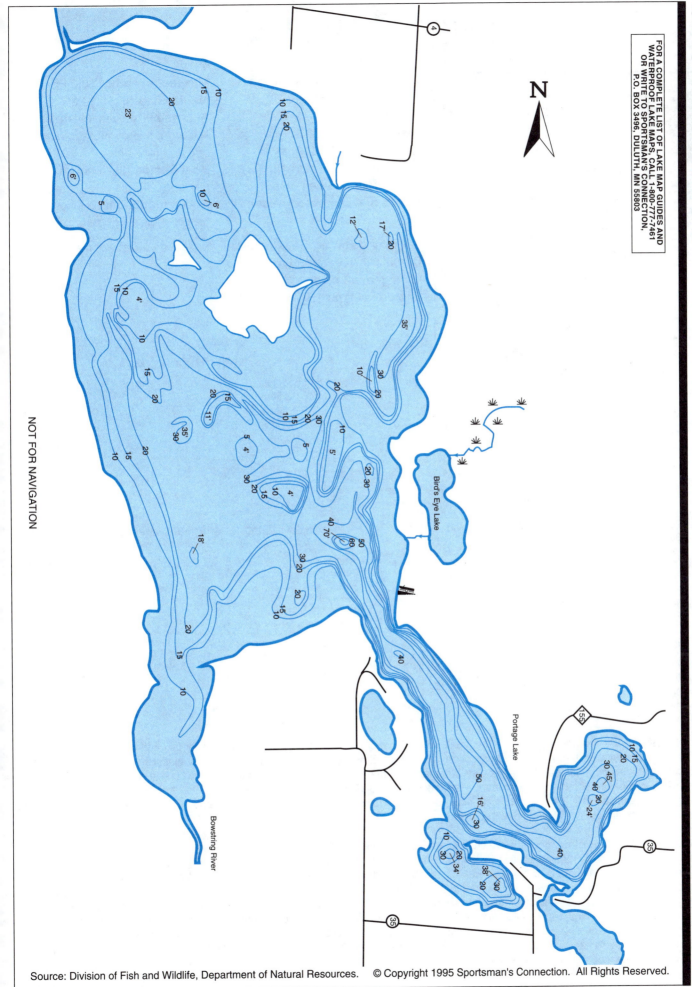

N

SPORTSMAN'S
connection ®

NOT FOR NAVIGATION

Bird's Eye Lake

Portage Lake

Bowstring River

BOWSTRING LAKE

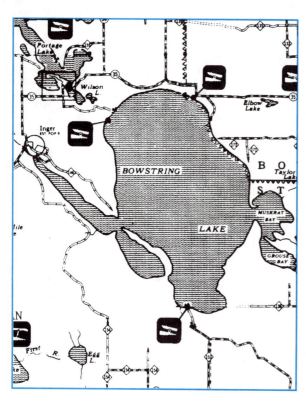

Location: Township 146, 147 Range 25, 26
Watershed: Big Fork
Size of lake: 8,900 Acres
Shorelength: 21.0 Miles
Secchi disk (water clarity): 3.3 Ft.
Water color: Green
Cause of water color: Algae

Maximum depth: 30.0 Ft.
Median depth: 15.0 Ft.
Accessibility: One located on NW side; one on NE shore and one on the S side
Boat Ramp: (3) Concrete
Parking: Ample
Accommodations: Resorts, picnic grounds, campground.

Shoreland zoning classification: Recreational Development
Dominant forest/soil type: NA
Management class: Walleye
Ecological type: Hard-water Walleye

FISH STOCKING DATA

year	species	size	# released
85	Walleye	Fry	8,900,000
87	Walleye	Fry	8,900,000
89	Walleye	Fry	8,900,000
91	Walleye	Fry	8,900,000

NET CATCH DATA

survey date: 7/13/92

species	Gill Nets # per net	Gill Nets avg fish wt. (lbs.)	Trap Nets # per set	Trap Nets avg fish wt. (lbs.)
Yellow Perch	29.4	0.39	0.9	0.29
Yellow Bullhead	0.1	0.80	-	-
White Sucker	4.3	1.99	0.1	2.30
Walleye	12.3	1.36	0.1	2.90
Tullibee (incl. Cisco)	0.3	0.20	-	-
Silver Redhorse	0.1	5.40	0.1	4.75
Shorthead Redhorse	0.8	2.26	0.4	2.57
Rock Bass	0.1	0.10	-	-
Northern Pike	12.6	1.49	0.9	0.94
Brown Bullhead	5.9	0.95	2.1	0.81
Bowfin (Dogfish)	0.2	3.75	0.5	3.97
Black Crappie	1.2	0.58	0.9	0.67
Black Bullhead	0.2	0.45	1.0	0.49
Pumpkin. Sunfish	-	-	0.7	0.42
Hybrid Sunfish	-	-	0.1	0.10
Bluegill	-	-	0.1	0.40

LENGTH OF SELECTED SPECIES SAMPLED FROM ALL GEAR

Number of fish caught for the following length categories (inches):

species	0-5	6-8	9-11	12-14	15-19	20-24	25-29	>30	Total
Yellow Perch	1	16	99	19	-	-	-	-	135
Yellow Bullhead	-	-	-	1	-	-	-	-	1
Walleye	-	12	8	35	76	18	1	-	150
Tullibee (incl. Cisco)	-	-	4	-	-	-	-	-	4
Rock Bass	2	-	-	-	-	-	-	-	2
Northern Pike	-	-	-	-	76	71	3	1	151
Brown Bullhead	-	-	11	59	1	-	-	-	71
Black Crappie	2	6	2	6	-	-	-	-	16
Black Bullhead	-	-	2	-	-	-	-	-	2

DNR COMMENTS: Northern Pike abundant but small, with gill net catches indicating a large number of fish in the 17-19" range; growth good till age 4, then slower; good natural reproduction, as evidenced by samplings from unstocked year classes; vast stands of wild rice provide excellent spawning habitat. Walleyes very abundant and above third quartile values for lake class; size range good, with a large portion of fish in the 15-19" range; good natural reproduction, as evidenced by strong presence of fish from unstocked years; growth good. Samplings indicate this lake also contains high numbers of quality-size crappies. Tullibee numbers low. Yellow Perch sampled in good numbers, with about 70% of sample being quality-size fish of 9" or larger.

FISHING INFORMATION: Bowstring is a classic Walleye fishery, being relatively large, shallow, wind-swept and sandy in character. Its dark waters warm up quickly making it a good early lake. The DNR's stocking efforts, along with good natural reproduction provide excellent Walleye fishing. It is also fairly easy to fish with its sandbars and rock piles being good magnets for Walleye and Crappie. The Northern end of the lake is full of weedbeds, which attract Northern Pike, Crappie and Perch. Northern average around 3 pounds with some reaching the 20 pound-class. In addition to the weedbed area, Inger Bay, on the east side by the Bowstring River outlet, is good for large Pike. Perch are found throughout the lake with some jumbos 9" and up. The Crappie fishing in Bowstring can be phenomenal. Good numbers of slabs, in the 1 to 2 pound range, are caught throughout the year. Rarely do you catch a papermouth that isn't a keeper. Fishing pressure for them seems to be at its peak during the winter. The eastern shoreline of the lake has a relatively steep dropoff and is rocky. The north side's bottom structure is primarily sand, mixed with areas of rock.

Bowstring Lake

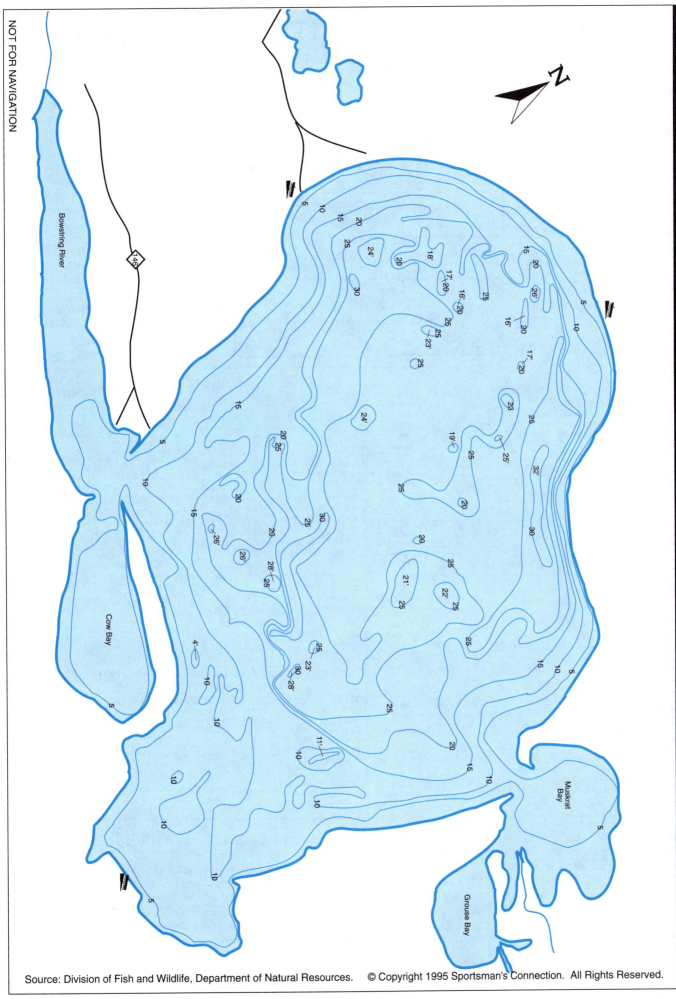

NOT FOR NAVIGATION

Bowstring River

Cow Bay

Muskrat Bay

Grouse Bay

JESSIE LAKE   LITTLE JESSIE LAKE

Location: Township 147, 148   Range 25
Watershed: Big Fork

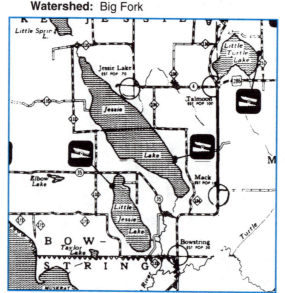

JESSIE LAKE

Size of lake: 1,782 Acres
Shorelength: 9.2 Miles
Secchi disk (water clarity): 5.9 Ft.
Water color: Green
Maximum depth: 42.0 Ft.
Median depth: 22.0 Ft.
Accessibility: State-owned access located on SE side
Boat Ramp: Concrete
Parking: Ample
Accommodations: Resorts
Shoreland zoning classif.: Rec. Dev.
Dominant forest/soil type: Decid/Sand
Cause of water color: Algae
Management class: Walleye
Ecological type: Hard-water Walleye

LITTLE JESSIE LAKE

Size of lake: 613 Acres
Shorelength: 4.7 Miles
Secchi disk (water clarity): NA
Water color: Blue-green
Maximum depth: 49.0 Ft.
Median depth: 28.0 Ft.
Accessibility: State-owned access on the NW corner
Boat Ramp: Concrete
Parking: Ample
Accommodations: Resort
Shoreland zoning classif.: Rec. Dev.
Dominant forest/soil type: Decid/Sand
Cause of water color: Calcium carbonate
Management class: Walleye-Centrarchid
Ecological type: Centrarchid-Walleye

DNR COMMENTS:
Northern Pike pop. about avg. for lake class; size distribution wide; ages 3,4 most prevalent in sample; growth above avg. Walleyes about avg. in numbers; growth rate avg. through age 5: Black Crappies numerous; growth about avg. for lake class. Yellow Perch and White Sucker populations at 3rd quartile levels. Tullibees near median in numbers.

FISH STOCKING DATA

year	species	size	# released
89	Walleye	Fry	1,800,000
91	Walleye	Fry	1,800,000
93	Walleye	Fry	1,800,000

survey date: 08/27/90

NET CATCH DATA

	Gill Nets		Trap Nets	
species	# per net	avg fish wt. (lbs)	# per set	avg fish wt. (lbs)
Yellow Perch	46.7	0.12	12.3	0.13
White Sucker	4.6	1.39	0.2	2.10
Walleye	4.1	1.84	0.5	0.95
Tullibee (incl. Cisco)	2.3	0.85	-	-
Rock Bass	0.1	0.30	0.7	0.14
Northern Pike	3.7	3.75	0.4	1.10
Black Crappie	0.1	0.80	2.1	0.38
Pumpkin. Sunfish	-	-	4.9	0.13
Largemouth Bass	-	-	1.7	0.11
Brown Bullhead	-	-	0.1	1.00
Bowfin (Dogfish)	-	-	0.8	3.68
Bluegill	-	-	0.2	0.10

LENGTH OF SELECTED SPECIES SAMPLED FROM ALL GEAR
Number of fish caught for the following length categories (inches):

species	0-5	6-8	9-11	12-14	15-19	20-24	25-29	>30	Total
Yellow Perch	1	124	1	-	-	-	-	-	126
Walleye	-	-	-	22	21	13	5	-	61
Tullibee (incl. Cisco)	-	4	2	25	4	-	-	-	35
Rock Bass	-	1	-	-	-	-	-	-	1
Northern Pike	-	-	1	7	20	22	5	55
Black Crappie	-	1	-	-	-	-	-	-	1

FISH STOCKING DATA

year	species	size	# released
90	Walleye	Fingerling	11,554
92	Walleye	Fingerling	9,270
94	Walleye	Fry	5,428

survey date: 07/23/90

NET CATCH DATA

	Gill Nets		Trap Nets	
species	# per net	avg fish wt. (lbs)	# per set	avg fish wt. (lbs)
Yellow Perch	16.0	0.11	1.0	0.10
White Sucker	2.9	1.32	-	-
Walleye	3.8	2.05	0.2	0.50
Tullibee (incl. Cisco)	17.4	0.45	-	-
Smallmouth Bass	0.1	1.80	-	-
Rock Bass	1.3	0.72	4.2	0.19
Pumpkin. Sunfish	0.2	0.20	1.8	0.16
Northern Pike	4.6	2.51	0.2	2.00
Largemouth Bass	0.1	1.80	0.2	0.10
Black Crappie	0.1	1.00	-	-
Yellow Bullhead	-	-	0.2	1.20
Hybrid Sunfish	-	-	0.2	0.30
Bluegill	-	-	1.8	0.10

LENGTH OF SELECTED SPECIES SAMPLED FROM ALL GEAR
Number of fish caught for the following length categories (inches):

species	0-5	6-8	9-11	12-14	15-19	20-24	25-29	>30	Total
Yellow Perch	-	113	7	-	-	-	-	-	120
Walleye	-	-	-	5	19	8	2	-	34
Tullibee (incl. Cisco)	-	27	37	44	-	-	-	-	108
Smallmouth Bass	-	-	-	-	1	-	-	-	1
Rock Bass	-	2	8	2	-	-	-	-	12
Pumpkin. Sunfish	1	1	-	-	-	-	-	-	2
Northern Pike	-	-	-	-	12	19	8	-	39
Largemouth Bass	-	-	-	-	-	1	-	-	1
Black Crappie	-	-	-	-	1	-	-	-	1

DNR COMMENTS:
Northern Pike pop. about equal to median for lake class; good reproduction, and sample contains wide range of sizes; lengths range from 14-29"; growth rates good through age 4. Walleyes present in about avg. numbers for lake class; lengths from 11.5-24"; growth about avg.; some natural reproduction. Largemouth and Smallmouth Bass present in small numbers. Yellow Perch, Tullibees abundant.

FISHING INFORMATION: Jessie and Little Jessie Lakes are located within the Chippewa National Forest providing a picturesque setting for anglers and recreational boaters. Both lakes give up some nice 2 to 3 pound Walleyes and an occasional trophy. Walleye can be found around the sunken islands, reefs and bars in Big Jessie. Joe, at the River Rat Trading Post in Cohasset, said that Crappies averaging around 3/4 pound can provide some fast action on spring evenings. Try the inlet area of the north bay of Big Jessie after ice out through early summer and move out to the sand bottom flats and deeper water dropoffs later in the year. Northerns don't receive much pressure on either lake, but the average sizes are good with plenty of 10 pound-class fish present. A good forage base of Tullibee and Perch contribute to the rapid growth rate of this voracious predator. Little Jessie's fishery is similar to its larger namesake and receives less attention. Its smaller size makes it easier to locate structure. Smallmouth Bass have been caught with some frequency on Little Jessie in recent years. Largemouth Bass are also present in both lakes, although they are virtually unfished.

Jessie & Little Jessie Lakes

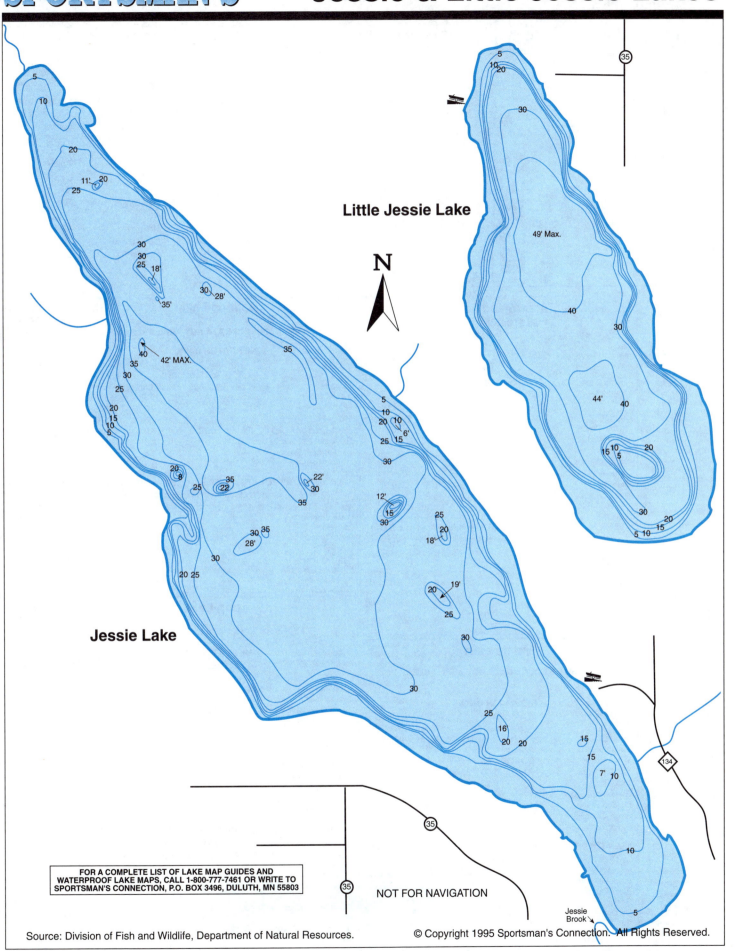

Little Jessie Lake

N

49' Max.

44'

Jessie Lake

42' MAX.

NOT FOR NAVIGATION

Jessie Brook

Source: Division of Fish and Wildlife, Department of Natural Resources.

Location: Township 149   Range 25
Watershed: Big Fork

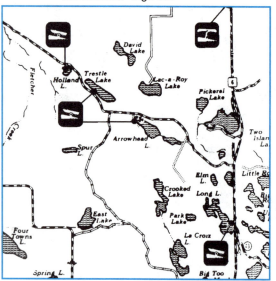

	ARROWHEAD (SAND) LAKE	LONG LAKE	TRESTLE LAKE	HOLLAND LAKE
Size of lake:	129 Acres	121 Acres	105 Acres	24 Acres
Shorelength:	2.0 Miles	3.3 Miles	2.0 Miles	0.6 Miles
Secchi disk (water clarity):	NA	NA	NA	NA
Water color:	Light green	Clear	Clear	Brown-green
Maximum depth:	30.0 Ft.	75.0 Ft.	30.0 Ft.	45.0 Ft.
Median depth:	15.0 Ft.	27.0 Ft.	18.1 Ft.	18.1 Ft.
Accessibility:	USFS-owned public access on W side	SE shore, state boat access and campground off Hwy. 6	7 miles N of Talmoon on Hwy. 6, then approx. 2 miles W on USFS Rd. 2187	Federal-owned access at NW corner from USFS Rd. 2187
Boat Ramp:	Earth	Gravel	Concrete	Earth
Parking:	Ample	Ample	Ample	Limited
Accommodations:	NA	Campground	NA	NA
Shoreland zoning classif.:	Nat. Envt.	Nat. Envt.	Nat. Envt.	Nat. Envt.
Dominant forest/soil type:	NA	NA	NA	NA
Cause of water color:	Algae bloom	NA	NA	Algae/bog stain
Management class:	Walleye-Centrarchid	Centrarchid	Centrarchid	Centrarchid
Ecological type:	Centrarchid	Centrarchid	Centrarchid	Centrarchid

DNR COMMENTS:
The most abundant fish species include Northern Pike, Yellow Perch, and Bluegills. 100,000 Walleye fry were stocked in 1986 which is the only introduction of this species since 1974. Some of these fry survived to provide 14 to 17 inch Walleyes in two years. This fast growth rate may be attributed to lack of any Walleyes in the lake from the previous 1974 initial introduction.

FISHING INFO:
Arrowhead (aka Sand) is an excellent spring Crappie lake, according to Joe at the River Rat Trading Post, providing 40 to 45 fish on a good evening. Some plump Bluegills, Walleyes, and Northerns round out this lake's fishery.

Arrowhead Lake

FISH STOCKING DATA

year	species	size	# released
89	Walleye	Fry	200,000
90	Walleye	Yearling	24
91	Walleye	Fry	90,000

NET CATCH DATA
survey date: 08/22/88

	Gill Nets		Trap Nets	
species	# per net	avg fish wt. (lbs)	# per set	avg fish wt. (lbs)
Yellow Perch	22.8	0.12	2.0	0.20
White Sucker	0.5	3.25	-	-
Walleye	2.3	1.61	-	-
Northern Pike	5.8	3.01	0.5	2.65
Largemouth Bass	0.3	0.50	-	-
Bluegill	4.8	0.22	5.5	0.07
Black Crappie	1.8	0.60	1.8	0.37
Pumpkin. Sunfish	-	-	1.0	0.20

LENGTH OF SELECTED SPECIES SAMPLED FROM ALL GEAR
Number of fish caught for the following length categories (inches):

species	0-5	6-8	9-11	12-14	15-19	20-24	25-29	>30	Total
Yellow Perch	2	88	1	-	-	-	-	-	91
Walleye	-	-	-	-	9	-	-	-	9
Northern Pike	-	-	-	-	2	18	3	-	23
Largemouth Bass	-	-	1	-	-	-	-	-	1
Bluegill	9	9	1	-	-	-	-	-	19
Black Crappie	-	3	1	3	-	-	-	-	7

DNR COMMENTS:
Northern Pike and Bluegill numbers are much higher than state and local catch medians. The abundance of other fish is within normal limits for this type of lake.

FISHING INFO:
Trestle (aka Fox) is a good Northern lake with some 20 pound-class fish present.

Trestle Lake

FISH STOCKING DATA NOT AVAILABLE

NET CATCH DATA
survey date: 06/22/83

	Gill Nets		Trap Nets	
species	# per net	avg fish wt. (lbs)	# per set	avg fish wt. (lbs)
Yellow Perch	4.8	0.10	4.3	0.12
White Sucker	0.5	1.75	-	-
Northern Pike	17.5	1.53	1.5	0.23
Bluegill	3.5	0.10	79.3	0.09
Pumpkin. Sunfish	-	-	1.5	0.23
Golden Shiner	-	-	0.3	0.20
Black Crappie	-	-	2.8	0.39
Black Bullhead	-	-	0.5	1.25

LENGTH OF SELECTED SPECIES SAMPLED FROM ALL GEAR
Number of fish caught for the following length categories (inches):

species	0-5	6-8	9-11	12-14	15-19	20-24	25-29	>30	Total
Black Bullhead	-	-	-	2	-	-	-	-	2
Black Crappie	-	3	5	3	-	-	-	-	11
Bluegill	23	57	5	-	-	-	-	-	85
Northern Pike	-	-	1	1	30	36	5	-	73
Pumpkin. Sunfish	-	6	-	-	-	-	-	-	6
Yellow Perch	-	33	3	-	-	-	-	-	36

Holland Lake

FISH STOCKING DATA NOT AVAILABLE

NET CATCH DATA
survey date: 07/05/79

	Gill Nets		Trap Nets	
species	# per net	avg fish wt. (lbs)	# per set	avg fish wt. (lbs)
Yellow Perch	45.5	0.11	1.8	0.21
Northern Pike	11.5	2.37	0.8	0.83
Bluegill	1.0	0.10	57.8	0.18
Black Crappie	0.5	0.20	7.0	0.05
Pumpkin. Sunfish	-	-	2.3	0.28
Largemouth Bass	-	-	0.8	0.27
Brown Bullhead	-	-	0.3	1.00

LENGTH OF SELECTED SPECIES SAMPLED FROM ALL GEAR
Number of fish caught for the following length categories (inches):

species	0-5	6-8	9-11	12-14	15-19	20-24	25-29	>30	Total
Black Crappie	-	2	25	-	-	-	-	-	27
Bluegill	-	29	3	-	-	-	-	-	32
Brown Bullhead	-	-	-	1	-	-	-	-	1
Largemouth Bass	-	3	-	-	-	-	-	-	3
Northern Pike	-	-	-	1	3	19	3	-	26
Pumpkin. Sunfish	-	8	1	-	-	-	-	-	9
Yellow Perch	-	30	4	-	-	-	-	-	34

DNR COMMENTS:
Northern Pike, Perch and Bluegill populations are at fairly high levels. All other fish populations appear to be within normal limits for this type of lake.

FISHING INFO:
Holland, tiny but deep, holds some 1/2 to 3/4 pound Crappie and lots of Bluegills. Largemouth Bass, averaging 2 pounds, can also be found. Catch and release of the Bass is highly recommended in order to help preserve the resource.

Long Lake

FISH STOCKING DATA NOT AVAILABLE

NET CATCH DATA
survey date: 08/03/83

	Gill Nets		Trap Nets	
species	# per net	avg fish wt. (lbs)	# per set	avg fish wt. (lbs)
White Sucker	0.3	4.00	-	-
Tullibee (incl. Cisco)	13.3	0.48	-	-
Northern Pike	8.8	1.70	0.5	0.75
Largemouth Bass	0.3	0.50	0.3	0.50
Bluegill	1.0	0.18	12.8	0.15
Black Bullhead	0.3	0.20	-	-
Yellow Perch	-	-	1.0	0.10
Yellow Bullhead	-	-	0.3	0.80
Rock Bass	-	-	0.5	0.25
Pumpkin. Sunfish	-	-	1.3	0.12
Black Crappie	-	-	3.6	0.27

LENGTH OF SELECTED SPECIES SAMPLED FROM ALL GEAR
Number of fish caught for the following length categories (inches):

species	0-5	6-8	9-11	12-14	15-19	20-24	25-29	>30	Total
Black Crappie	-	8	6	-	-	-	-	-	14
Bluegill	13	42	-	-	-	-	-	-	55
Largemouth Bass	-	-	1	1	-	-	-	-	2
Northern Pike	-	-	1	1	20	11	4	1	37
Pumpkin. Sunfish	2	3	1	-	-	-	-	-	5
Rock Bass	-	1	1	-	-	-	-	-	2
Tullibee (incl. Cisco)	-	2	29	15	7	-	-	-	53
Yellow Perch	-	1	3	-	-	-	-	-	4

DNR COMMENTS:
Cisco and Northern Pike population are well above state and local medians. All other fish numbers seem to be within normal limits for this type of lake.

FISHING INFO:
Long Lake, deep and clear, is another good Panfish lake in the area and it has a nice campground and a good gravel boat landing. Northerns and Largemouth Bass are also present, but the Crappies and Bluegills provide most of the action.

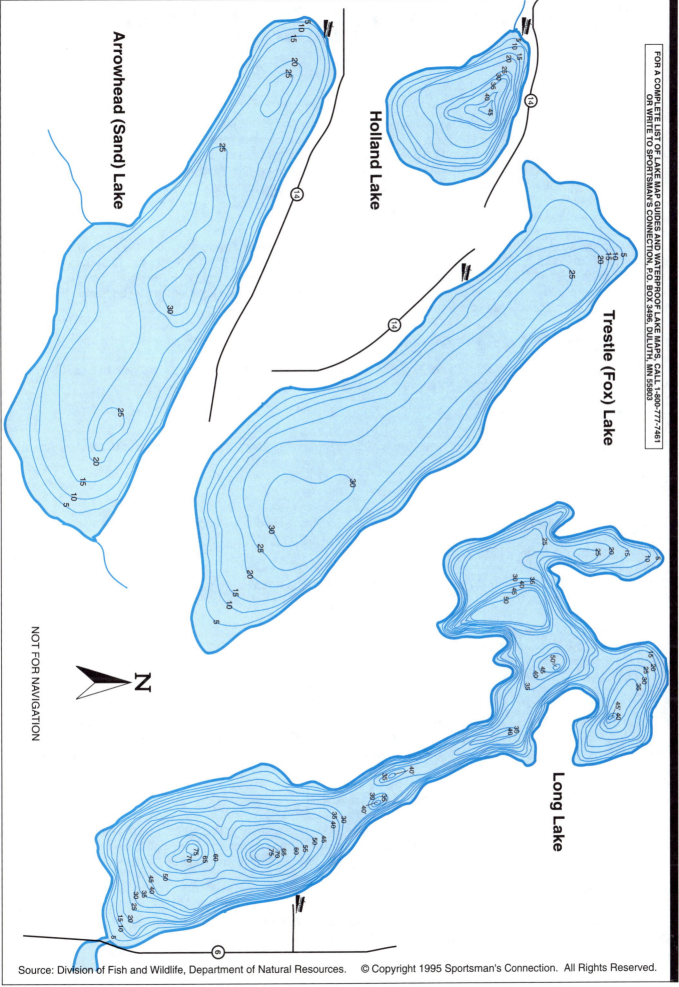

FOR A COMPLETE LIST OF LAKE MAP GUIDES AND WATERPROOF LAKE MAPS, CALL 1-800-777-7461 OR WRITE TO SPORTSMAN'S CONNECTION, P.O. BOX 3496, DULUTH, MN 55803

Arrowhead (Sand) Lake

Holland Lake

Trestle (Fox) Lake

Long Lake

N

NOT FOR NAVIGATION

LAKE WINNIBIGOSHISH

(Continued from page 6)

Auger: One to two pounders. In the fall and midsummer off of Bena Bar you catch a lot of five and six pounders. Up towards the top past Big Bend where the bar starts breaking northwest, you can find some nice ones in late summer. Tamarack Point is good around early spring in around 7-12 feet of water. Straight out from the satellite dishes there is a submerged point that gives up some fish in 8 - 12 feet of water. There's a pretty good breakline there with some weeds; pretty much a mixed bottom which seems to work pretty good.

Sportsman's Connection: How's the area off of Third River Flowage?

Auger: Again, the fish seem to follow a regular migratory pattern; coming out of the flowage up along the north shore, out on Stony Point and onto the Humps. The Humps are good all year once the fish get there - a week or two after the opener. If there are a lot of boats don't be afraid to go a little bit deeper and right along the edge. The Rock Piles are a good spot to fish with sand bottom changing to rock, back to sand and back to rock again. Out from The Gap there are weed humps that come up in the middle of summer that you can go out to and cast for Walleyes late in the evening.

Sportsman's Connection: So you can actually see the weeds; they're up above water?

Auger: Right. They're pencil weeds. Right out of The Gap towards Tamarack Point. You can't miss them because they are ringed with buoys. Some of the best fishing is right along the buoys.

Sportsman's Connection: How about Crappies?

Auger: Some in Sugar Lake but not a lot. McAvity Bay is good in the winter. Bena Bar, Highbanks and Horseshoe Bar are good for Perch in the winter.

Sportsman's Connection: What are the sizes of the Perch?

Auger: Some years are better than others. A good year will yield some up to about 14" - about a pound and a half.

Sportsman's Connection: Do they get a lot of Muskies out here?

Auger: Not a lot of Muskie. One about 46 pounds was caught recently with a Walleye rig. Seeley Point on Cut foot Sioux is a good early and late season spot.

Sportsman's Connection: How deep?

Auger: Run the breakline from 10-17 feet.

Sportsman's Connection: Big Northerns?

Auger: Out of the Winnie/Cut Foot area? Not really. A lot of 4 - 10 pounders mixed in with the snakes. There's not really enough cover for them. Sugar Lake has some. As far as the Perch go, fish the top of the Bena Bar with a jig and chub. Fish Highbanks and Bowlen in about 7 feet of water with jigs and chubs too. Winter or summer. Instead of fishing the breakline, fish the top or bottom of the bars.

Sportsman's Connection: How about the Third River Flowage itself?

Auger: I haven't fished it a heck of a lot. I know they get a lot of Northerns and some Walleyes. Down on the opposite end of the lake around the Reclaim you can find some Walleyes that move in early to spawn. They call it the Reclaim because they're reclaiming the shore there, putting in huge rocks to cut down erosion. The fish are in about 7 - 12 feet in spring.

Sportsman's Connection: How about in the summer; are they still laying in there?

Auger: They go deeper as the summer progresses, or as boat traffic increases. Like in any lake, the Walleyes shy away from light or other disturbances. Adjust the depth that you fish for them accordingly.

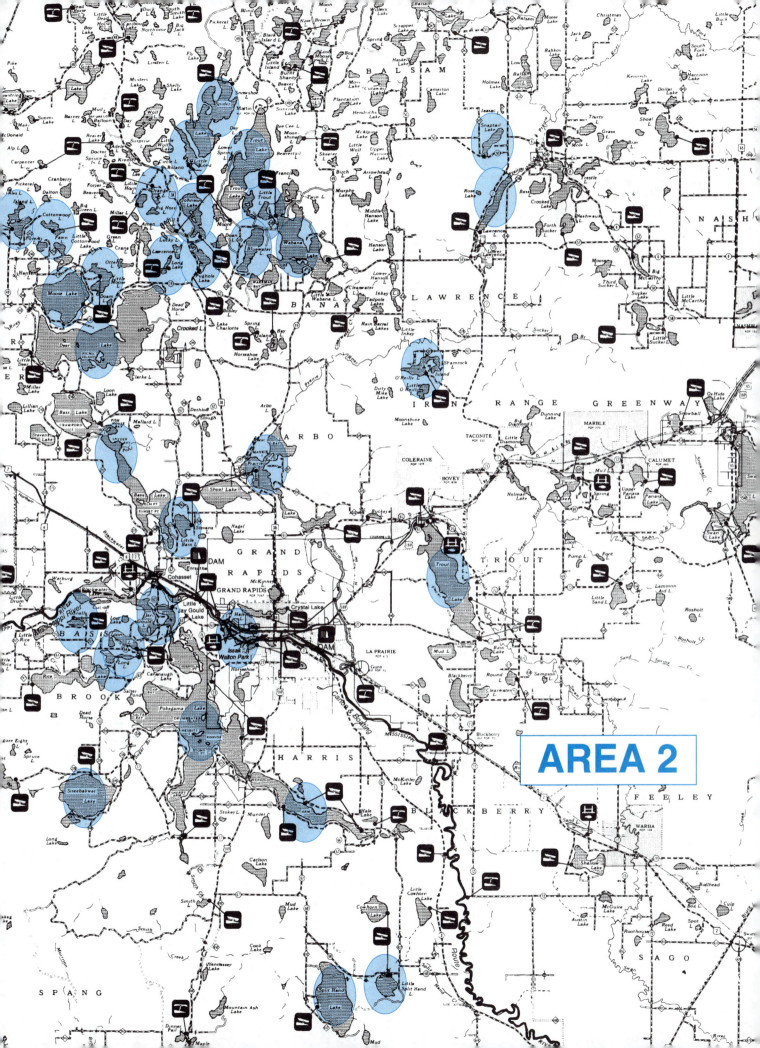

AREA 2

DEER LAKE

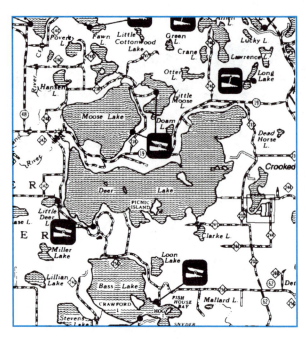

Location: Township 56, 57
Range 26, 27
Watershed: Mississippi Headwaters
Size of lake: 3,926 Acres
Shorelength: 22.3 Miles
Secchi disk (water clarity): 14.6 Ft.
Water color: Green
Cause of water color: Algae

Maximum depth: 120.0 Ft.
Median depth: NA
Accessibility: County-owned access, with ramp and dock, on SW bay
Boat Ramp: Concrete
Parking: Ample
Accommodations: Resorts

Shoreland zoning classification: Recreational Development
Dominant forest/soil type: Decid/Loam
Management class: Walleye-Centrarchid
Ecological type: Hard-water Walleye

FISH STOCKING DATA

year	species	size	# released
89	Walleye	Adult	9
89	Walleye	Fingerling	1,074
89	Walleye	Yearling	3,693
91	Walleye	Yearling	1,271
93	Walleye	Fingerling	3,724
93	Walleye	Fingerling	2,505

NET CATCH DATA

survey date: 07/23/90

species	Gill Nets # per net	Gill Nets avg fish wt. (lbs.)	Trap Nets # per set	Trap Nets avg fish wt. (lbs.)
Yellow Perch	15.9	0.23	1.2	0.18
White Sucker	1.9	1.62	-	-
Walleye	4.7	2.11	-	-
Tullibee (incl. Cisco)	0.1	0.25	-	-
Smallmouth Bass	5.3	1.31	-	-
Shorthead Red.	0.1	3.00	-	-
Rock Bass	25.6	0.37	2.2	0.22
Pumpkin. Sunfish	0.5	0.27	4.0	0.18
Northern Pike	0.8	5.85	-	-
Muskellunge	0.1	3.80	-	-
Largemouth Bass	1.1	0.69	3.1	0.34
Lake Whitefish	0.1	1.50	-	-
Common Shiner	0.1	0.10	0.1	0.10
Brown Bullhead	0.1	1.00	0.1	1.20
Bluegill	0.3	0.20	21.0	0.12
Yellow Bullhead	-	-	0.3	0.63
Bowfin (Dogfish)	-	-	0.1	6.50

LENGTH OF SELECTED SPECIES SAMPLED FROM ALL GEAR

Number of fish caught for the following length categories (inches):

species	0-5	6-8	9-11	12-14	15-19	20-24	25-29	>30	Total
Yellow Perch	-	76	61	4	-	-	-	-	141
Walleye	-	-	6	-	54	6	4	-	70
Tullibee (incl. Cisco)	-	-	2	-	-	-	-	-	2
Smallmouth Bass	-	6	19	31	23	-	-	-	79
Rock Bass	14	93	56	-	-	-	-	-	163
Pumpkin. Sunfish	2	3	-	-	-	-	-	-	5
Northern Pike	-	-	-	-	-	6	3	2	11
Muskellunge	-	-	-	-	-	-	2	-	2
Largemouth Bas	-	2	6	8	-	-	-	-	16
Lake Whitefish	-	-	-	-	1	1	-	-	2
Brown Bullhead	-	-	-	1	-	-	-	-	1
Bluegill	2	2	-	-	-	-	-	-	4

DNR COMMENTS: Northern Pike numbers stable and below statewide median. Walleye pop. down, but near median value for lake class; avg. size up to 2.1 lb; both length and age distributions good, with fair numbers of large fish. Largemouth Bass abundant, with pop. level above 3rd quartile level for lake class; good size and age distributions. Rock Bass pop. up significantly and above 3rd quartile values; size has remained constant. Bluegill and Pumpkinseed numbers up.

FISHING INFORMATION: We talked to Brian Krecklau, Pole Bender Guide Service, who guides on Deer Lake for Muskie, Walleye and Bass on a regular basis. Walleye, averaging about 1 3/4 pounds, with some up to 11 pounds, are fished with lindy rigs and minnows around the points and sunken islands found throughout the middle of the lake, including the area near Battleship Island in 18 to 23 feet of water. Slip bobber setups rigged with minnows or leeches over the underwater islands produce well at night. Floating Rapalas trolled over the mid-lake bars and shoreline structure also yield some Walleyes. Smallmouth Bass, averaging around 2 pounds, with some up to 5 pounds are also found around some of these same areas. Some 20 pound-class Northerns are caught in Deer, usually by anglers chasing Muskies, which is what the lake is known for. Weekend fishing can be relatively crowded with Muskie fishermen, but early in the week is fairly quiet. Krecklau told us that an average Deer Lake Muskie runs about 37 inches (40" is the legal minimum length), but he has seen 40 pound-class fish. The best time to chase Muskies in Deer, according to Brian, is from opening fishing, in late June into early July and again in September through early November. Brian has good success on light colored bucktails cast near the cabbage weeds. Jerk baits will raise some fish, but follows outnumber strikes when using wood. Trolling crankbaits through schools of Ciscoes can also produce some nice fish. A knowledgeable guide can increase your Muskie fishing success and improve your knowledge immensely. Give Pole Bender Guide Service a call at 1-800-622-3590 or contact Brian Krecklau at the Forest Lake Motel in Grand Rapids for your personal guided half day or whole day outing.

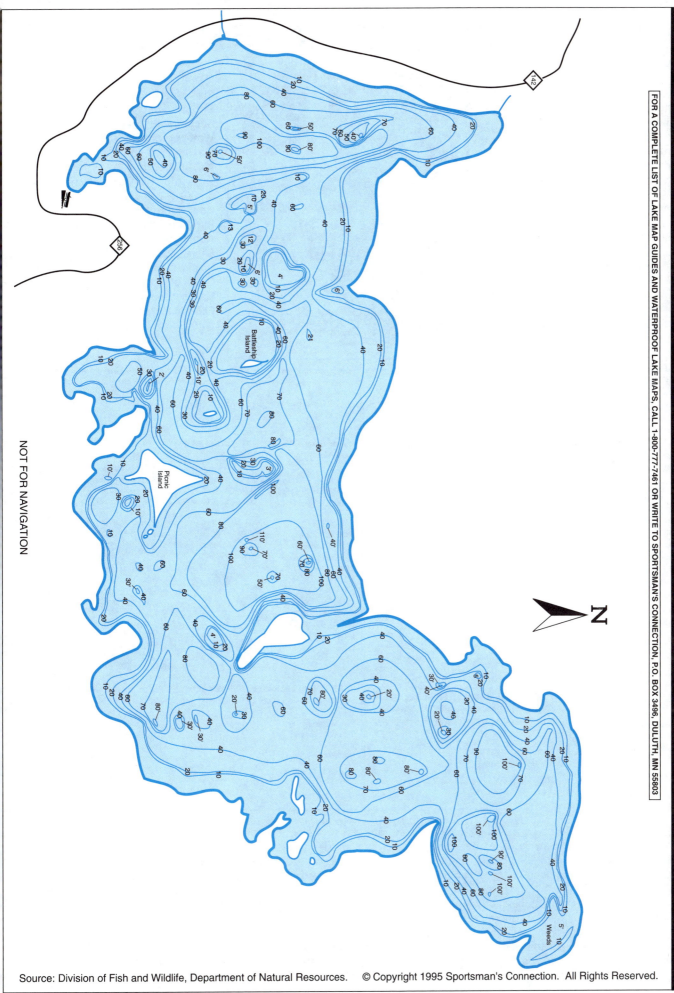

NOT FOR NAVIGATION

Battleship Island

Picnic Island

Weeds

N

FOR A COMPLETE LIST OF LAKE MAP GUIDES AND WATERPROOF LAKE MAPS, CALL 1-800-777-7461 OR WRITE TO SPORTSMAN'S CONNECTION, P.O. BOX 3496, DULUTH, MN 55803

Deer Lake

MOOSE LAKE   LITTLE MOOSE LAKE

Location: Township 57   Range 26, 27
Watershed: Mississippi Headwaters

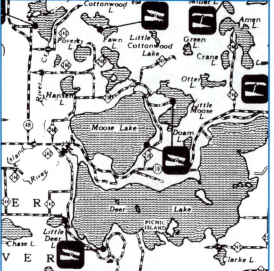

Size of lake: 1140 Acres
Shorelength: 6.7 Miles
Secchi disk (water clarity): 11.2 Ft.
Water color: Clear
Maximum depth: 61.0 Ft.
Median depth: 30.0 Ft.
Accessibility: State-owned access on E side
Boat Ramp: Concrete
Parking: Ample
Accommodations: Resorts, Campground
Shoreland zoning classif.: Rec. Dev.
Dominant forest/soil type: Decid/Loam
Cause of water color: NA
Management class: Walleye
Ecological type: Hard-water Walleye

Size of lake: 259 Acres
Shorelength: 4.1 Miles
Secchi disk (water clarity): 5.2 Ft.
Water color: NA
Maximum depth: 23.0 Ft.
Median depth: NA
Accessibility: County-owned access on W side, off Cty. Rd. 238
Boat Ramp: Earth
Parking: Limited
Accommodations: None
Shoreland zoning classif.: Rec. Dev.
Dominant forest/soil type: Decid/Loam
Cause of water color: NA
Management class: Walleye-Centrarchid
Ecological type: Centrarchid-Walleye

DNR COMMENTS:
Northern Pike pop. stable and very low with very good growth. Walleyes numerous, with excellent natural reproduction; growth good. Earlier samplings have indicated an excellent, self-sustaining Muskellunge pop. Yellow Perch, Tullibees and Crayfish remain numerous.

FISH STOCKING DATA

year	species	size	# released
89	Walleye	Fry	1,100,000
91	Walleye	Fry	1,100,000

NET CATCH DATA
survey date: 08/19/91

species	Gill Nets # per net	avg fish wt. (lbs)	Trap Nets # per set	avg fish wt. (lbs)
Yellow Perch	49.6	0.18	2.3	0.01
White Sucker	1.8	2.03	0.1	5.60
Walleye	10.4	1.17	0.9	0.80
Tullibee (incl. Cisco)	10.6	0.56	-	-
Rock Bass	3.4	0.47	1.7	0.30
Pumpkin. Sunfish	0.1	0.10	2.0	0.12
Northern Pike	1.1	3.40	0.1	3.10
Muskellunge	0.2	4.60	0.1	0.20
Largemouth Bass	-	-	0.7	0.18
Bowfin (Dogfish)	-	-	0.1	9.20
Bluegill	-	-	7.6	0.24
Black Crappie	-	-	0.7	0.20

LENGTH OF SELECTED SPECIES SAMPLED FROM ALL GEAR
Number of fish caught for the following length categories (inches):

species	0-5	6-8	9-11	12-14	15-19	20-24	25-29	>30	Total
Yellow Perch	-	101	15	-	-	-	-	-	116
Walleye	-	8	23	23	26	12	2	-	94
Tullibee (incl. Cisco)	-	13	36	32	9	-	-	-	90
Rock Bass	1	20	9	1	-	-	-	-	31
Pumpkin. Sunfish	1	-	-	-	-	-	-	-	1
Northern Pike	-	-	-	-	-	8	3	-	11
Muskellunge	-	-	-	-	-	-	1	-	1

FISH STOCKING DATA NOT AVAILABLE

NET CATCH DATA
survey date: 08/26/91

species	Gill Nets # per net	avg fish wt. (lbs)	Trap Nets # per set	avg fish wt. (lbs)
Yellow Perch	13.6	0.11	5.3	0.08
Yellow Bullhead	0.2	2.10	-	-
White Sucker	3.0	2.91	-	-
Walleye	1.8	1.18	0.3	0.50
Northern Pike	12.2	2.19	0.7	1.30
Muskellunge	0.2	3.40	-	-
Bluegill	1.2	0.60	13.7	0.29
Tiger Muskellunge	-	-	0.2	trace
Rock Bass	-	-	1.0	0.38
Pumpkin. Sunfish	-	-	3.2	0.25
Largemouth Bass	-	-	0.2	0.10
Brown Bullhead	-	-	1.0	1.55
Bowfin (Dogfish)	-	-	0.3	6.85
Black Crappie	-	-	5.3	0.59

LENGTH OF SELECTED SPECIES SAMPLED FROM ALL GEAR
Number of fish caught for the following length categories (inches):

species	0-5	6-8	9-11	12-14	15-19	20-24	25-29	>30	Total
Yellow Perch	-	67	1	-	-	-	-	-	68
Yellow Bullhead	-	-	-	1	-	-	-	-	1
Walleye	-	-	1	5	1	2	-	-	9
Northern Pike	-	-	-	-	6	52	3	-	61
Muskellunge	-	-	-	-	-	-	1	1	1
Bluegill	-	1	5	-	-	-	-	-	6

DNR COMMENTS:
Northern Pike numbers and avg. weight high; growth rates above avg. Muskellunge samplings inconclusive, but natural reproduction and hybridization may be taking place. Walleye pop. about at lake class median; spawning success has been sufficient to maintain pop. Largemouth Bass, Pumpkinseed pop.s low and stable. Bluegills up, but below lake class median; size above avg. Rock Bass pop. declining. White Suckers numerous. Bullhead pop.s low.

FISHING INFORMATION: Moose Lake and Little Moose Lake are Muskie waters that also produce some nice Northern Pike. Brian Krecklau, of Pole Bender Guide Service, fishes Deer and Moose Lake's Muskies and feels that he has better success with wood baits such as jerk baits on Moose while Deer Lake's Muskies generally prefer bucktails. Moose has a lot of shoreline cabbage weeds running out to about 14 feet of water that are productive by casting parallel to the breakline. Krecklau also told us that Moose has a reputation for larger numbers of Muskies than Deer with some in the 30 to 40 pound-class. Little Moose produces some Muskies by working the shoreline cabbage weeds and the bar in the north bay just off the creek to Moose. Northern Pike provide some excitement on both lakes between Muskie strikes (which, as any Muskie fisherman knows, can be few and far between). The lakes' forage bases and general ecological make-up seem to provide conditions for larger average sizes of fish. Walleye fishermen also fare well on Moose by working its numerous underwater islands, bars and points. Some nice Largemouth, reaching the 4 pound category, are also caught. Little Moose also has some Walleye but its Crappies, ranging in the 3/4 to 1-1/2 pound-class, provide the most action, especially right after ice out.

FOR A COMPLETE LIST OF LAKE MAP GUIDES AND WATERPROOF LAKE MAPS, CALL 1-800-777-7461 OR WRITE TO SPORTSMAN'S CONNECTION, P.O. BOX 3496, DULUTH, MN 55803

NOT FOR NAVIGATION

Moose & Little Moose Lakes

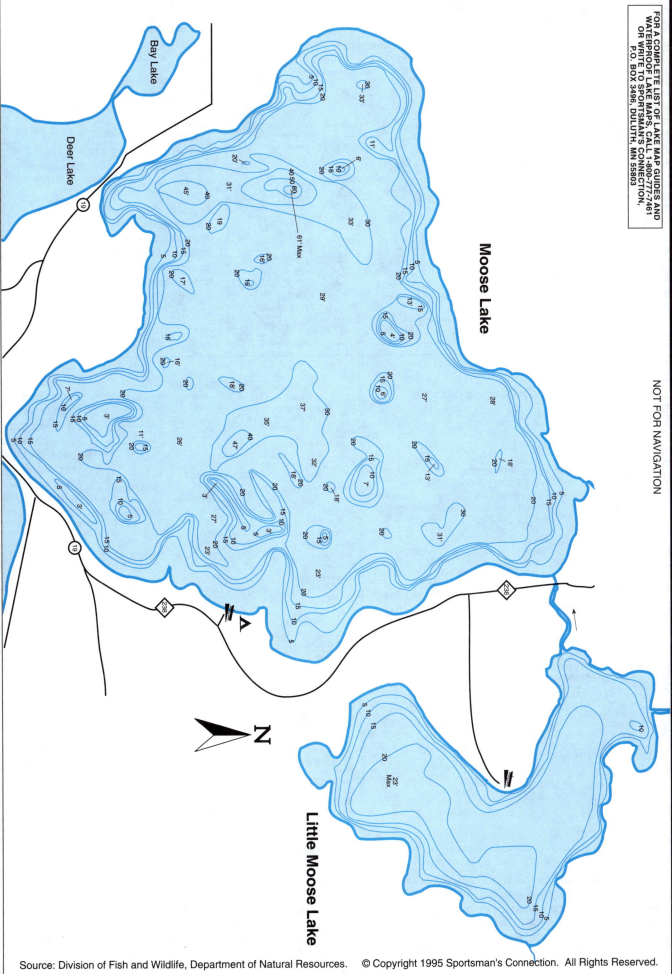

Bay Lake

Deer Lake

Moose Lake

Little Moose Lake

COTTONWOOD LAKE   ISLAND LAKE

Location: Township 57   Range 26, 27
Watershed: Mississippi Headwaters

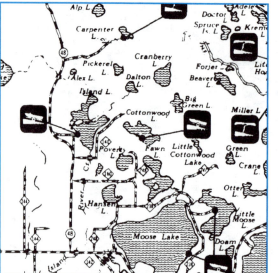

Size of lake: 109 Acres
Shorelength: 2.5 Miles
Secchi disk (water clarity): NA
Water color: Brown
Maximum depth: 40.0 Ft.
Median depth: 15.0 Ft.
Accessibility: State-owned access at campground on S side
Boat Ramp: Concrete
Parking: Ample
Accommodations: Campground
Shoreland zoning classif.: Nat. Envt.
Dominant forest/soil type: NA
Cause of water color: Bog stain
Management class: Centrarchid
Ecological type: Centrarchid

Size of lake: 256 Acres
Shorelength: 5.2 Miles
Secchi disk (water clarity): NA
Water color: Yellow-brown
Maximum depth: 31.0 Ft.
Median depth: 13.0 Ft.
Accessibility: USFS access off Co. Rd. #48
Boat Ramp: Earth
Parking: Ample
Accommodations: Resorts
Shoreland zoning classif.: Rec. Dev.
Dominant forest/soil type: Decid/Loam
Cause of water color: Swamp drainage
Management class: Walleye-Centrarchid
Ecological type: Centrarchid-Walleye

DNR COMMENTS:
Northern Pike abundance is at a high level while Perch numbers are fairly low. Panfish numbers are typical for this type of lake.

FISH STOCKING DATA NOT AVAILABLE

survey date: 06/27/83

NET CATCH DATA

species	Gill Nets # per net	Gill Nets avg fish wt. (lbs)	Trap Nets # per set	Trap Nets avg fish wt. (lbs)
Yellow Perch	4.3	0.16	0.3	0.30
Yellow Bullhead	0.3	0.70	1.5	0.58
Rock Bass	2.0	0.14	0.3	0.10
Northern Pike	16.8	1.66	1.3	0.52
Brown Bullhead	0.5	0.35	0.8	0.50
Bowfin (Dogfish)	0.3	1.80	0.8	4.73
Bluegill	0.5	0.35	5.8	0.15
Black Crappie	1.0	0.93	2.8	0.22
Pumpkin. Sunfish	-	-	2.8	0.13

LENGTH OF SELECTED SPECIES SAMPLED FROM ALL GEAR
Number of fish caught for the following length categories (inches):

species	0-5	6-8	9-11	12-14	15-19	20-24	25-29	>30	Total
Black Crappie	1	12	6	-	-	-	-	-	19
Bluegill	12	9	4	-	-	-	-	-	25
Brown Bullhead	-	2	2	1	-	-	-	-	5
Northern Pike	-	-	1	10	40	15	3	3	72
Pumpkin. Sunfish	6	5	-	-	-	-	-	-	11
Rock Bass	2	2	1	-	-	-	-	-	5
Yellow Bullhead	-	1	3	3	-	-	-	-	7
Yellow Perch	6	5	-	-	-	-	-	-	11

FISH STOCKING DATA

year	species	size	# released
91	Walleye	Fry	285,000
93	Walleye	Fry	296,400

survey date: 08/26/91

NET CATCH DATA

species	Gill Nets # per net	Gill Nets avg fish wt. (lbs)	Trap Nets # per set	Trap Nets avg fish wt. (lbs)
Yellow Perch	102.2	0.17	11.7	0.13
Yellow Bullhead	0.8	0.68	0.3	0.50
White Sucker	1.0	1.94	-	-
Walleye	1.0	3.10	0.2	0.80
Northern Pike	11.0	3.36	1.3	0.90
Brown Bullhead	1.4	1.19	0.2	1.60
Bowfin (Dogfish)	0.4	4.45	1.0	5.20
Bluegill	1.0	0.98	1.8	0.65
Black Bullhead	4.2	0.83	0.2	1.30
Pumpkin. Sunfish	-	-	0.8	0.28
Largemouth Bass	-	-	0.2	0.20
Hybrid Sunfish	-	-	0.2	0.40
Black Crappie	-	-	1.5	0.81

LENGTH OF SELECTED SPECIES SAMPLED FROM ALL GEAR
Number of fish caught for the following length categories (inches):

species	0-5	6-8	9-11	12-14	15-19	20-24	25-29	>30	Total
Yellow Perch	-	134	11	-	-	-	-	-	145
Yellow Bullhead	-	-	3	1	-	-	-	-	4
Walleye	-	-	-	2	2	1	-	-	5
Northern Pike	-	-	-	-	3	39	9	4	55
Brown Bullhead	-	-	1	6	-	-	-	-	7
Bluegill	-	-	5	-	-	-	-	-	5
Black Bullhead	-	3	9	9	-	-	-	-	21

DNR COMMENTS:
Northern Pike increasing in both numbers and size due to large forage base. Walleye pop. near median for lake class; natural reproduction poor; growth slow. Good natural reproduction taking place among Largemouth Bass. Bluegills few, but normal for Island Lake. Black Crappie near lake class median. Rough fish populations remain stable at near lake class medians.

FISHING INFORMATION: Just north of the big popular waters of Deer and Moose Lakes lie two small bodies of water that you don't hear much about. Cottonwood has a small campground that is well secluded and doesn't get much use. The lake is basically a Bass, Panfish, Northern fishery with some decent sized Crappie and Bluegill. The blowdowns and brush piles provide some exciting Largemouth and Northern fishing when the bait fish are in shallow. The Bass aren't large, typically around the 1-1/2 pound size, but there are a lot of them. Northern Pike are also numerous with some in the 8 to 10 pound-class. Island Lake is larger than Cottonwood and has some Walleye in it. Prior to the DNR's stocking efforts, Northern Pike and Perch were about the only things caught with any regularity.

Island & Cottonwood Lakes

NOT FOR NAVIGATION

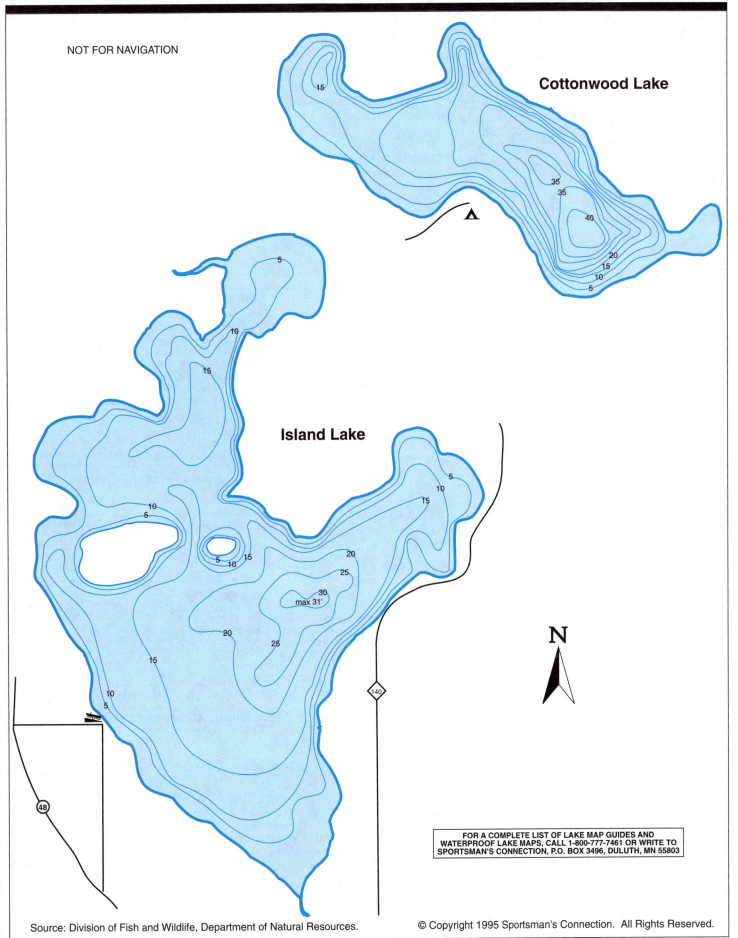

Cottonwood Lake

Island Lake

max 31'

N

Source: Division of Fish and Wildlife, Department of Natural Resources.

Location: Township 57, 58 Range 26
Watershed: Mississippi Headwaters

	PUGHOLE LAKE	LONG LAKE	ORANGE LAKE
Size of lake:	113 Acres	81 Acres	96 Acres
Shorelength:	2.4 Miles	1.5 Miles	1.8 Miles
Secchi disk (water clarity):	NA	NA	NA
Water color:	Brown	Light brown	NA
Maximum depth:	20.0 Ft.	48.0 Ft.	30.0 Ft.
Median depth:	8.0 Ft.	10.0 Ft.	11.0 Ft.
Accessibility:	State-owned public access off state Hwy. 38	Public access off Cty. Rd. 19	USFS walk-in access from Orange Lake Road
Boat Ramp:	Earth	Carry Down	Carry Down
Parking:	Ample	Side of road	Lot down on Hwy 38
Accommodations:	Wayside Rest	None	Campsite
Shoreland zoning classif.:	Rec. Dev.	Nat. Envt.	Rec. Dev.
Dominant forest/soil type:	NA	NA	NA
Cause of water color:	Bog stain	Bog Stain	NA
Management class:	Walleye-Centrarchid	Centrarchid	Centrarchid
Ecological type:	Centrarchid-Walleye	Centrarchid	Centrarchid

DNR COMMENTS:
Northern Pike have been, and remain at, very high levels. Black Crappie and Bluegill abundance, as indicated by trapnet catch, have increased dramatically from the past two assessments. Walleye fry stocking has been ineffective in recent years. Only one was caught during this assessment. It appears that fry stocking was only successful after the 1962 winterkill.

Pughole Lake

FISH STOCKING DATA

year	species	size	# released
91	Walleye	Adult	366
94	Walleye	Fingerling	2,115

NET CATCH DATA
survey date: 07/05/89

	Gill Nets		Trap Nets	
species	# per net	avg fish wt. (lbs)	# per set	avg fish wt. (lbs)
Yellow Perch	18.0	0.10	1.0	0.13
White Sucker	1.4	3.36	-	-
Walleye	0.2	6.20	-	-
Pumpkin. Sunfish	0.2	0.20	3.8	0.19
Northern Pike	12.0	2.76	1.0	1.70
Largemouth Bass	0.4	1.40	-	-
Bluegill	17.2	0.08	33.8	0.07
Black Crappie	2.0	0.14	10.8	0.26

LENGTH OF SELECTED SPECIES SAMPLED FROM ALL GEAR
Number of fish caught for the following length categories (inches):

species	0-5	6-8	9-11	12-14	15-19	20-24	25-29	>30	Total
Yellow Perch	-	89	1	-	-	-	-	-	90
Walleye	-	-	-	-	-	-	1	-	1
Pumpkin. Sunfish	-	1	-	-	-	-	-	-	1
Northern Pike	-	-	-	1	46	9	2	-	58
Largemouth Bass	-	-	1	1	-	-	-	-	2
Bluegill	54	32	-	-	-	-	-	-	86
Black Crappie	1	9	-	-	-	-	-	-	10

Long Lake

FISH STOCKING DATA NOT AVAILABLE

NET CATCH DATA
survey date: 07/01/91

	Gill Nets		Trap Nets	
species	# per net	avg fish wt. (lbs)	# per set	avg fish wt. (lbs)
Yellow Perch	13.3	0.18	2.8	0.26
White Sucker	0.3	2.50	-	-
Largemouth Bass	0.5	0.25	0.5	0.10
Bluegill	0.8	0.23	1.8	0.09
Black Crappie	-	-	0.5	0.10

LENGTH OF SELECTED SPECIES SAMPLED FROM ALL GEAR
Number of fish caught for the following length categories (inches):

species	0-5	6-8	9-11	12-14	15-19	20-24	>30	Total
Yellow Perch	-	35	20	-	-	-	-	55
Largemouth Bass	-	-	2	-	-	-	-	2
Bluegill	-	3	-	-	-	-	-	3

DNR COMMENTS:
Muskellunge have not been sampled since 1980, and it appears that stockings in 1968 and 1970 failed to produce a self-sustaining pop. Largemouth Bass sampling slightly below lake class median; catch rates down since Muskellunge introduction. Bluegills well below lake class medians. Yellow Perch present at above-median levels; however, the pop. still reflects Muskellunge predation.

Orange Lake

FISH STOCKING DATA NOT AVAILABLE

NET CATCH DATA
survey date: 08/18/92

	Gill Nets		Trap Nets	
species	# per net	avg fish wt. (lbs)	# per set	avg fish wt. (lbs)
Yellow Perch	39.8	0.36	0.3	0.30
Muskellunge	0.3	8.50	-	-
Largemouth Bass	5.8	0.57	0.3	2.80
Bluegill	03	0.50	0.8	0.27
Black Crappie	0.3	0.10	-	-
White Sucker	-	-	0.3	4.20

LENGTH OF SELECTED SPECIES SAMPLED FROM ALL GEAR
Number of fish caught for the following length categories (inches):

species	0-5	6-8	9-11	12-14	15-19	20-24	25-29	>30	Total
Yellow Perch	-	6	89	10	-	-	-	-	105
Muskellunge	-	-	-	-	-	-	1	-	1
Largemouth Bass	-	-	3	18	-	-	-	-	21
Bluegill	-	-	2	-	-	-	-	-	2
Black Crappie	1	1	-	-	-	-	-	-	2

DNR COMMENTS:
Largemouth Bass pop. up sharply to values above those for 3rd quartile; lengths in 12-19" range. Smallmouth Bass sampled only by shoreline seining. Black Crappies scarce. Bluegills below 1st quartile values. This lake contains no Northern Pike or Walleyes.

FISHING INFORMATION: These three gems are located on either side of Highway 38 and have at least one thing in common: Muskies. Years ago, Pughole held some good Muskies and locals claim that some still roam the lake's dark waters. Pughole used to be regarded as an outstanding lake but has declined in recent years. Some good Crappies can still be found and some nice Northerns are caught with one weighing in at God's Country Outfitters at 14 pounds. Orange is located in the Suomi Hills Recreation Area which is a semi-primitive non-motorized area (SMA) and is restricted accordingly with no boat motors or motorized vehicles allowed. Shoepack strain Muskies are still quite abundant in this fascinating lake. Largemouth Bass up to 5 pounds and nice Smallmouth Bass are also found. Bluegills average around 1/2 pound. We haven't heard any reports about the 1984 Crappie planting. By canoeing down to the south end of the lake you can portage a short trail to Little Horn Lake for some more excellent Largemouth Bass fishing. Long Lake's north end is also located in the SMA. It too has a history of Muskies although the fish are rare now. Largemouth fishing can be pretty good with decent numbers and sizes caught.

SPORTSMAN'S® connection Long, Orange & Pughole Lakes

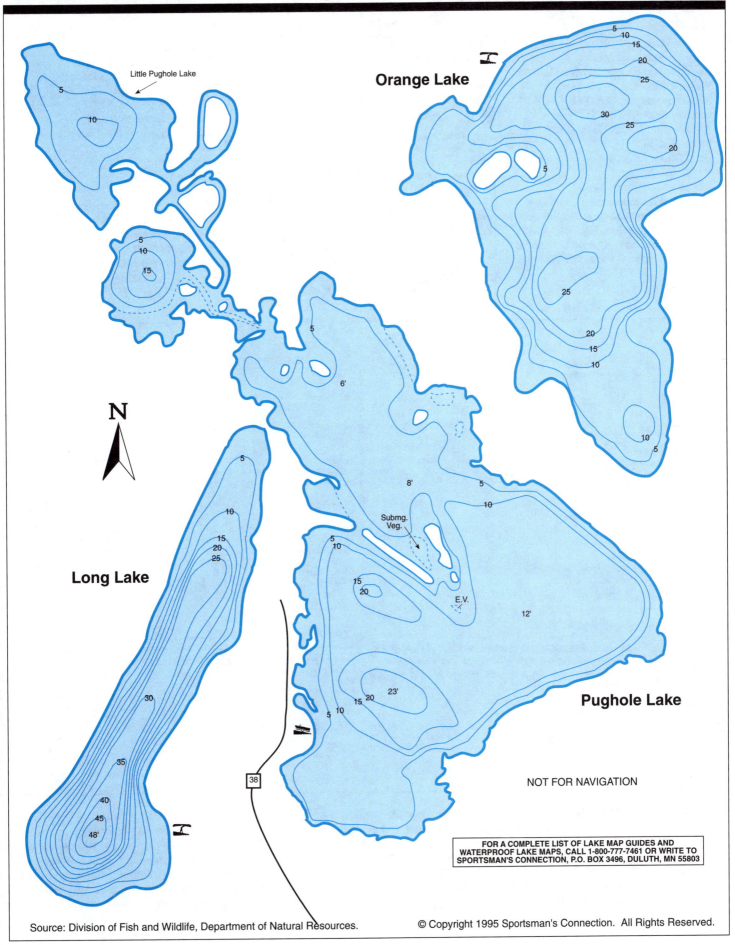

Little Pughole Lake

Orange Lake

Long Lake

N

Pughole Lake

Submg. Veg.

E.V.

38

NOT FOR NAVIGATION

Source: Division of Fish and Wildlife, Department of Natural Resources.

JOHNSON LAKE   LITTLE LONG LAKE

Size of lake: 437 Acres
Shorelength: 5.1 Miles
Secchi disk (water clarity): 15.2 Ft.
Water color: Clear
Maximum depth: 88.0 Ft.
Median depth: 20.5 Ft.
Accessibility: USFS access off Hwy. 38 on S. side
Boat Ramp: Concrete
Parking: Ample
Accommodations: None
Shoreland zoning classif.: Rec. Dev.
Dominant forest/soil type: Decid/Loam
Cause of water color: NA
Management class: Walleye-Centrarchid
Ecological type: Centrarchid-Walleye

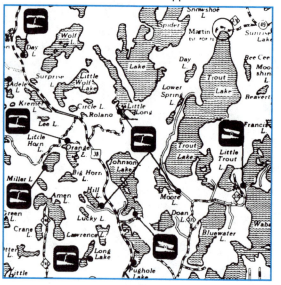

Size of lake: 274 Acres
Shorelength: 7.4 Miles
Secchi disk (water clarity): NA
Water color: Clear
Maximum depth: 61.0 Ft.
Median depth: NA
Accessibility: State-owned access on the SW side
Boat Ramp: Carry-down
Parking: Limited
Accommodations: None
Shoreland zoning classif.: Rec. Dev.
Dominant forest/soil type: Decid/Loam
Cause of water color: NA
Management class: Centrarchid
Ecological type: Centrarchid

DNR COMMENTS:
Northern Pike pop. within 1st and 3rd quartile values and stable; most fish small; growth about avg. Walleyes scarce despite fingerling stockings; growth appears very good. Largemouth Bass pop. normal for lake class; young fish compose entire sample; growth avg. Smallmouth Bass numerous, above 3rd quartile values; size small. Black Crappie likewise numerous in wide range of sizes. Bluegills small and slow-growing.

FISH STOCKING DATA

year	species	size	# released
90	Walleye	Fingerling	3,010

survey date: 8/9/91

NET CATCH DATA

	Gill Nets		Trap Nets	
species	# per net	avg fish wt. (lbs)	# per set	avg fish wt. (lbs)
Yellow Perch	0.3	0.10	0.3	0.10
White Sucker	0.3	1.80	-	-
Walleye	0.6	1.68	0.1	6.80
Smallmouth Bass	1.1	2.68	-	-
Rock Bass	2.1	0.62	0.8	0.27
Northern Pike	5.1	1.89	0.6	2.50
Largemouth Bass	1.9	0.58	1.1	0.28
Bluegill	1.1	0.20	8.0	0.11
Black Crappie	1.9	0.62	2.6	0.19
Pumpkin. Sunfish	-	-	0.3	0.10
Hybrid Sunfish	-	-	3.1	0.26

LENGTH OF SELECTED SPECIES SAMPLED FROM ALL GEAR
Number of fish caught for the following length categories (inches):

species	0-5	6-8	9-11	12-14	15-19	20-24	25-29	>30	Total
Yellow Perch	-	2	-	-	-	-	-	-	2
Walleye	-	-	1	2	1	-	-	-	4
Smallmouth Bass	-	-	-	2	5	1	-	-	8
Rock Bass	1	4	10	-	-	-	-	-	15
Northern Pike	-	-	-	-	11	22	3	-	36
Largemouth Bass	-	6	1	4	2	-	-	-	13
Bluegill	4	4	-	-	-	-	-	-	8
Black Crappie	1	3	3	6	-	-	-	-	13

FISH STOCKING DATA NOT AVAILABLE

survey date: 7/6/92

NET CATCH DATA

	Gill Nets		Trap Nets	
species	# per net	avg fish wt. (lbs)	# per set	avg fish wt. (lbs)
Yellow Perch	21.5	0.11	2.8	0.10
White Sucker	1.0	2.97	-	-
Walleye	0.8	3.46	0.1	7.50
Rock Bass	2.2	0.18	1.2	0.33
Pumpkin. Sunfish	1.5	0.17	9.8	0.17
Northern Pike	8.5	2.10	0.8	2.73
Largemouth Bass	0.3	1.55	0.3	1.43
Hybrid Sunfish	0.3	0.40	2.7	0.17
Bluegill	12.2	0.17	49.1	0.14
Black Crappie	1.5	0.37	1.3	0.41
Golden Shiner	-	-	0.1	0.10

LENGTH OF SELECTED SPECIES SAMPLED FROM ALL GEAR
Number of fish caught for the following length categories (inches):

species	0-5	6-8	9-11	12-14	15-19	20-24	25-29	>30	Total
Yellow Perch	-	110	3	-	-	-	-	-	113
Walleye	-	-	-	-	5	-	-	-	5
Rock Bass	2	12	-	-	-	-	-	-	14
Pumpkin. Sunfish	-	10	-	-	-	-	-	-	10
Northern Pike	-	-	-	-	9	39	3	-	51
Largemouth Bass	-	-	-	2	-	-	-	-	2
Hybrid Sunfish	-	2	1	-	-	-	-	-	3
Bluegill	1	30	2	-	-	-	-	-	33
Black Crappie	-	6	1	1	-	-	-	-	8

DNR COMMENTS:
Northern Pike fairly numerous at 3rd quartile level; good natural reproduction and good growth. Some Walleyes sampled. Largemouth Bass sample not believed reliable. Black Crappies present in near-avg. numbers; growth about avg. for lake class. Bluegills relatively numerous at 3rd quartile values; growth poor, however. Yellow Perch pop. at 3rd quartile level.

FISHING INFORMATION: Walleye fishing has taken off in Johnson with some 4-pound fish caught right into the summer months. Try working the north end with a jig and minnow early in the year and move onto the secondary breakline in about 15-20 feet with a leech as summer progresses. Muskies are rumored to be in the lake but not of fishable numbers. The Northerns are respectable with 3-pound fish common. Pokegama Sports weighed a 5-pound, 12-ounce Largemouth Bass a few seasons ago and Smallmouth numbers and size are good. Early in the year boats congregated on the north end of the lake fishing for 1/2 to 3/4 pound Crappies can be seen when traveling along Highway 38. Little Long Lake used to be a Muskie-rearing pond years ago and some fish still remain. The lake is better known for its Northern Pike fishing with 3-pound averages and some 15-pound-class fish. Largemouth Bass are also fairly abundant in good spawning habitat.

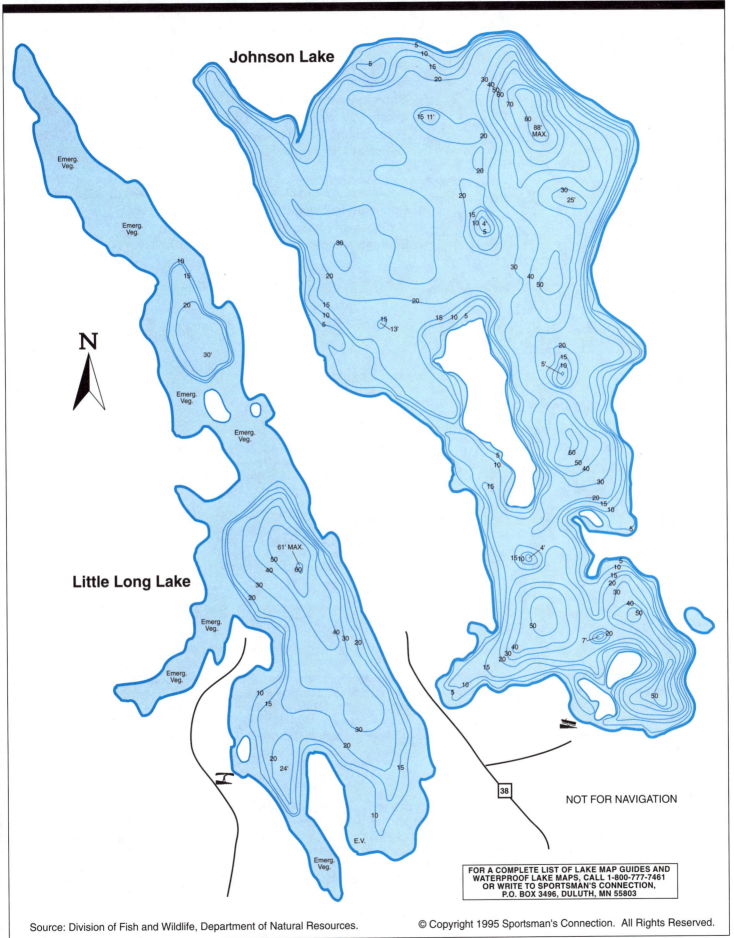

Johnson Lake

Little Long Lake

Emerg. Veg.

Emerg. Veg.

Emerg. Veg.

Emerg. Veg.

Emerg. Veg.

Emerg. Veg.

Emerg. Veg.

Emerg. Veg.

E.V.

88' MAX.

61' MAX.

N

38

NOT FOR NAVIGATION

Source: Division of Fish and Wildlife, Department of Natural Resources.

SPIDER LAKE

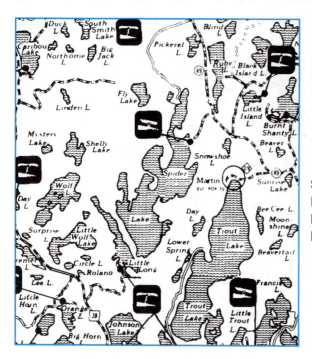

Location: Township 58
Range 25,26
Watershed: Mississippi Headwaters
Size of lake: 1,266 Acres
Shorelength: 16.0 Miles
Secchi disk (water clarity): 9.4 Ft.
Water color: Green-brown
Cause of water color: Algae

Maximum depth: 35.0 Ft.
Median depth: 12.1 Ft.
Accessibility: USFS-owned public access - NE corner
Boat Ramp: Concrete
Parking: Ample
Accommodations: Resorts

Shoreland zoning classification: Recreational Development
Dominant forest/soil type: Decid/Loam
Management class: Walleye-Centrarchid
Ecological type: Centrarchid-Walleye

FISH STOCKING DATA

year	species	size	# released
89	Walleye	Adult	4
89	Walleye	Fingerling	5,275
89	Walleye	Yearling	548
90	Walleye	Fry	1,500,000
91	Walleye	Fingerling	1,494
91	Walleye	Yearling	1,478
92	Walleye	Fry	1,400,000

NET CATCH DATA

survey date: 08/07/89

species	Gill Nets # per net	Gill Nets avg fish wt. (lbs.)	Trap Nets # per set	Trap Nets avg fish wt. (lbs.)
Yellow Perch	23.8	0.14	1.0	0.21
White Sucker	3.8	2.15	0.1	3.00
Walleye	3.7	2.05	0.1	1.20
Smallmouth Bass	3.5	0.78	0.4	0.23
Rock Bass	0.4	0.32	0.1	0.20
Pumpkin. Sunfish	4.0	0.22	4.8	0.19
Northern Pike	3.9	2.89	0.1	1.00
Muskellunge	0.3	6.27	-	-
Brown Bullhead	0.6	0.79	1.0	1.04
Bluegill	25.3	0.15	29.6	0.20
Black Crappie	1.2	0.26	18.3	0.29
Black Bullhead	0.3	0.53	-	-
Largemouth Bass	-	-	0.6	0.22

LENGTH OF SELECTED SPECIES SAMPLED FROM ALL GEAR

Number of fish caught for the following length categories (inches):

species	0-5	6-8	9-11	12-14	15-19	20-24	25-29	>30	Total
Yellow Perch	-	102	18	-	-	-	-	-	120
Walleye	-	-	1	12	16	13	2	-	44
Smallmouth Bass	-	11	8	16	7	-	-	-	42
Rock Bass	-	4	1	-	-	-	-	-	5
Pumpkin. Sunfish	9	39	-	-	-	-	-	-	48
Northern Pike	-	-	-	-	4	32	10	1	47
Muskellunge	-	-	-	-	-	-	1	1	2
Brown Bullhead	-	-	-	8	-	-	-	-	8
Bluegill	27	90	1	-	-	-	-	-	118
Black Crappie	3	6	5	-	-	-	-	-	14
Black Bullhead	-	1	2	-	-	-	-	-	3

DNR COMMENTS: Northern Pike down about 40% from previous samplings; avg. weight, 2.6 lb.; growth good; Walleyes on the increase; most of sample corresponds to years in which stockings occurred; growth rate about avg. for all age groups. Smallmouth Bass pop. increasing; sample catch is highest ever recorded for this lake; weight, 0.8 lb.; growth rates slightly below avg. Black Crappie and Bluegills at all-time highs; Crappies at 7.5-8.9"; Bluegills, 3.5-8.4"; growth rates below avg.; Pumpkinseed pop. about normal for lake class. White Sucker, Yellow Perch pop.s down, likely due to increases in predator species. Black and Brown Bullheads and Rock Bass pop.s small.

FISHING INFORMATION: Spider Lake has a long history of being an all-around good fishing lake with good numbers and sizes of Walleye, Bass, Northern, Muskie and Panfish. Brian Krecklau, of Pole Bender Guide Service, who guides on the lake, stated that fishing is usually either on or off, depending upon when you're there. He has guided parties that filled out on 1-1/2 to 6 pound Walleyes and he's been there when you can't buy a bite. When Walleye fishing is slow, the plump Crappies and Bluegills can usually be enticed into biting. Crappies in the 1-pound class are pretty abundant. The Smallies are real nice and Largemouth are also caught, although less frequently. Spider is a designated Muskie lake with some of respectable size while Northern Pike, many in the 5 to 10 pound-class and some 20 pounders, provide some steady action.

NOT FOR NAVIGATION

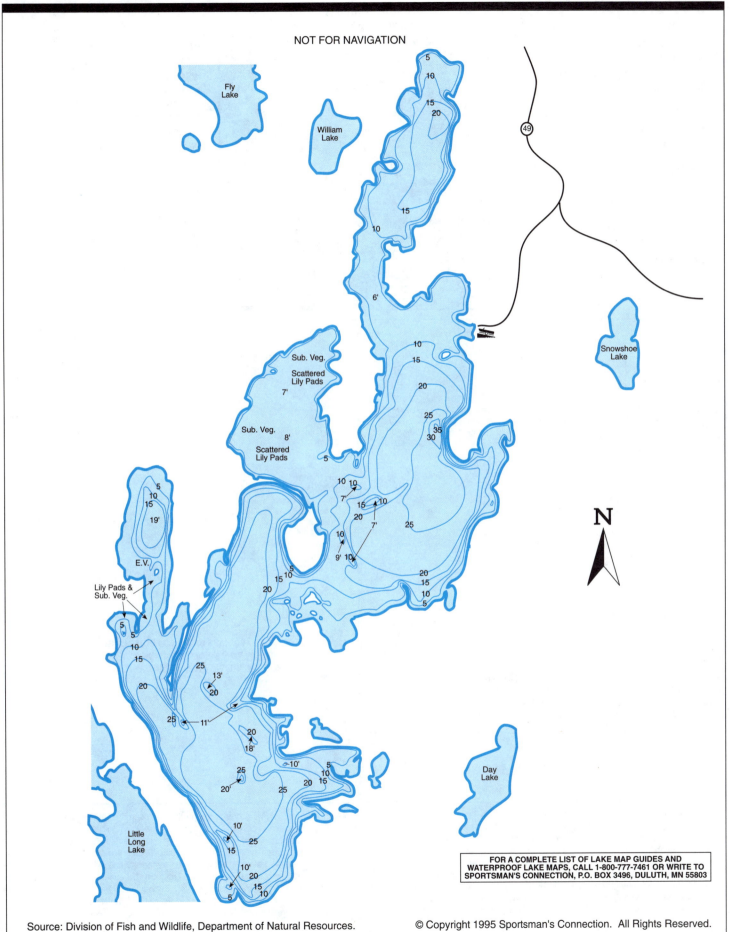

Source: Division of Fish and Wildlife, Department of Natural Resources.

TROUT LAKE   LITTLE TROUT LAKE

Location: Township 57, 58   Range 25
Watershed: Prairie-Willow

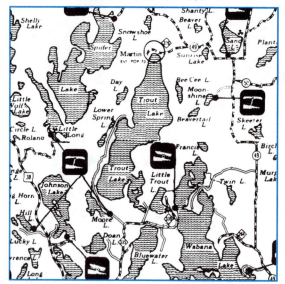

Size of lake: 1,792 Acres
Shorelength: 13.1 Miles
Secchi disk (water clarity): 12.6 Ft.
Water color: Blue-green
Maximum depth: 157.0 Ft.
Median depth: 48.0 Ft.
Accessibility: County-owned access at Kastner's Resort on N side
Boat Ramp: Earth
Parking: Toll on parking
Accommodations: Resort, 3 Chippewa Natl. Forest campsites
Shoreland zoning classif.: Rec. Dev.
Dominant forest/soil type: Decid/Loam
Cause of water color: Carbonates
Management class: Lake Trout
Ecological type: Trout

Size of lake: 78 Acres
Shorelength: 1.6 Miles
Secchi disk (water clarity): 19.6 Ft.
Water color: Clear
Maximum depth: 90.0 Ft.
Median depth: 33.0 Ft.
Accessibility: Access from road over inlet; access from Wabana Lake through inlet
Boat Ramp: None
Parking: Limited
Accommodations: None
Shoreland zoning classif.: Rec. Dev.
Dominant forest/soil type: NA
Cause of water color: NA
Management class: Centrarchid
Ecological type: Centrarchid

DNR COMMENTS:
Gillnet sampling achieved a Catch Per Unit of Effort pf 2.2 fish; because previous samplings were dissimilar, comparisons cannot be made; natural reproduction appears to be taking place, but accuracy of samples is in question. Splake sampled at 0.6 fish/gillnet set; sizes range from 21.8-26.5". Bluegills relatively numerous for this lake; mean length small and growth slow. Tullibees numerous.

FISH STOCKING DATA

year	species	size	# released
89	Lake Trout	Yearling	10,008
89	Splake	Fingerling	28,272
90	Lake Trout	Yearling	11,000
91	Lake Trout	Yearling	16,000
91	Splake	Fingerling	43,690
92	Splake	Fingerling	45,000
93	Lake Trout	Yearling	8,874
93	Splake	Fingerling	30,640
94	Splake	Fingerling	43,820

NET CATCH DATA
survey date: 08/13/90

species	Gill Nets # per net	Gill Nets avg fish wt. (lbs)	Trap Nets # per set	Trap Nets avg fish wt. (lbs)
Yellow Perch	0.1	0.20	0.6	0.22
White Sucker	0.5	2.84	-	-
Walleye	0.1	4.75	-	-
Tullibee (incl. Cisco)	41.9	0.10	-	-
Splake	0.6	5.30	-	-
Rock Bass	0.1	0.40	3.4	0.18
Northern Pike	0.5	5.08	0.1	4.00
Largemouth Bass	0.3	1.85	2.0	0.33
Lake Trout	2.2	3.17	-	-
Pumpkin. Sunfish	-	-	0.5	0.14
Hybrid Sunfish	-	-	2.6	0.21
Green Sunfish	-	-	0.6	0.13
Bluegill	-	-	19.8	0.19
Black Crappie	-	-	0.1	0.20

LENGTH OF SELECTED SPECIES SAMPLED FROM ALL GEAR
Number of fish caught for the following length categories (inches):

species	0-5	6-8	9-11	12-14	15-19	20-24	25-29	>30	Total
Yellow Perch	-	2	-	-	-	-	-	-	2
Walleye	-	-	-	-	2	-	-	-	2
Tullibee (incl. Cisco)	-	117	2	-	-	-	-	-	119
Splake	-	1	-	-	-	3	5	-	9
Rock Bass	-	1	1	-	-	-	-	-	2
Northern Pike	-	-	-	-	-	2	3	1	6
Largemouth Bass	-	-	2	2	-	-	-	-	4
Lake Trout	-	6	6	-	6	6	6	2	32

FISH STOCKING DATA NOT AVAILABLE

NET CATCH DATA
survey date: 07/13/81

species	Gill Nets # per net	Gill Nets avg fish wt. (lbs)	Trap Nets # per set	Trap Nets avg fish wt. (lbs)
Yellow Perch	0.5	0.15	-	-
White Sucker	0.5	2.10	-	-
Tullibee (incl. Cisco)	34.3	0.22	-	-
Splake	0.3	0.50	-	-
Rock Bass	0.3	0.10	4.0	0.22
Northern Pike	0.3	4.50	0.3	1.50
Largemouth Bass	0.3	0.20	2.0	0.43
Lake Trout	0.3	5.60	-	-
Pumpkin. Sunfish	-	-	4.0	0.18
Bluegill	-	-	48.5	0.13

LENGTH OF SELECTED SPECIES SAMPLED FROM ALL GEAR
Number of fish caught for the following length categories (inches):

species	0-5	6-8	9-11	12-14	15-19	20-24	25-29	>30	Total
Bluegill	26	109	1	-	-	-	-	-	136
Lake Trout	-	-	-	-	-	1	-	-	1
Largemouth Bass	-	7	-	2	-	-	-	-	9
Northern Pike	-	-	-	-	-	1	1	-	2
Pumpkin. Sunfish	-	16	-	-	-	-	-	-	16
Rock Bass	3	13	1	-	-	-	-	-	17
Splake	-	-	-	1	-	-	-	-	1
Tullibee (incl. Cisco)	-	21	113	3	-	-	-	-	137
Yellow Perch	-	2	-	-	-	-	-	-	2

DNR COMMENTS:
Little Trout has a very good population of Cisco. Bluegills are way over state and local averages. Northern Pike are under the medians. Bass population is at a good level.

FISHING INFORMATION: Trout Lake, located within the Trout Lake Semi-primitive Non-motorized Area (SNA), is one of the prettiest lakes in the Chippewa National Forest with very little development and clear blue water. There are three primitive campsites on the lake. The lake is accessible by motorized vehicles on the north end, but a four wheel drive and small boats are recommended due to the steep ramp and sugar sand landing. A small parking fee is required at Kastner's Resort. Many people access the lake by launching at one of Wabana Lake's landings and traveling through Little Trout. During the summer months, Lake Trout and Splake are caught in Trout Lake by anglers using downriggers to get down deep, with spoons and floating rapalas. Earlier in the year, when the Lakers' preferred water temperature is still near the surface, jigging dead smelt or trolling rapalas and spoons behind planer boards works well. Brian, at the Forest Lake Motel, told us that Trout can be easier to locate in the winter through the ice by jigging or live bait fishing with shiners. Walleyes don't receive much attention from anglers, but they average 2 to 3 pounds and there are some trophy sized fish. Northerns fattening up on the Tullibees average 5 to 6 pounds according to Brian, who also guides on several of the lakes in the area. Twenty-pound class Northerns are taken occasionally. Little Trout Lake also gives up some Lakers and Splake. Largemouth Bass and Panfish are plentiful, although the Bluegills run on the small side.

Trout & Little Trout Lakes

N

FOR A COMPLETE LIST OF LAKE MAP GUIDES AND WATERPROOF LAKE MAPS, CALL 1-800-777-7461 OR WRITE TO SPORTSMAN'S CONNECTION, P.O. BOX 3496, DULUTH, MN 55803

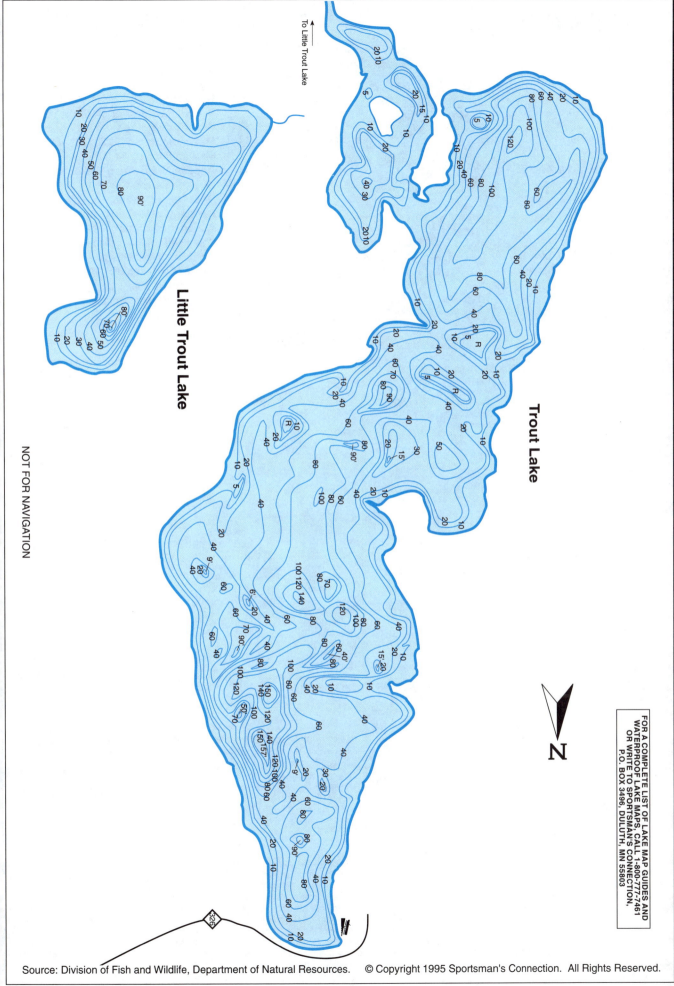

Little Trout Lake

Trout Lake

To Little Trout Lake

NOT FOR NAVIGATION

Source: Division of Fish and Wildlife, Department of Natural Resources.

WABANA LAKE   BLUEWATER LAKE

Location: Township 57   Range 25
Watershed: Prairie-Willow

Size of lake: 2,146 Acres
Shorelength: 23.2 Miles
Secchi disk (water clarity): 12.6 Ft.
Water color: Clear
Maximum depth: 115.0 Ft.
Median depth: 26.0 Ft.
Accessibility: State-owned access on NW and SE corners
Boat Ramp: (2) Earth
Parking: SE: 6-8 vehicles
         N: 3-4 vehicles
Accommodations: Resorts
Shoreland zoning classif.: Rec. Dev.
Dominant forest/soil type: Decid/Loam
Cause of water color: NA
Management class: Walleye-Centrarchid
Ecological type: Centrarchid-Walleye

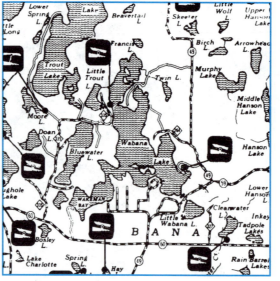

Size of lake: 356 Acres
Shorelength: 4.2 Miles
Secchi disk (water clarity): 16.7 Ft.
Water color: Clear
Maximum depth: 120.0 Ft.
Median depth: 54.2 Ft.
Accessibility: From Wakeman Bay, Wabana Lake
Boat Ramp: None
Parking: At Wabana Lake
Accommodations: Resort
Shoreland zoning classif.: Rec. Dev.
Dominant forest/soil type: Decid/Loam
Cause of water color: NA
Management class: Lake Trout
Ecological type: Trout

DNR COMMENTS: Northern Pike pop. between 1st and 3rd quartile values for lake class; wide range of sizes, with mode at 25"; growth very fast through age 4, then avg. Walleye pop. between 1st and 3rd quartile values for lake class; size range wide, with mode at 16"; growth good. Largemouth Bass very abundant, but small; growth about avg. Smallmouth Bass sampled in small numbers. Bluegills very abundant; growth well below avg.

FISH STOCKING DATA

year	species	size	# released
90	Walleye	Fingerling	1,413
90	Walleye	Yearling	1,541
92	Walleye	Fingerling	22,813
92	Walleye	Yearling	16
94	Walleye	Fingerling	9,620

NET CATCH DATA
survey date: 07/16/90

species	Gill Nets # per net	Gill Nets avg fish wt. (lbs)	Trap Nets # per set	Trap Nets avg fish wt. (lbs)
Yellow Perch	4.0	0.16	0.1	0.10
Yellow Bullhead	0.1	1.00	0.1	0.80
White Sucker	0.5	2.19	-	-
Walleye	4.3	1.97	0.2	3.25
Tullibee (incl. Cisco)	5.3	0.35	-	-
Smallmouth Bass	0.3	1.24	-	-
Rock Bass	12.3	0.28	2.2	0.30
Pumpkin. Sunfish	2.5	0.23	0.5	0.36
Northern Pike	3.5	3.94	0.1	5.00
Largemouth Bass	3.6	0.51	0.4	0.28
Hybrid Sunfish	0.2	0.23	3.1	0.20
Green Sunfish	0.2	0.07	-	-
Bluegill	16.7	0.20	0.1	0.10
Black Crappie	0.6	0.30	-	-
Black Bullhead	0.1	0.55	-	-
Coho Salmon	-	-	0.1	0.10

LENGTH OF SELECTED SPECIES SAMPLED FROM ALL GEAR
Number of fish caught for the following length categories (inches):

species	0-5	6-8	9-11	12-14	15-19	20-24	25-29	>30	Total
Yellow Perch	-	39	20	-	-	-	-	-	59
Yellow Bullhead	-	-	-	1	-	-	-	-	1
Walleye	-	-	10	1	35	14	1	-	61
Tullibee (incl. Cisco)	-	24	27	29	-	-	-	-	80
Smallmouth Bass	-	-	-	3	2	-	-	-	5
Rock Bass	11	88	26	-	-	-	-	-	125
Pumpkin. Sunfish	5	33	-	-	-	-	-	-	38
Northern Pike	-	-	-	-	1	17	28	5	51
Largemouth Bass	-	4	38	11	-	-	-	-	53
Hybrid Sunfish	1	2	-	-	-	-	-	-	3
Green Sunfish	3	-	-	-	-	-	-	-	3
Bluegill	11	86	3	-	-	-	-	-	100
Black Crappie	1	3	5	-	-	-	-	-	9
Black Bullhead	-	1	1	-	-	-	-	-	2

FISH STOCKING DATA

year	species	size	# released
89	Lake Trout	Yearling	808
90	Lake Trout	Yearling	700
91	Lake Trout	Yearling	1,000
93	Lake Trout	Yearling	1,820

NET CATCH DATA
survey date: 08/05/91

species	Gill Nets # per net	Gill Nets avg fish wt. (lbs)	Trap Nets # per set	Trap Nets avg fish wt. (lbs)
White Sucker	0.4	3.16	-	-
Tullibee (incl. Cisco)	0.5	0.17	-	-
Smallmouth Bass	0.1	0.10	0.3	0.15
Lake Trout	1.3	4.55	-	-
Green Sunfish	0.8	1.61	-	-
Yellow Perch	-	-	0.7	0.22
Rock Bass	-	-	0.9	0.32
Largemouth Bass	-	-	1.1	0.50
Hybrid Sunfish	-	-	3.9	0.19
Bluegill	-	-	8.1	0.15
Black Bullhead	-	-	0.1	0.10

LENGTH OF SELECTED SPECIES SAMPLED FROM ALL GEAR
Number of fish caught for the following length categories (inches):

species	0-5	6-8	9-11	12-14	15-19	20-24	25-29	>30	Total
Tullibee (incl. Cisco)	-	4	1	-	1	-	-	-	6
Smallmouth Bass	-	-	2	2	6	-	-	-	10
Lake Trout	-	-	2	2	2	2	7	-	15
Green Sunfish	1	-	-	-	-	-	-	-	1

DNR COMMENTS: Lake Trout pop. down and below management target level; cause of decline unclear. Largemouth Bass and Green Sunfish levels above statewide means, with Largemouth growing faster than normal. Smallmouth Bass near median levels, with slow growth. Hybrid Sunfish catch above statewide mean. Tullibees, White Suckers, Black Bullheads, Rock Bass, and Bluegills below statewide means.

FISHING INFORMATION: Wabana's deep, clear waters hold a wide variety of fish species including some nice Bass (both Largemouth and Smallmouth), Walleyes averaging 1-1/2 pounds, with some 8 to 9 pounders, good Northern in the 5 pound-plus class and some nice-sized Crappies. Although Wabana has depths reaching 115 feet, Lake Trout are not present. Steep dropoffs and clear water can make the lake difficult to fish. Anglers have better success catching Walleyes in low-light conditions and at night. Wabana's Bass fishing is excellent with good numbers and nice sizes of Largemouth and Smallmouth. Underwater islands and other structure on the lake can be overwhelming. You can save yourself a lot of time and improve your fishing success by hiring a guide the first time or two on the lake. Brian, of the Pole Bender Guide Service, who knows Wabana and other lakes in the region very well, provides half and full day trips at reasonable rates (see directory of services near the end of this book for phone numbers and addresses). Bluewater can be reached via the channel from Wabana's Wakeman Bay. Lake Trout can be found in Bluewater by following its preferred water temperature range of around 50 degrees F as the season progresses. Early in the season, when area lakes' Walleyes may still be in their post-spawn funk, Lake Trout are often still in shallow water where they can be more easily located. Later in the season, getting down deep is the key. Two ounce jigs on braided line or downriggers rigged with spoons, floating Rapalas and other attractants can be effective.

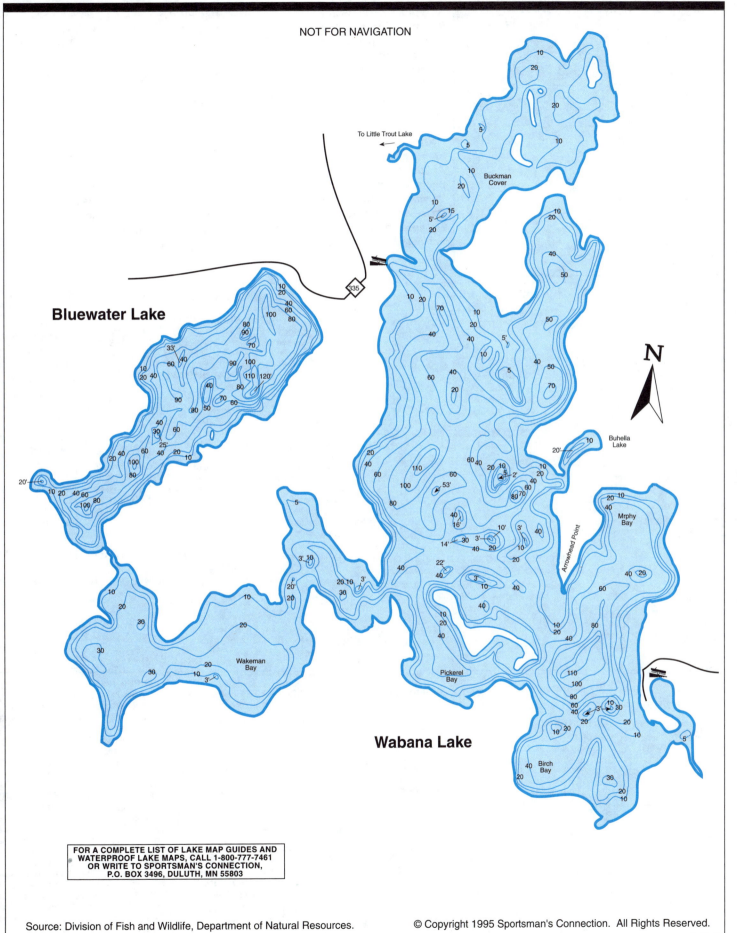

NOT FOR NAVIGATION

Source: Division of Fish and Wildlife, Department of Natural Resources.

Location: Township 56, 57, 58   Range 24
Watershed: Prairie-Willow

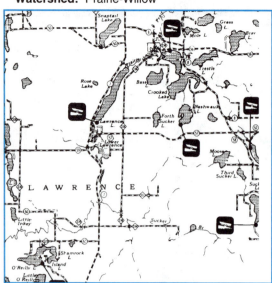

	LAWRENCE LAKE	SNAPTAIL LAKE	O'REILLY LAKE
Size of lake:	382 Acres	156 Acres	198 Acres
Shorelength:	5.7 Miles	5.0 Miles	3.1 Miles
Secchi disk (water clarity):	5.9 Ft.	NA	7.2 Ft.
Water color:	Brown	Light brown	Clear
Maximum depth:	32.0 Ft.	68.0 Ft.	79.0 Ft.
Median depth:	NA	28.0 Ft.	22.0 Ft.
Accessibility:	9 miles N of Taconite, MN; state-owned	State-owned access on S side off Cty. Rd. 50	State-owned public access on S side off Hwy. 7.
Boat Ramp:	Earth	Gravel	Earth
Parking:	Ample	Side of road	Ample
Accommodations:	Resort	None	Park
Shoreland zoning classif.:	Rec. Dev.	Rec. Dev.	Rec. Dev.
Dominant forest/soil type:	Decid/Wet	NA	Decid/Loam
Cause of water color:	Bog drainage	Bog stain	None
Management class:	Walleye-Centrarchid	Walleye-Centrarchid	Centrarchid
Ecological type:	Centrarchid-Walleye	Centrarchid	Centrarchid

DNR COMMENTS:
The Northern Pike net catch is below 1st quartile range. Yellow Bullhead and Pumpkinseed pop.s below 1st quartile. Bluegill pop. low as well, and previous samplings show a low and stable pop. for this species.

Lawrence Lake

FISH STOCKING DATA

year	species	size	# released
90	Walleye	Fingerling	3,875
92	Walleye	Fingerling	17,979
92	Walleye	Yearling	120

survey date: 07/15/91

NET CATCH DATA

	Gill Nets		Trap Nets	
species	# per net	avg fish wt. (lbs)	# per set	avg fish wt. (lbs)
Yellow Perch	10.5	0.11	1.5	0.17
White Sucker	1.5	1.11	0.4	2.73
Walleye	1.5	1.00	0.1	2.50
Silver Redhorse	0.3	2.05	-	-
Rock Bass	0.2	0.90	-	-
Northern Pike	2.5	2.12	0.6	2.00
Bluegill	0.2	0.20	3.8	0.23
Black Crappie	2.8	0.21	5.0	0.22
Yellow Bullhead	-	-	0.1	1.10
Pumpkin. Sunfish	-	-	0.3	0.15
Hybrid Sunfish	-	-	0.1	0.60

LENGTH OF SELECTED SPECIES SAMPLED FROM ALL GEAR
Number of fish caught for the following length categories (inches):

species	0-5	6-8	9-11	12-14	15-19	20-24	25-29	>30	Total
Yellow Perch	-	58	5	-	-	-	-	-	63
Walleye	-	-	1	6	1	1	-	-	9
Rock Bass	-	-	1	-	-	-	-	-	1
Northern Pike	-	-	-	-	4	9	2	-	15
Bluegill	-	1	-	-	-	-	-	-	1
Black Crappie	-	15	2	-	-	-	-	-	17

Snaptail Lake

FISH STOCKING DATA

year	species	size	# released
90	Walleye	Yearling	165
92	Walleye	Fingerling	2,700

survey date: 06/20/88

NET CATCH DATA

	Gill Nets		Trap Nets	
species	# per net	avg fish wt. (lbs)	# per set	avg fish wt. (lbs)
Yellow Perch	9.5	0.09	-	-
White Sucker	0.5	1.50	-	-
Walleye	0.3	0.30	0.3	3.50
Tullibee (incl. Cisco)	1.5	2.80	-	-
Northern Pike	4.5	3.48	0.5	0.45
Largemouth Bass	0.3	0.30	0.3	0.30
Bluegill	1.0	0.10	42.3	0.08
Black Crappie	1.5	0.28	1.8	0.26
Yellow Bullhead	-	-	5.0	0.73
Pumpkin. Sunfish	-	-	3.3	0.12
Hybrid Sunfish	-	-	0.5	0.25

LENGTH OF SELECTED SPECIES SAMPLED FROM ALL GEAR
Number of fish caught for the following length categories (inches):

species	0-5	6-8	9-11	12-14	15-19	20-24	25-29	>30	Total
Yellow Perch	-	38	-	-	-	-	-	-	38
Walleye	-	-	1	-	-	-	-	-	1
Tullibee (incl. Cisco)	-	-	-	-	6	-	-	-	6
Northern Pike	-	-	-	-	5	4	9	-	18
Largemouth Bass	-	-	1	-	-	-	-	-	1
Bluegill	1	3	-	-	-	-	-	-	4
Black Crappie	-	4	2	-	-	-	-	-	6

DNR COMMENTS:
Northern Pike population above state and local medians. Bluegills are abundant but very small. Northern Cisco and Yellow Perch numbers are down, compared to 1978 survey. Bullheads are common. Walleye population appears to be low.

O'Reilly Lake

FISH STOCKING DATA NOT AVAILABLE

survey date: 08/31/92

NET CATCH DATA

	Gill Nets		Trap Nets	
species	# per net	avg fish wt. (lbs)	# per set	avg fish wt. (lbs)
Yellow Perch	0.2	0.10	0.3	0.40
White Sucker	2.4	2.63	-	-
Walleye	0.2	1.80	-	-
Tullibee (incl. Cisco)	0.8	0.28	-	-
Smallmouth Bass	0.2	1.00	-	-
Rock Bass	6.2	0.38	2.5	0.15
Pumpkin. Sunfish	0.2	0.10	-	-
Northern Pike	2.8	3.61	0.3	3.00
Largemouth Bass	1.4	0.90	1.3	0.76
Hybrid Sunfish	0.2	0.50	-	-
Bluegill	5.4	0.07	12.5	0.11
Black Crappie	3.4	0.21	1.0	0.20
Common Shiner	-	-	0.3	1.20

LENGTH OF SELECTED SPECIES SAMPLED FROM ALL GEAR
Number of fish caught for the following length categories (inches):

species	0-5	6-8	9-11	12-14	15-19	20-24	25-29	>30	Total
Yellow Perch	2	-	-	-	-	-	-	-	2
Walleye	-	-	-	-	1	-	-	-	1
Tullibee (incl. Cisco)	-	-	4	-	-	-	-	-	4
Smallmouth Bass	-	-	-	1	-	-	-	-	1
Rock Bass	1	21	9	-	-	-	-	-	31
Pumpkin. Sunfish	2	-	-	-	-	-	-	-	2
Northern Pike	-	-	-	-	-	6	8	-	14
Largemouth Bass	-	2	4	1	2	-	-	-	9
Hybrid Sunfish	-	1	1	-	-	-	-	-	2
Bluegill	24	4	-	-	-	-	-	-	28
Black Crappie	-	14	5	-	-	-	-	-	19

DNR COMMENTS: Northern Pike pop. is below median for lake class; growth normal and good fish size, with avg. weight of 3.6 lb. Walleye pop. is marginal even though fry were stocked in 1986, '88; low Yellow Perch pop. may be limiting Walleye forage and viability. Tullibee pop. below 1st quartile values.

FISHING INFORMATION: Lawrence Lake has been receiving significant plantings of fry, fingerling and yearling Walleye over the last several years, which are providing anglers with some steady, if not spectacular, Walleye fishing. One to 2 pounders are the norm. Crappies average about 1/2 pound and some of the Bluegills run to 3/4 pound. The lake's structure is fairly basic; most anglers work the subtle points and dropoffs. Snaptail is beginning to produce a few Walleyes. Crappies run about 3 to the pound. Northern fishing can be pretty good with good numbers of 3 pound-plus fish. Bass might also be worth trying. O'Reilly is a pretty lake with some good Largemouth and Northern Pike. The folks at Hollywood Bait in Coleraine told us that the lake's heavy Cisco population keeps the fish well fed and tough to catch. Try fishing early in the morning before the fish have had a chance to gorge themselves.

Lawrence, Snaptail, & O'Reilly Lakes

NOT FOR NAVIGATION

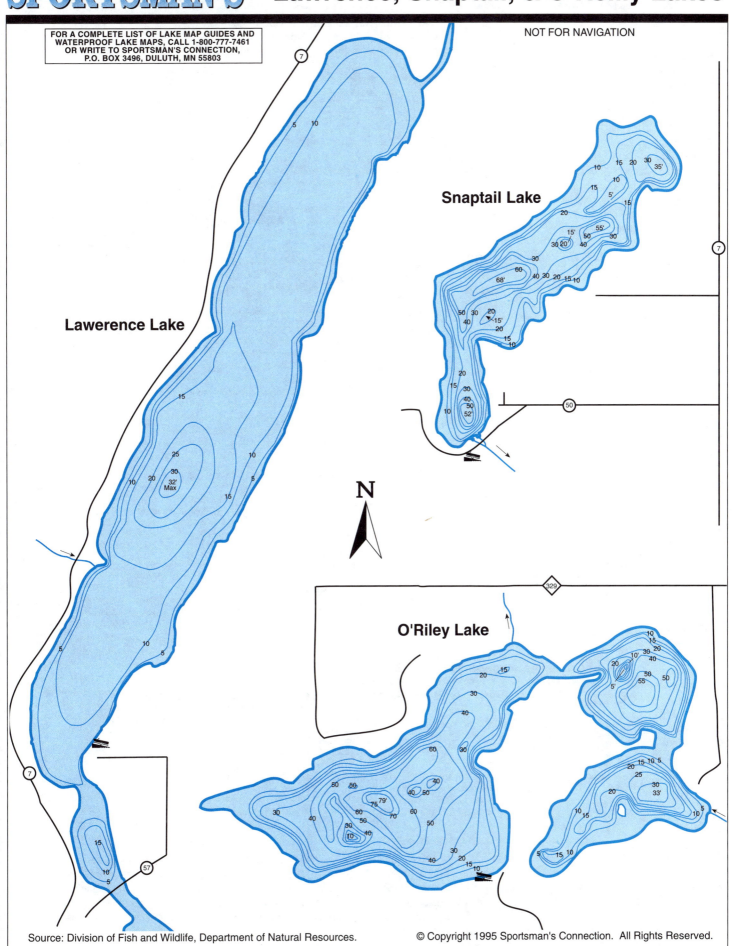

BASS LAKE   LITTLE BASS LAKE

Location: Township 55, 56 Range 26
Watershed: Mississippi Headwaters

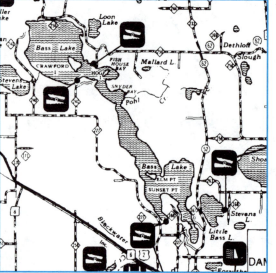

Size of lake: 2,844 Acres
Shorelength: 14.5 Miles
Secchi disk (water clarity): 6.9 Ft.
Water color: Light green
Maximum depth: 76.0 Ft.
Median depth: NA
Accessibility: County-owned access on NE side in Fish House Bay; DNR access on S side of N basin; access on S side of lake
Boat Ramps: (2) Earth; (1) Concrete
Parking: Ample
Accommodations: Resorts
Shoreland zoning classif.: Rec. Dev.
Dominant forest/soil type: Decid/Loam
Cause of water color: Light algae bloom
Management class: Walleye-Centrarchid
Ecological type: Centrarchid-Walleye

Size of lake: 158 Acres
Shorelength: 2.4 Miles
Secchi disk (water clarity): NA
Water color: Green
Maximum depth: 62.0 Ft.
Median depth: 35.0 Ft.
Accessibility: State-owned access on the E side
Boat Ramp: Earth
Parking: Ample
Accommodations: Resorts
Shoreland zoning classif.: Rec. Dev.
Dominant forest/soil type: Decid/Loam
Cause of water color: Algae
Management class: Centrarchid
Ecological type: Centrarchid

DNR COMMENTS:
Tullibee abundance is lower than in the 1977 and 1982 studies. Walleye and Northern Pike numbers are similar to those in previous studies. Bluegill and Yellow Perch abundance has risen slightly. The abundance rate for all Bullhead species has risen slightly since 1982, but Bullhead abundance is still much lower than it was before commercial removal from 1978 to 1980.

FISH STOCKING DATA

year	species	size	# released
89	Walleye	Fry	3,000,000
91	Walleye	Fry	3,000,000
93	Walleye	Fry	2,496,000

NET CATCH DATA
survey date: 07/18/88

| | Gill Nets | | Trap Nets | |
species	# per net	avg fish wt. (lbs)	# per set	avg fish wt. (lbs)
Yellow Perch	10.5	0.23	3.5	0.15
Yellow Bullhead	0.9	1.17	0.2	1.00
White Sucker	0.5	2.11	-	-
Walleye	4.5	1.79	0.4	1.44
Tullibee (incl. Cisco)	1.2	1.05	-	-
Rock Bass	2.6	0.73	2.3	0.28
Pumpkin. Sunfish	1.6	0.24	2.8	0.15
Northern Pike	6.2	1.69	0.6	0.63
Brown Bullhead	1.6	1.43	0.1	2.20
Bluegill	0.3	0.83	3.2	0.22
Black Bullhead	1.2	1.12	-	-

LENGTH OF SELECTED SPECIES SAMPLED FROM ALL GEAR
Number of fish caught for the following length categories (inches):

species	0-5	6-8	9-11	12-14	15-19	20-24	25-29	>30	Total
Yellow Perch	-	115	16	6	-	-	-	-	137
Yellow Bullhead	-	-	1	11	-	-	-	-	12
Walleye	-	-	7	14	26	10	2	-	59
Tullibee (incl. Cisco)	-	1	1	10	3	-	-	-	15
Rock Bass	2	6	24	2	-	-	-	-	34
Pumpkin. Sunfish	9	12	-	-	-	-	-	-	21
Northern Pike	-	-	-	8	43	23	7	-	81
Brown Bullhead	-	1	2	15	3	-	-	-	21
Bluegill	-	-	4	-	-	-	-	-	4
Black Bullhead	-	-	-	15	-	-	-	-	15

FISH STOCKING DATA

year	species	size	# released
93	Black Crappie	Adult	373

NET CATCH DATA
survey date: 06/25/90

| | Gill Nets | | Trap Nets | |
species	# per net	avg fish wt. (lbs)	# per set	avg fish wt. (lbs)
Yellow Perch	9.7	0.10	0.3	0.10
White Sucker	1.0	2.30	-	-
Walleye	1.0	3.47	0.3	0.10
Tullibee (incl. Cisco)	2.7	1.91	-	-
Northern Pike	4.7	2.02	0.3	3.00
Yellow Bullhead	-	-	1.3	0.64
Rock Bass	-	-	2.3	0.23
Pumpkin. Sunfish	-	-	3.3	0.18
Largemouth Bass	-	-	0.5	2.00
Bluegill	-	-	31.8	0.15

LENGTH OF SELECTED SPECIES SAMPLED FROM ALL GEAR
Number of fish caught for the following length categories (inches):

species	0-5	6-8	9-11	12-14	15-19	20-24	25-29	>30	Total
Yellow Perch	-	29	-	-	-	-	-	-	29
Walleye	-	-	-	1	-	1	1	-	3
Tullibee (incl. Cisco)	-	-	-	4	3	1	-	-	8
Northern Pike	-	-	-	-	6	8	-	-	14

DNR COMMENTS:
Northern Pike decreasing from historically high numbers; age classes 2-6 represented; growth good till age 4. Walleyes few; natural reproduction appears to be occurring. Bluegills present at above-avg. levels. Tullibee about avg. in numbers, with a wide range of sizes. Yellow Perch pop. stable.

FISHING INFORMATION: Bass Lake does hold some Largemouth Bass, but its big Walleyes, Northerns and Sunfish get most of the attention. Brian Krecklau, of Pole Bender Guide Service in Grand Rapids, said that anglers' stringers of 1-1/2 to 2 pound Walleyes will often include some 3 to 6 pounders. Northern Pike up to 20 pounds are also found, although 3 to 4 pound fish are the norm. The north and south lobes of the lake are separated by a large, long, shallow, weedy stretch that produces some nice plate-sized Bluegills and large Pumpkinseeds. The Bass, Northerns and Walleyes are fished primarily off the points and underwater islands in the north and south lobes. Little Bass Lake also holds some good Largemouth Bass and lots of Northern Pike. Walleye fishing can be spotty but the average size is good. Panfish run small.

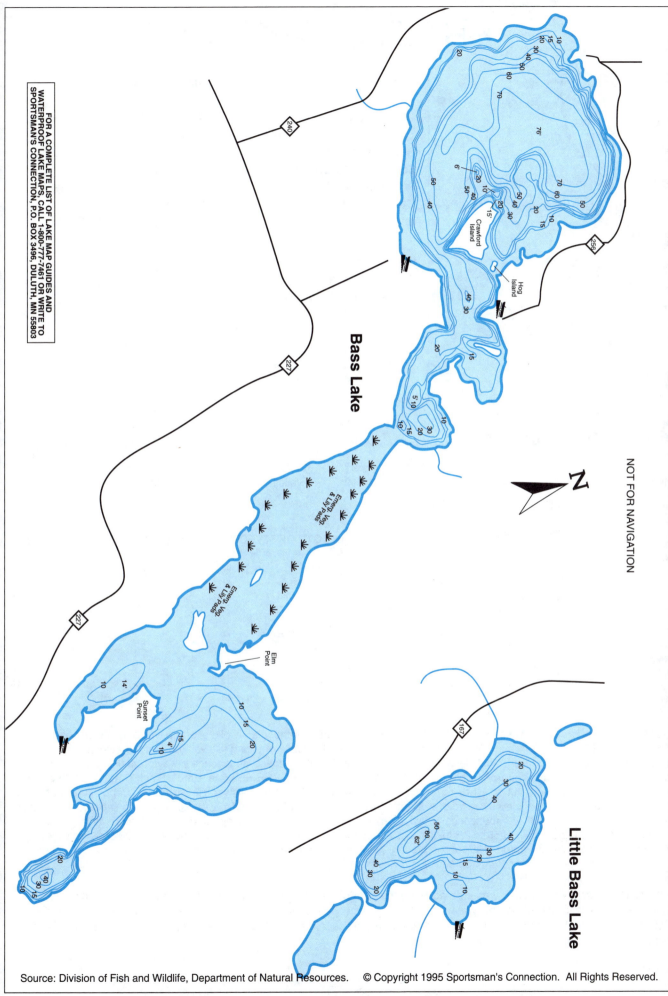

Bass & Little Bass Lakes

SPORTSMAN'S Connection ®

NOT FOR NAVIGATION

N

Bass Lake

Little Bass Lake

Crawford Island

Hog Island

Emerg. Veg. & Lily Pads

Emerg. Veg. & Lily Pads

Elm Point

Sunset Point

240

256

227

227

167

PRAIRIE LAKE

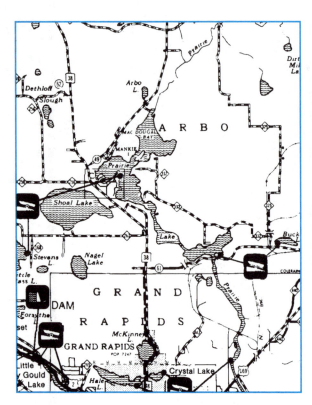

Location: Township 56
Range 25
Watershed: Prairie-Willow
Size of lake: 1,279 Acres
Shorelength: 16.6 Miles
Secchi disk (water clarity): 3.9 Ft.
Water color: Brown
Cause of water color: Bog stain and suspended silt

Maximum depth: 31.0 Ft.
Median depth: 12.0 Ft.
Accessibility: Township-owned on W side off Millard Pt. Road; access can also be gained on lower Prairie Lake
Boat Ramp: (2) Concrete
Parking: Ample
Accommodations: Resorts, Campground

Shoreland zoning classification: Recreational Development
Dominant forest/soil type: Decid/Loam
Management class: Walleye-Centrarchid
Ecological type: Centrarchid-Walleye

FISH STOCKING DATA

year	species	size	# released
89	Walleye	Fry	2,000,000
90	Walleye	Fingerling	11,044
91	Walleye	Fry	2,000,000
92	Walleye	Fingerling	7,087
92	Walleye	Yearling	81
92	Walleye	Fingerling	3,479
92	Walleye	Yearling	2
92	Walleye	Adult	78

NET CATCH DATA

survey date: 07/09/90

species	Gill Nets # per net	Gill Nets avg fish wt. (lbs.)	Trap Nets # per set	Trap Nets avg fish wt. (lbs.)
Yellow Perch	1.1	0.11	5.1	0.15
Yellow Bullhead	0.5	0.90	0.2	1.15
White Sucker	0.3	2.20	2.5	1.55
Walleye	2.3	2.25	-	-
Shorthead Red.	3.5	2.45	-	-
Rock Bass	0.3	0.20	0.8	0.34
Pumpkin. Sunfish	1.8	0.16	0.6	0.13
Northern Pike	1.1	1.93	4.8	2.03
Largemouth Bass	0.2	0.70	-	-
Golden Redhorse	0.1	6.50	0.1	5.10
Brown Bullhead	0.4	1.07	0.3	1.10
Bluegill	4.5	0.22	1.4	0.27
Black Crappie	3.8	0.16	9.4	0.22

LENGTH OF SELECTED SPECIES SAMPLED FROM ALL GEAR

Number of fish caught for the following length categories (inches):

species	0-5	6-8	9-11	12-14	15-19	20-24	25-29	>30	Total
Yellow Perch	-	58	3	-	-	-	-	-	61
Yellow Bullhead	-	-	-	2	-	-	-	-	2
Walleye	-	-	-	3	15	8	1	-	27
Rock Bass	2	6	2	-	-	-	-	-	10
Pumpkin. Sunfish	2	5	-	-	-	-	-	-	7
Northern Pike	-	-	-	-	22	30	6	-	58
Largemouth Bass	-	-	1	1	-	-	-	-	2
Brown Bullhead	-	-	1	2	-	-	-	-	3
Bluegill	2	15	1	-	-	-	-	-	18
Black Crappie	28	61	25	-	-	-	-	-	114

DNR COMMENTS: The Northern Pike population has fluctuated somewhat over the years while average weight has increased steadily from 1.5 lb./fish in 1955 to 2.0 lb./fish in 1990. This population is made up mostly of young fish with 96% of the samples taken being age class IV's and below. Rough fish populations vary slightly over time with Bullhead abundance always remaining low and Shorthead Redhorse populations increasing from a gillnet CPUE of 1.0 in 1980 to a CPUE of 3.5 in 1990. Black Crappie CPUEs swing widely through the years sampled, but size has remained constant with small fish and slower growth rates. Populations of Yellow Perch dropped considerably in the late 1970s from a gillnet CPUE of 18.6 in 1975 to a CPUE of 3.6 in 1980. The abundance has remained low since that time. Walleye abundance is fairly constant compared to past netting information although average size has steadily increased from 1.0 lbs./fish in 1955 to 2.2 lb./fish in 1990. Both fry and fingerling stocking done before 1982 failed to show any recognizable year classes. Stocking from 1982 to the present has been done every year with a mixture of fry, fingerling, and yearling making evaluation of stocked fish and natural reproduction difficult.

FISHING INFORMATION: Prairie Lake was created when the river of the same name was dammed for hydroelectric power generation. Its relatively shallow, bog-stained waters are teeming with Crappies which provide steady action year round. Good numbers of Northerns and Largemouth Bass are also found in the reservoir, and Walleyes averaging about 1-1/2 pounds have resulted from DNR stocking.

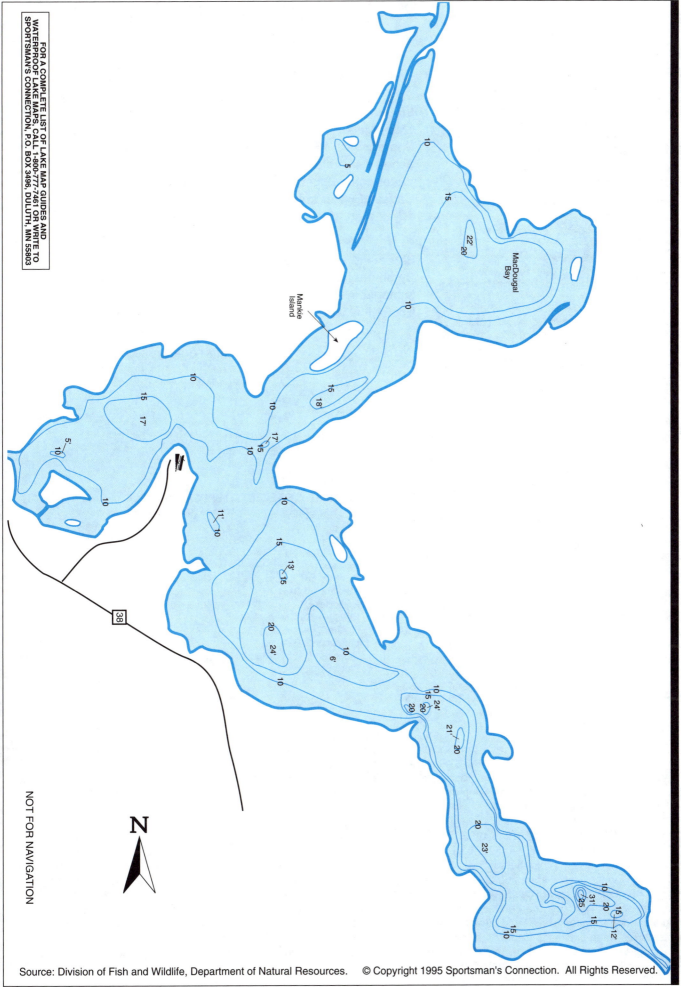

MacDougal
Bay

Mankie
Island

38

N

NOT FOR NAVIGATION

FOR A COMPLETE LIST OF LAKE MAP GUIDES AND WATERPROOF LAKE MAPS, CALL 1-800-777-7461 OR WRITE TO SPORTSMAN'S CONNECTION, P.O. BOX 3496, DULUTH, MN 55803

Source: Division of Fish and Wildlife, Department of Natural Resources.   © Copyright 1995 Sportsman's Connection. All Rights Reserved.

TROUT LAKE

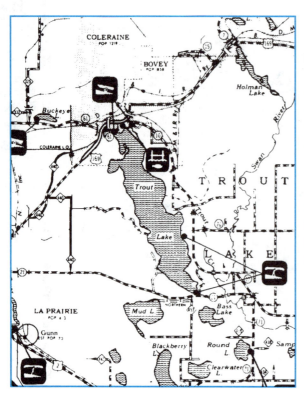

Location: Township 55, 56 Range 24
Watershed: Prairie-Willow
Size of lake: 1,953 Acres
Shorelength: 13.0 Miles
Secchi disk (water clarity): 10.3 Ft.
Water color: Light green
Cause of water color: Algae

Maximum depth: 115.0 Ft.
Median depth: NA
Accessibility: Two city-owned accesses with concrete ramps on N side of lake; also at Komenen Park and S side
Boat Ramp: Concrete (3), Gravel (1)
Parking: Ample
Accommodations: Park

Shoreland zoning classification: Recreational Development
Dominant forest/soil type: Decid/Loam
Management class: Walleye
Ecological type: Hard-water Walleye

FISH STOCKING DATA

year	species	size	# released
89	Walleye	Fry	2,000,000
91	Walleye	Fry	2,000,000
93	Walleye	Fry	2,085,200

NET CATCH DATA

survey date: 08/14/89

	Gill Nets		Trap Nets	
species	# per net	avg fish wt. (lbs.)	# per set	avg fish wt. (lbs.)
Yellow Perch	29.8	0.21	1.1	0.14
Yellow Bullhead	0.3	1.00	0.2	0.95
White Sucker	4.1	1.43	0.2	2.00
Walleye	6.1	2.32	-	-
Tullibee (incl. Cisco)	3.8	0.38	-	-
Smallmouth Bass	0.2	3.00	-	-
Rock Bass	5.4	0.58	0.8	0.50
Pumpkin. Sunfish	5.8	0.18	3.3	0.15
Northern Pike	5.9	2.91	0.8	2.29
Largemouth Bass	0.7	1.20	0.1	0.10
Common Shiner	0.3	0.10	-	-
Bowfin (Dogfish)	0.2	4.95	-	-
Bluegill	1.6	0.24	1.5	0.22
Black Crappie	2.3	0.37	1.0	0.23
Bigmouth Buffalo	0.1	35.00	-	-
Golden Shiner	-	-	0.1	0.10

LENGTH OF SELECTED SPECIES SAMPLED FROM ALL GEAR

Number of fish caught for the following length categories (inches):

species	0-5	6-8	9-11	12-14	15-19	20-24	25-29	>30	Total
Yellow Perch	-	81	32	9	-	-	-	-	122
Yellow Bullhead	-	-	1	2	-	-	-	-	3
Walleye	-	2	-	13	34	19	5	-	73
Tullibee (incl. Cisco)	-	-	39	4	2	-	-	-	45
Smallmouth Bass	-	-	-	-	2	-	-	-	2
Rock Bass	18	10	29	8	-	-	-	-	65
Pumpkin. Sunfish	29	41	-	-	-	-	-	-	70
Northern Pike	-	-	-	-	8	47	16	-	71
Largemouth Bass	-	-	1	5	2	-	-	-	8
Bluegill	6	12	1	-	-	-	-	-	19
Black Crappie	-	24	-	3	-	-	-	-	27

DNR COMMENTS: The Walleye gillnet catch rate was 6.1 fish/net and meets the long range goal of the management plan. The mean length has increased from 13.3" in 1984 to 17.0". For this sample the mean total length for most Walleye age groups was about 1" longer than the state average. Northern Pike gillnet catch rate was 5.9 fish/net which exceeds the long range goal of 4 fish/net in the management plan. The mean length of the sample was 22.4" which is excellent for lakes in this area. Northern Pike were mainly age 1 and 2 fish which had excellent growth rates.

FISHING INFORMATION: In the 1930's to 1950's Trout Lake (near Coleraine) was filled with Lake Trout, many in the 30 to 35 pound range. The folks at Hollywood Bait, near the lake, told us of stories about lakers being so plentiful that you could walk across their backs when they were spawning in the shallower bays in the autumn. However, those days have passed; years of siltation buildup essentially destroyed the Trouts' spawning areas. The lake has been managed for Walleyes in more recent times and is receiving regular stocking by the DNR. Walleyes can be found along the underwater islands and points throughout the lake. Northern Pike appear to be fattening up on the Tullibees and Perch with reports of 20-pound fish being caught. Bass, both Largemouth and Smallmouth, are also found around the sunken islands and other irregular structure. Crappies up to 1-1/2 pounds are fished in the winter and spring, but virtually disappear in the summer. Electronic fish-finding gear is a must in locating the structure on Trout. You don't hear much about Lakers on Trout Lake these days, but some spear fishermen have reported seeing them swim past their holes and the one 35-pound fish listed only as "unidentified species" is intriguing.

Trout Lake

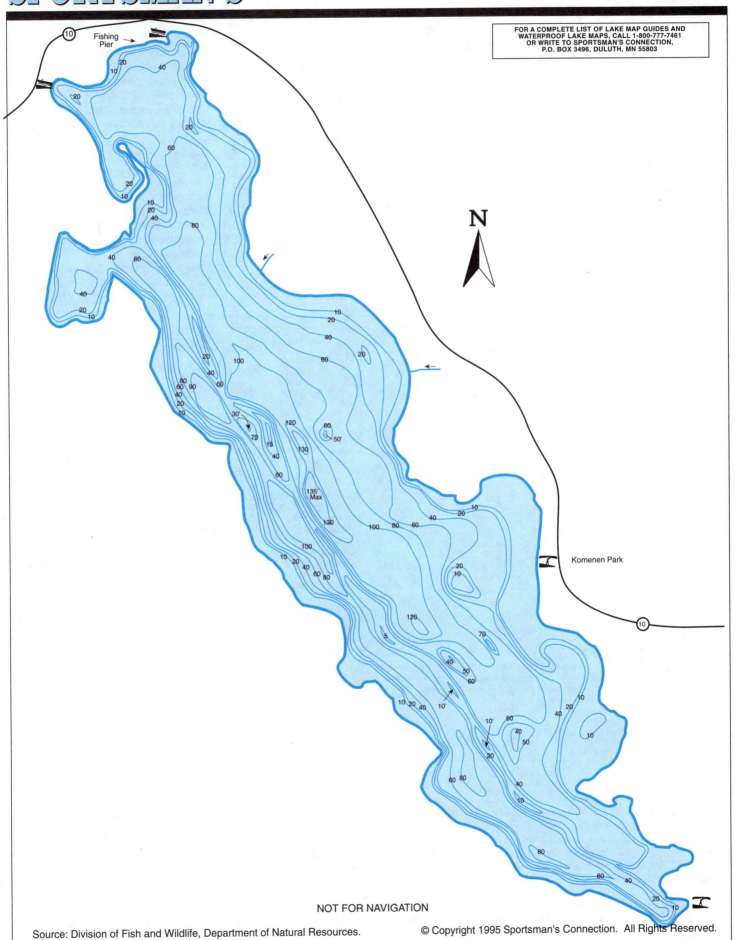

NOT FOR NAVIGATION

Source: Division of Fish and Wildlife, Department of Natural Resources.

SPLIT HAND LAKE   LITTLE SPLIT HAND LAKE

Location: Township 53   Range 24, 25
Watershed: Prairie-Willow

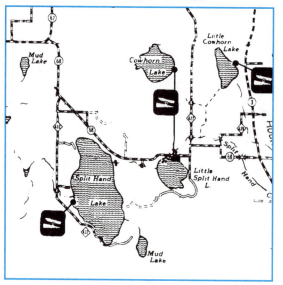

Size of lake: 1,352 Acres
Shorelength: 7.1 Miles
Secchi disk (water clarity): 3.9 Ft.
Water color: Green
Maximum depth: 34.0 Ft.
Median depth: NA
Accessibility: State-owned access on W side
Boat Ramp: Concrete
Parking: Ample
Accommodations: Resort
Shoreland zoning classif.: Rec. Dev.
Dominant forest/soil type: Decid/Wet
Cause of water color: Algae bloom
Management class: Walleye
Ecological type: Hard-water Walleye

Size of lake: 243 Acres
Shorelength: 2.5 Miles
Secchi disk (water clarity): 3.6 Ft.
Water color: Brown-green
Maximum depth: 23.0 Ft.
Median depth: 13.0 Ft.
Accessibility: State-owned public access on N side
Boat Ramp: Earth
Parking: Ample
Accommodations: Resorts
Shoreland zoning classif.: Rec. Dev.
Dominant forest/soil type: No tree/Wet
Cause of water color: Suspended silt and algae bloom
Management class: Centrarchid
Ecological type: Centrarchid

DNR COMMENTS:
Northern Pike pop. below statewide median; growth above avg. Walleyes about avg. in numbers; sample indicates a good population of acceptable-size fish for angling. Black Crappies above lake class median values; entire sample is aged 1; hence, the pop. is dominated by small fish. Bluegills below avg. in numbers; pop. consists mainly of small, young fish. White Sucker, Tullibees and Yellow Perch above avg. in numbers. Yellow Bullheads scarce.

FISH STOCKING DATA

year	species	size	# released
89	Walleye	Fry	1,300,000
91	Walleye	Fry	1,300,000
93	Walleye	Fry	1,398,880

NET CATCH DATA
survey date: 08/20/90

species	Gill Nets # per net	avg fish wt. (lbs)	Trap Nets # per set	avg fish wt. (lbs)
Yellow Perch	38.1	0.22	1.6	0.18
Yellow Bullhead	0.1	1.20	0.5	1.60
White Sucker	9.0	1.43	1.3	2.82
Walleye	7.4	2.41	-	-
Tullibee (incl. Cisco)	3.1	1.75	-	-
Northern Pike	3.1	4.19	0.5	2.13
Largemouth Bass	0.1	0.20	0.3	5.05
Black Crappie	2.9	0.12	0.6	0.14
Rock Bass	-	-	0.1	0.30
Pumpkin. Sunfish	-	-	4.1	0.17
Bowfin (Dogfish)	-	-	0.1	7.50
Bluegill	-	-	3.8	0.11
Bigmouth Buffalo	-	-	0.3	22.60

LENGTH OF SELECTED SPECIES SAMPLED FROM ALL GEAR
Number of fish caught for the following length categories (inches):

species	0-5	6-8	9-11	12-14	15-19	20-24	25-29	>30	Total
Yellow Perch	8	75	23	-	-	-	-	-	106
Yellow Bullhead	-	-	1	-	-	-	-	-	1
Walleye	-	-	12	44	16	2	-	-	74
Tullibee (incl. Cisco)	-	-	1	-	30	-	-	-	31
Northern Pike	-	-	-	2	18	8	2	-	30
Largemouth Bass	-	1	-	-	-	-	-	-	1
Bluegill	21	9	-	-	-	-	-	-	30
Black Crappie	10	19	-	-	-	-	-	-	29

FISH STOCKING DATA

year	species	size	# released
90	Walleye	Yearling	392
92	Walleye	Yearling	52
92	Walleye	Fingerling	200
92	Walleye	Yearling	227
92	Walleye	Adult	114

NET CATCH DATA
survey date: 06/17/91

species	Gill Nets # per net	avg fish wt. (lbs)	Trap Nets # per set	avg fish wt. (lbs)
Yellow Perch	18.4	0.09	1.3	0.10
Yellow Bullhead	0.4	0.35	-	-
White Sucker	2.2	2.34	-	-
Walleye	0.8	3.23	-	-
Tullibee (incl. Cisco)	0.2	2.50	-	-
Pumpkin. Sunfish	1.0	0.20	2.5	0.18
Northern Pike	9.4	2.19	-	-
Brown Bullhead	1.0	1.30	-	-
Bowfin (Dogfish)	0.2	8.00	1.0	4.55
Black Crappie	11.6	0.18	1.8	0.26
Silver Redhorse	-	-	0.3	4.00
Bluegill	-	-	6.3	0.24

LENGTH OF SELECTED SPECIES SAMPLED FROM ALL GEAR
Number of fish caught for the following length categories (inches):

species	0-5	6-8	9-11	12-14	15-19	20-24	25-29	>30	Total
Yellow Perch	-	89	3	-	-	-	-	-	92
Yellow Bullhead	-	1	1	-	-	-	-	-	2
Walleye	-	-	-	-	-	4	-	-	4
Tullibee (incl. Cisco)	-	-	-	-	1	-	-	-	1
Pumpkin. Sunfish	-	5	-	-	-	-	-	-	5
Northern Pike	-	-	-	1	10	30	6	-	47
Brown Bullhead	-	-	5	-	-	-	-	-	5
Black Crappie	9	40	7	2	-	-	-	-	58

DNR COMMENTS:
Northern Pike remain abundant, though down somewhat from their historic high level of 1980. Walleyes, meanwhile, remain at very low pop. level, despite frequent stockings. Black Crappie pop. well above lake class median; growth avg. Bluegills and Pumpkinseeds present in small numbers. Shoreline seining yielded many small Largemouth Bass. Yellow Perch pop. down, but still high for lake class.

FISHING INFORMATION: Mike Auger, Blue Horizon Guide Service out of Ken's Pokegama Sports fishes Splithand Lake regularly and offered these tips: Crappie fishing is excellent with typical fish running from 1/2 pound on up to 1 3/4 pounds. The east end of the lake between the creeks is good in the winter. Start on the north end of this area after ice up and move down to the south beds as winter progresses on into spring. The 20 foot bar in the middle of the lake actually comes up to about 18 feet and is good for Walleyes. Splithand's relatively murky waters can be productive all day for Walleyes. The 10 foot island off of the center bar comes up to about 7 feet and is good for Crappie off the deep sides. Move up into the shallower water over the island as night falls. Fish the edges for Walleyes also. The north bay is good for spring Crappie. Bluegills in the 1/2 pound to pound range can also be found around 10-15 feet in this area, a little shallower than the Crappies. You can usually count on consistently catching good Sunnies in Splithand throughout the year. Fish the shoreline weeds in the spring and summer for Northerns, many in the 8-12 pound range. Little Splithand has some good early Walleye and Crappie fishing. Recent years' Walleye stockings of fingerlings and older fish seem to be successful.

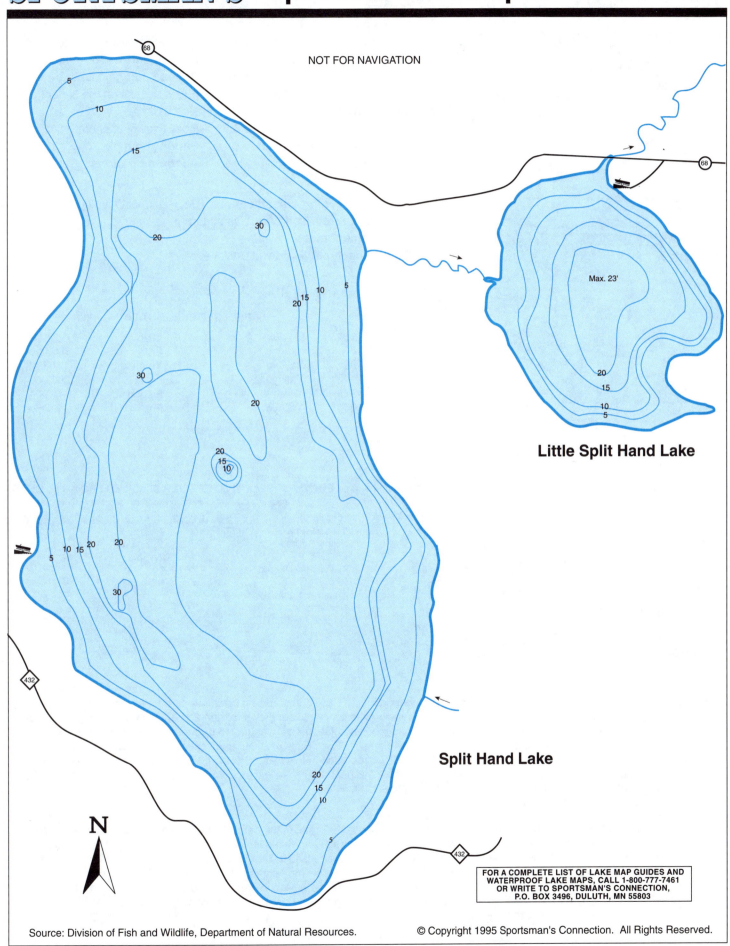

NOT FOR NAVIGATION

Max. 23'

Little Split Hand Lake

Split Hand Lake

N

Source: Division of Fish and Wildlife, Department of Natural Resources.

SISEEBAKWET (Sugar) LAKE

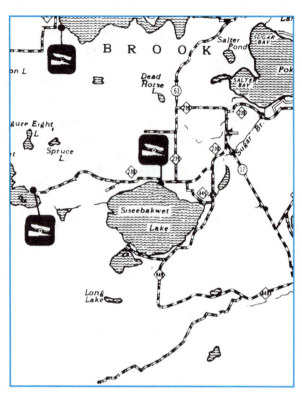

Location: Township 54
Range 26
Watershed: Mississippi Headwaters
Size of lake: 1,350 Acres
Shorelength: 7.7 Miles
Secchi disk (water clarity): 13.8 Ft.
Water color: Clear
Cause of water color: NA

Maximum depth: 105.0 Ft.
Median depth: NA
Accessibility: County-owned public access on the N-central side of lake.
Boat Ramp: Concrete
Parking: Ample
Accommodations: Resort

Shoreland zoning classification: Recreational Development
Dominant forest/soil type: Decid/Loam
Management class: Walleye
Ecological type: Hard-water Walleye

FISH STOCKING DATA

year	species	size	# released
89	Walleye	Fry	1,300,000
90	Walleye	Yearling	1,138
91	Walleye	Fry	1,300,000
92	Walleye	Fingerling	4,964
94	Walleye	Fry	1,300,000

NET CATCH DATA

survey date: 08/19/91

species	Gill Nets # per net	Gill Nets avg fish wt. (lbs.)	Trap Nets # per set	Trap Nets avg fish wt. (lbs.)
Yellow Perch	31.4	0.24	-	-
Yellow Bullhead	0.1	1.50	-	-
White Sucker	0.7	1.42	-	-
Walleye	10.2	1.61	-	-
Tullibee (incl. Cisco)	0.1	0.40	-	-
Rock Bass	42.1	0.47	0.7	0.25
Pumpkin. Sunfish	1.8	0.19	1.8	0.21
Northern Pike	1.3	4.12	-	-
Largemouth Bass	1.1	1.61	0.2	0.31
Bluegill	0.7	0.10	19.2	0.16
Hybrid Sunfish	-	-	0.3	0.25

LENGTH OF SELECTED SPECIES SAMPLED FROM ALL GEAR

Number of fish caught for the following length categories (inches):

species	0-5	6-8	9-11	12-14	15-19	20-24	25-29	>30	Total
Yellow Perch	-	40	58	4	-	-	-	-	102
Yellow Bullhead	-	-	-	1	-	-	-	-	1
Walleye	-	-	-	22	53	16	1	-	92
Tullibee (incl. Cisco)	-	-	-	1	-	-	-	-	1
Rock Bass	3	41	55	1	-	-	-	-	100
Pumpkin. Sunfish	3	12	1	-	-	-	-	-	16
Northern Pike	-	-	-	-	-	8	3	1	12
Largemouth Bass	-	-	-	4	6	-	-	-	10
Bluegill	4	2	-	-	-	-	-	-	6

DNR COMMENTS: Northern Pike have never been very abundant in this lake. The current catch rate falls below 1st quartile values for lake class and is the lowest ever recorded for the lake; three year classes identified; growth of age 2 nearly 44% above avg. Walleyes slightly under historical mean for lake, but still twice lake class median value; median length, 15.6"; mean weight, 1.6 lb.; growth rates nearly at statewide avg., and over-all pop. is of size desirable to angler. Rock Bass most common species sampled, composing 40% of the catch; pop. is 18 times lake class median and the highest ever recorded in this lake. Bluegill pop. slightly above lake class median and three times the previous high for lake; growth rates for ages 2,3 nearly 20% below avg. Yellow Perch double lake class median value, with wide representation of year classes; median length, 8.1".

FISHING INFORMATION: Siseebakwet Lake, also known as Sugar Lake, is one of the best Walleye lakes in the entire region. Its clear water holds some plump fish including wall hangers. The key to catching old marble eyes in Sugar, according to Ken Patterson, owner of Pokegama Sports in Grand Rapids, is night fishing. Shad raps and other shallow crank baits trolled along the shoreline or across the sunken islands can be very productive. Sugar's notoriety as a good night fishing lake is creating some traffic at night so be sure that your boat's lights are in good working order. Daytime fishing for Walleye can be tough, but light line with small hooks and weights will produce fish; especially in low-light conditions such as overcast skies and choppy water. Serious Bass fishermen pull some nice Largemouth out of the lake. Panfish don't receive much attention.

NOT FOR NAVIGATION

Siseebakwet (Sugar) Lake

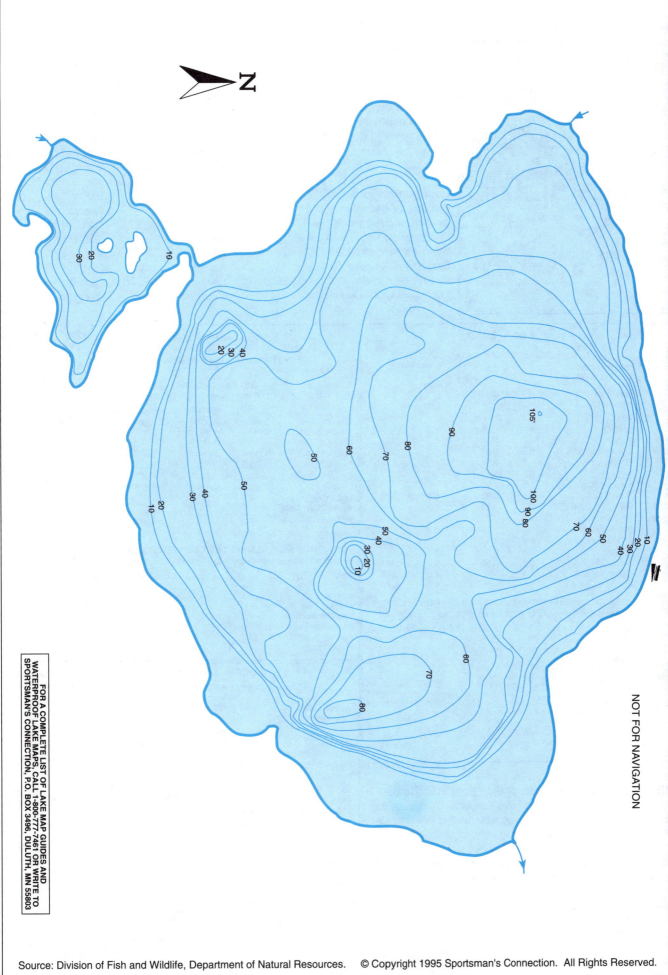

Source: Division of Fish and Wildlife, Department of Natural Resources.   © Copyright 1995 Sportsman's Connection. All Rights Reserved.

Location: Township 55   Range 26
Watershed: Mississippi Headwaters

LOON LAKE

	LOON LAKE	SNELLS LAKE	LONG LAKE
Size of lake:	220 Acres	86 Acres	117 Acres
Shorelength:	3.5 Miles	1.1 Miles	1.1 Miles
Secchi disk (water clarity):	NA	NA	NA
Water color:	Clear	Green	Clear
Maximum depth:	69.0 Ft.	50.0 Ft.	75.0 Ft.
Median depth:	35.0 Ft.	NA	9.0 Ft.
Accessibility:	County-owned public access on E side	County-owned access on the NE side of lake; off Cty. Rd. 257	Newly developed access on extreme E arm off Cty. Rd. 63
Boat Ramp:	Earth	Earth	Earth
Parking:	Adequate	Adequate	Adequate
Accommodations:	NA	NA	NA
Shoreland zoning classif.:	Rec. Dev.	Rec. Dev.	Nat. Envt.
Dominant forest/soil type:	Decid/Sand	NA	NA
Cause of water color:	NA	Algae bloom	NA
Management class:	Walleye-Centrarchid	Centrarchid	Centrarchid
Ecological type:	Centrarchid	Centrarchid	Centrarchid

DNR COMMENTS: Northern Pike pop. near median levels. Walleyes scarce, but rising Yellow Perch pop. could increase the numbers of Walleyes. Bluegill and Pumpkinseed pop.s above lake class medians; growth rates slow. Largemouth Bass pop. increasing; many seen in shallows during assessment. Yellow Perch pop. up to twice 3rd quartile values. Tullibees well above lake class 3rd quartile. Bowfin up as well.

Loon Lake

FISH STOCKING DATA

year	species	size	# released
90	Walleye	Yearling	319

NET CATCH DATA
survey date: 06/08/92

	Gill Nets		Trap Nets	
species	# per net	avg fish wt. (lbs)	# per set	avg fish wt. (lbs)
Yellow Perch	30.7	0.09	0.3	0.17
Yellow Bullhead	0.5	0.67	0.9	0.65
White Sucker	0.2	2.50	-	-
Walleye	0.3	1.70	-	-
Tullibee (incl. Cisco)	7.5	1.20	-	-
Rock Bass	0.5	0.23	0.9	0.28
Pumpkin. Sunfish	0.3	0.10	10.3	0.16
Northern Pike	4.0	2.33	-	-
Largemouth Bass	0.7	1.73	0.3	1.13
Brown Bullhead	0.2	0.40	0.2	0.30
Bluegill	2.5	0.07	57.3	0.13
Black Crappie	0.2	0.30	0.7	0.40
Hybrid Sunfish	-	-	1.0	0.13
Bowfin (Dogfish)	-	-	1.2	4.65

LENGTH OF SELECTED SPECIES SAMPLED FROM ALL GEAR
Number of fish caught for the following length categories (inches):

species	0-5	6-8	9-11	12-14	15-19	20-24	25-29	>30	Total
Yellow Perch	-	89	-	-	-	-	-	-	89
Yellow Bullhead	-	-	3	-	-	-	-	-	3
Walleye	-	-	-	1	-	1	-	-	2
Tullibee (incl. Cisco)	-	-	-	7	38	-	-	-	45
Rock Bass	2	2	2	-	-	-	-	-	6
Pumpkin. Sunfish	1	-	-	-	-	-	-	-	1
Northern Pike	-	-	-	5	16	3	-	-	24
Largemouth Bass	1	1	-	-	1	1	-	-	4
Brown Bullhead	-	-	1	-	-	-	-	-	1
Bluegill	14	1	-	-	-	-	-	-	15
Black Crappie	-	-	1	-	-	-	-	-	1

Snells (Giles) Lake

FISH STOCKING DATA NOT AVAILABLE

NET CATCH DATA
survey date: 07/19/89

	Gill Nets		Trap Nets	
species	# per net	avg fish wt. (lbs)	# per set	avg fish wt. (lbs)
Yellow Bullhead	0.5	1.20	0.3	0.50
Walleye	0.3	5.90	-	-
Northern Pike	10.5	3.06	0.5	2.00
Largemouth Bass	0.3	3.90	-	-
Brown Bullhead	0.5	1.85	-	-
Bluegill	27.5	0.17	15.5	0.15
Black Crappie	0.3	0.30	-	-
Yellow Perch	-	-	0.5	0.20
Pumpkin. Sunfish	-	-	4.5	0.09

LENGTH OF SELECTED SPECIES SAMPLED FROM ALL GEAR
Number of fish caught for the following length categories (inches):

species	0-5	6-8	9-11	12-14	15-19	20-24	25-29	>30	Total
Yellow Bullhead	-	-	-	2	-	-	-	-	2
Walleye	-	-	-	-	-	-	1	-	1
Northern Pike	-	-	-	-	-	20	22	-	42
Largemouth Bass	-	-	-	1	-	-	-	-	1
Brown Bullhead	-	-	2	-	-	-	-	-	2
Bluegill	1	82	-	-	-	-	-	-	83
Black Crappie	-	-	1	-	-	-	-	-	1

DNR COMMENTS: Yellow Perch have decreased drastically. Northern Pike much more numerous. Bluegills up as well.

Long Lake

FISH STOCKING DATA NOT AVAILABLE

NET CATCH DATA
survey date: 08/03/77

	Gill Nets		Trap Nets	
species	# per net	avg fish wt. (lbs)	# per set	avg fish wt. (lbs)
Yellow Bullhead	6.0	0.54	4.5	0.58
Pumpkin. Sunfish	5.7	0.13	7.3	0.41
Northern Pike	10.3	1.48	1.5	1.33
Largemouth Bass	0.7	1.50	0.3	4.00
Crappie	0.7	0.10	0.8	0.33
Brown Bullhead	2.3	0.57	2.0	0.53
Bowfin (Dogfish)	0.3	4.50	2.3	5.06
Bluegill	6.0	0.18	22.3	0.31
Rock Bass	-	-	0.3	0.50

LENGTH OF SELECTED SPECIES SAMPLED FROM ALL GEAR
Number of fish caught for the following length categories (inches):

species	0-5	6-8	9-11	12-14	15-19	20-24	25-29	>30	Total
Bluegill	3	83	4	-	-	-	-	-	90
Brown Bullhead	-	2	9	4	-	-	-	-	15
Crappie	-	4	1	-	-	-	-	-	5
Largemouth Bass	-	-	-	1	1	1	-	-	3
Northern Pike	-	-	1	20	12	1	-	-	34
Pumpkin. Sunfish	6	40	1	-	-	-	-	-	47
Rock Bass	-	-	1	-	-	-	-	-	1
Yellow Bullhead	-	2	23	11	-	-	-	-	36

DNR COMMENTS: Northern Pike and Bluegill populations at quite high levels. All other fish populations within normal limits for this type of lake.

FISHING INFORMATION: Mike Auger, of Blue Horizon Guide Service, told us that Loon and Long Lakes have Largemouth Bass in the 2 to 3 pound range and Crappies averaging about 1/2 to 3/4 pounds. Crappie fishing is best from ice out until mid-July, especially just before nightfall. Loon has been receiving Walleye stockings in even number years, but we haven't heard about any being caught yet. Snells, aka Giles, yields good numbers and average sizes of Northern Pike, along with a few big Largemouth. Bluegills are thick, but most are stunted. Crappies are better sized, but less plentiful. Judging from the gill net survey in 1989, there are some lunker Walleyes hiding somewhere in the lake.

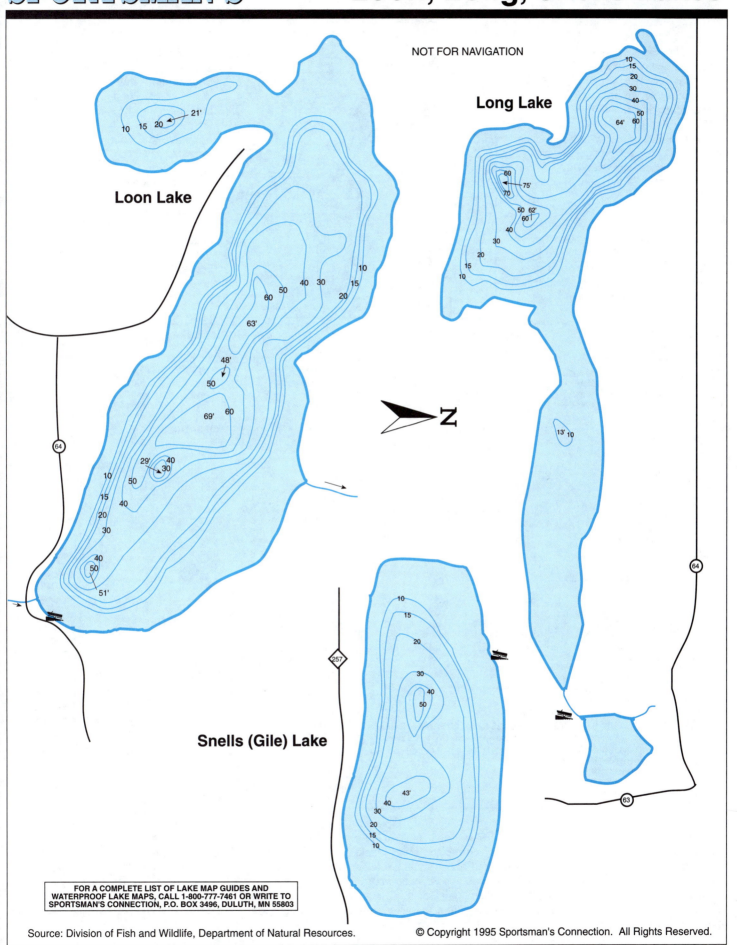

NOT FOR NAVIGATION

Long Lake

Loon Lake

Snells (Gile) Lake

Source: Division of Fish and Wildlife, Department of Natural Resources.

BLANDIN LAKE   JAY GOULD LAKE

Location: Township 55   Range 25, 26
Watershed: Prairie-Willow

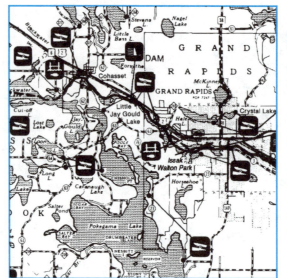

Size of lake: 455 Acres
Shorelength: 7.0 Miles
Secchi disk (water clarity): 6.6 Ft.
Water color: Amber
Maximum depth: 44.0 Ft.
Median depth: 20.0 Ft.
Accessibility: County-owned access off CSAH #63 near bridge, and city-owned access on Sylvan Bay
Boat Ramp: Earth (county); concrete (city)
Parking: Ample
Accommodations: County park
Shoreland zoning classif.: Gen. Dev.
Dominant forest/soil type: No tree/loam
Cause of water color: Slight bog stain
Management class: Walleye-Centrarchid
Ecological type: Centrarchid

Size of lake: 455 Acres
Shorelength: 5.0 Miles
Secchi disk (water clarity): NA
Water color: Green
Maximum depth: 33.0 Ft.
Median depth: NA
Accessibility: County-owned NE bay, also at L. Jay Gould
Boat Ramp: Concrete
Parking: Adequate
Accommodations: None
Shoreland zoning classif.: Rec. Dev.
Dominant forest/soil type: Decid/Sand
Cause of water color: Algae
Management class: Walleye-Centrarchid
Ecological type: Centrarchid-Walleye

DNR COMMENTS:

The Walleye gillnet CPUE has increased from 1983 and is at its highest point over all sampling periods and above lake class medians. Most year classes are represented although half the captured fish were the 1988 year class. There was no Walleye stocking done in 1988 but 1,789 yearlings were stocked in 1989 which could account for some of the high numbers of 2 year old fish. Northern Pike and White Sucker have had little fluctuation over the past 12 years and populations are below lake class medians. Muskellunge were not captured in this assessment and have rarely been taken in any summer netting while the Muskellunge assessment in 1988 took no fish and the 1983 Muskellunge assessment captured only 2 fish. In 1988, 360 Muskie fingerlings were stocked. Centrarchid species and Bullhead populations have fluctuated over the years but appear to be within normal ranges. Tullibee have never been observed in past nettings, but samples taken in this netting reflect a marginal population. Yellow Perch numbers have fallen by more than 50% in the last 12 years and have always been below state and lake class medians, although minnow species, as shown in the shoreline seining, contribute to the forage base.

Blandin Lake

FISH STOCKING DATA

year	species	size	# released
89	Walleye	Fingerling	6,088
89	Walleye	Yearling	699
91	Walleye	Fingerling	1,916
91	Walleye	Yearling	551
91	Walleye	Adult	31
91	Muskellunge	Fingerling	366
93	Walleye	Fingerling	8,264
94	Walleye	Fingerling	466

survey date:
08/13/90

NET CATCH DATA

	Gill Nets		Trap Nets	
		avg fish		avg fish
species	# per net	wt. (lbs)	# per set	wt. (lbs)
Yellow Perch	2.3	0.25	0.1	0.20
Yellow Bullhead	3.3	0.77	0.4	0.70
White Sucker	0.7	2.26	0.3	1.85
Walleye	2.9	0.93	-	-
Tullibee (incl. Cisco)	0.3	1.40	-	-
Shorthead Red.	1.6	2.45	-	-
Rock Bass	0.7	0.38	0.1	0.50
Pumpkin. Sunfish	6.6	0.16	0.5	0.13
Northern Pike	2.9	1.81	0.1	2.70
Largemouth Bass	0.4	0.93	-	-
Brown Bullhead	0.9	0.95	0.1	1.60
Bowfin (Dogfish)	0.1	6.20	0.4	5.63
Bluegill	2.6	0.32	0.4	0.25
Black Crappie	0.6	0.25	-	-
Black Bullhead	5.0	0.96	-	-
Hybrid Sunfish	-	-	0.1	0.40

LENGTH OF SELECTED SPECIES SAMPLED FROM ALL GEAR
Number of fish caught for the following length categories (inches):

species	0-5	6-8	9-11	12-14	15-19	20-24	25-29	>30	Total
Tullibee (incl. Cisco)	-	-	-	2	-	-	-	-	2
Rock Bass	1	3	1	-	-	-	-	-	5
Pumpkin. Sunfish	21	25	-	-	-	-	-	-	46
Northern Pike	-	-	-	-	11	9	-	-	20

Jay Gould Lake

FISH STOCKING DATA

year	species	size	# released
90	Walleye	Fry	500,000
92	Walleye	Fry	425,000
94	Walleye	Fry	425,000

survey date:
07/30/90

NET CATCH DATA

	Gill Nets		Trap Nets	
		avg fish		avg fish
species	# per net	wt. (lbs)	# per set	wt. (lbs)
Yellow Perch	31.4	0.22	3.1	0.19
Yellow Bullhead	2.9	0.61	2.3	1.01
White Sucker	1.7	2.68	0.1	1.60
Walleye	3.0	1.62	0.4	9.80
Tullibee (incl. Cisco)	0.1	0.10	-	-
Shorthead Red.	0.7	3.36	-	-
Rock Bass	2.4	0.54	0.4	0.57
Pumpkin. Sunfish	6.6	0.17	5.9	0.16
Northern Pike	4.1	1.70	1.5	1.27
Largemouth Bass	0.4	1.33	0.3	0.25
Brown Bullhead	1.3	1.03	0.4	0.83
Bowfin (Dogfish)	0.1	6.00	2.8	7.50
Bluegill	1.6	0.45	7.3	0.19
Black Crappie	1.0	1.00	-	-

LENGTH OF SELECTED SPECIES SAMPLED FROM ALL GEAR
Number of fish caught for the following length categories (inches):

species	0-5	6-8	9-11	12-14	15-19	20-24	25-29	>30	Total
Yellow Perch	-	81	23	-	-	-	-	-	104
Yellow Bullhead	-	2	12	6	-	-	-	-	20
Walleye	-	-	3	9	5	3	1	-	21
Tullibee (incl. Cisco)	-	1	-	-	9	-	-	-	10
Rock Bass	2	8	7	-	-	-	-	-	17
Pumpkin. Sunfish	27	19	-	-	-	-	-	-	46
Northern Pike	-	-	-	2	9	6	3	-	20
Largemouth Bass	-	-	1	-	1	-	-	-	2
Brown Bullhead	-	-	3	6	-	-	-	-	9
Bluegill	2	5	3	4	-	-	-	2	12
Black Crappie	-	-	3	4	-	-	-	-	7

DNR COMMENTS:

Walleye population is twice the lake classification median at 3 CPUE for gillnet. Yellow Perch population is three times lake classification median for gillnet and trapnet CPUE. Northern Pike population is one half of lake classification median for gillnet CPUE. Black Bullhead and Bowfin populations are higher than lake classification median. Bluegill population is low at one-third lake classification median. Every other species is close to lake classification median.

FISHING INFORMATION: Blandin Lake, better known as Paper Mill Reservoir, has a reputation for big Muskies, according to Brian Krecklau of Pole Bender Guide Service and Mike Auger of Blue Horizon Guide Service. While the Muskies reach the 30 to 40 pound-class, overall Muskie numbers are low compared to the other Muskie waters in the area. Ken's Pokegama Sports weighed in a 33-pounder last year. Patrons at the store talked about some excellent Largemouth Bass fishing on the reservoir. Walleye have been stocked with some success and anglers' catches appear to be improving. Early ice is excellent for Crappie fishing, especially in Sylvan Bay, where some 1 to 1-1/2 pounders are taken. Jay Gould is also part of the Mississippi River flowage. Krecklau has caught some 15 pound-class Northern and some decent Muskies from the lake. Walleye are caught with some regularity and the Crappies run in the pound-plus range. Largemouth and Smallmouth can also be found.

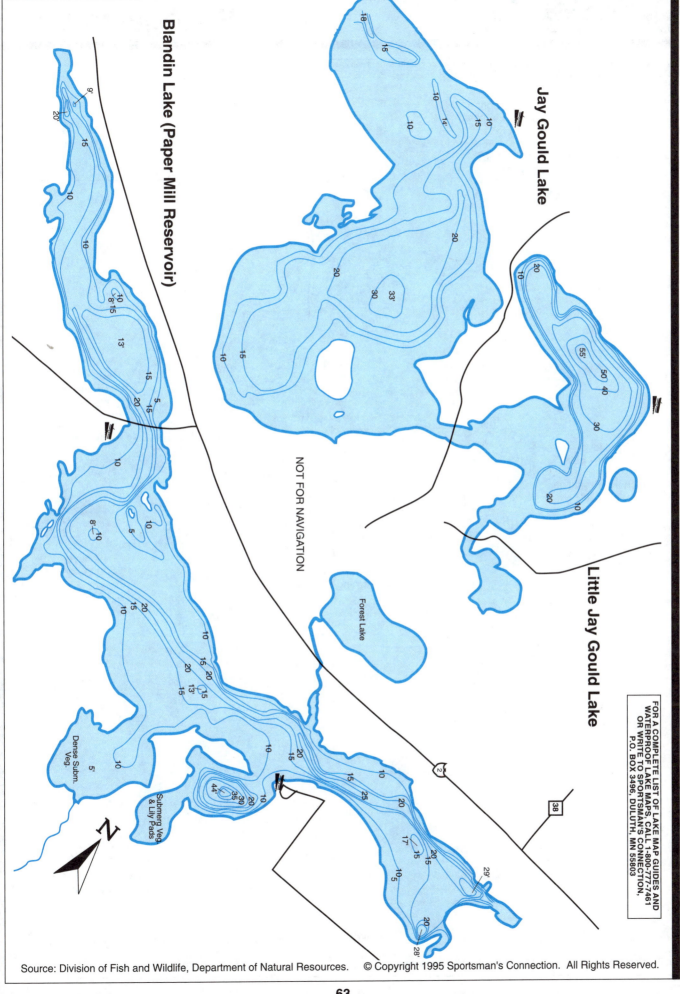

Blandin, Jay Gould, & L. Jay Gould Lakes

Jay Gould Lake

Blandin Lake (Paper Mill Reservoir)

Little Jay Gould Lake

NOT FOR NAVIGATION

Forest Lake

Dense Subm. Veg.

Submerg. Veg. & Lily Pads

N

FOR A COMPLETE LIST OF LAKE MAP GUIDES AND WATERPROOF LAKE MAPS, CALL 1-800-777-7461 OR WRITE TO SPORTSMAN'S CONNECTION, P.O. BOX 3496, DULUTH, MN 55803

Source: Division of Fish and Wildlife, Department of Natural Resources.

FOR A COMPLETE LIST OF LAKE MAP GUIDES AND WATERPROOF LAKE MAPS, CALL 1-800-777-7461
OR WRITE TO SPORTSMAN'S CONNECTION, P.O. BOX 3496, DULUTH, MN 55803

Spring
Crappie

Bass

Poole
Bay

Chisolm
Point

Walleye

Troll
Big Northern
Pike

Tioga
Bay

Wilder
Island

Drumbeater
Island

Crappie/Bass
Early Season

Walleye
Morning/
Night

King's
Bay

King's
Point

Winter
Spearing

Walleye/
Northern Pike

Sugar
Bay

Fish the Breakline
at Night

Newbitt
Island

Stony
Point

Spring
Smelt

Salter
Bay

Walleye
Night Fishing

Walleye
Morning/Evening

Sherry
Arm

Walleye
Spring/June

23

169

17

NOT FOR NAVIGATION

Source: Division of Fish and Wildlife, Department of Natural Resources.

FISHING INFORMATION: Mike Auger, who operates the Blue Horizon Guide Service out of Ken's Pokegama Sports, lives on the lake and knows it like the back of his hand. Mike shared some of Pokegama's fish-holding hot spots with us while marking our map. The lake is full of steep drops with more structure than any other lake in the area with weeds just about

(see map - "Walleye summer 17 ft. breakline") that is good for summer Walleye. The flat between Nesbitt Island and Drum-beater Island is real poor during the day due to the recreational boat traffic but night fishing with a weedless jig and minnow or a Rapala can be very productive. Walleyes can be found just about anywhere along the whole shore-

ging bright jigs in the afternoon. Some big Pike are also caught downrigging down to 30 feet of water where the thermocline and smelt can be found. Once in a blue moon some Lakers in the 8-12 pound range are picked up while Northern fishing this way. Crappies are nice with some 3/4 to 1 1/2 pound slabs present. Pokegama has a good Small-

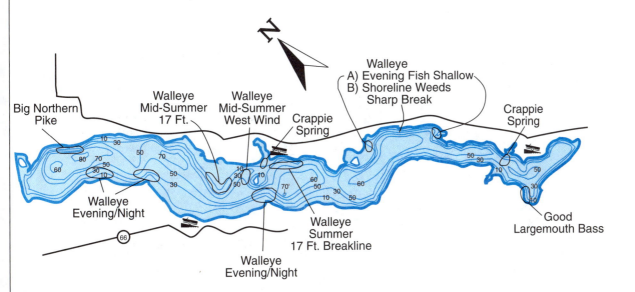

everywhere. The Walleyes seem to key on the 17 foot depth, according to Mike, because that is where the weed-line breaks. Due to its clear water and recreational boating, night fishing is best. Fish the shallows in the evenings. The island down in Wendigo Arm is good when there is a west wind, especially in the summer. The maps don't show it but there is a 17 foot breakline in the deep water to the west of the island

line but the steep breaks are tough. Find the gradual break-lines and start out in the evening in about 17 - 18 feet moving up into the flats as night falls. A lot of the Walleyes that you catch at night run between 2 to 4 pounds with some lunkers. Mike caught a 12 1/2 pounder a while back. Northern Pike in the 10 pound class are not uncommon with some 20 to 25 pounders caught. Fish the weedlines throughout the lake, trolling Rapalas or jig-

mouth Bass population and is under-established as a Large-mouth Bass Lake with many fish in the 3-6 pound range. Try the Largemouth in the evening by working the weeds and cabbage beds along the 17 foot weedline with jigs and worms or spinner baits. Pokegama even has an annual smelt run up the creek from Salter Bay.

(Please turn page for lake data).

POKEGAMA LAKE

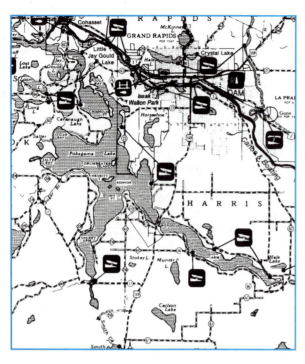

Location: Township 54, 55 Range 25, 26
Watershed: Mississippi Headwaters
Size of lake: 15,600 Acres
Shorelength: 50.8 Miles
Secchi disk (water clarity): 17.1 Ft.
Water color: Clear
Cause of water color: NA

Maximum depth: 110.0 Ft.
Median depth: NA
Accessibility: Access off Hwy. 17 on S side; off Hwy. 23 on E side; off of Hwy. 169 on E side; Tioga Beach on NW side; 3 accesses on Wendigo Arm
Boat Ramps: Concrete; Earth
Parking: Ample
Accommodations: Resorts, Campground

Shoreland zoning classification: General Development
Dominant forest/soil type: NA
Management class: Walleye-Centrarchid
Ecological type: Centrarchid-Walleye

FISH STOCKING DATA

year	species	size	# released
90	Walleye	Fingerling	7,395
90	Walleye	Yearling	6,235
91	Lake Trout	Yearling	25,000
92	Walleye	Fingerling	36,814
92	Walleye	Yearling	54
94	Walleye	Fingerling	15,098

NET CATCH DATA

survey date: 07/29/90

species	Gill Nets # per net	Gill Nets avg fish wt. (lbs.)	Trap Nets # per set	Trap Nets avg fish wt. (lbs.)
Yellow Perch	13.2	0.15	2.5	0.13
Yellow Bullhead	1.4	0.69	0.8	0.69
White Sucker	1.8	1.70	0.1	0.20
Walleye	7.1	1.89	0.4	3.90
Tullibee (incl. Cisco)	3.0	0.80	-	-
Smallmouth Bass	1.3	2.13	-	-
Rock Bass	8.5	0.51	2.0	0.30
Rainbow Smelt	0.8	0.07	-	-
Pumpkin. Sunfish	1.8	0.18	1.0	0.18
Northern Pike	5.3	2.66	0.4	2.88
Largemouth Bass	0.3	1.63	-	-
Lake Whitefish	0.6	1.76	-	-
Brown Bullhead	0.2	0.45	-	-
Bluegill	1.3	0.21	4.5	0.23
Black Crappie	0.6	0.39	0.2	0.25
Common Shiner	-	-	0.1	0.10
Bowfin (Dogfish)	-	-	0.7	5.74

LENGTH OF SELECTED SPECIES SAMPLED FROM ALL GEAR

Number of fish caught for the following length categories (inches):

species	0-5	6-8	9-11	12-14	15-19	20-24	25-29	>30	Total
Yellow Perch	-	109	18	1	-	-	-	-	128
Yellow Bullhead	-	4	8	5	-	-	-	-	17
Walleye	-	-	3	21	19	30	-	-	73
Tullibee (incl. Cisco)	-	-	-	35	1	-	-	-	36
Smallmouth Bass	-	-	2	17	7	-	-	-	26
Rock Bass	1	55	45	1	-	-	-	-	102
Pumpkin. Sunfish	10	11	-	-	-	-	-	-	21
Northern Pike	-	-	-	3	10	44	3	3	63
Largemouth Bass	-	-	1	2	1	-	-	-	4
Lake Whitefish	-	-	-	1	6	-	-	-	7
Brown Bullhead	-	1	1	-	-	-	-	-	2
Bluegill	4	11	-	-	-	-	-	-	15
Black Crappie	-	4	2	1	-	-	-	-	7

DNR COMMENTS: Northern Pike pop. stable and between 1st and 2rd quartile values, with about half of the fish 21" or greater; growth rates above statewide avg. Walleyes increasing, but still between 1st and 3rd quartiles; lengths range from 12-19.9", with strong age 2 and 4 year classes corresponding to lake stockings; growth rates above statewide means. Largemouth Bass within 1st-3rd quartile range; growth slightly faster than statewide avg. Smallmouth Bass fairly numerous at slightly above 3rd quartile values; most fish of quality size; growth rates above avg. Black Crappie pop. low, below 1st quartile range; growth slightly above statewide avg. Bluegills near avg.; pop. includes wide range of ages; growth slow. Yellow Perch between 1st and 3rd quartiles; pop. contains large number of small fish. Tullibee, Lake Whitefish, White Sucker, Brown Bullhead, Yellow Bullhead pop.s within 1st and 3rd quartile values. Lake Trout stocked in 1991, and anglers are taking some fish.

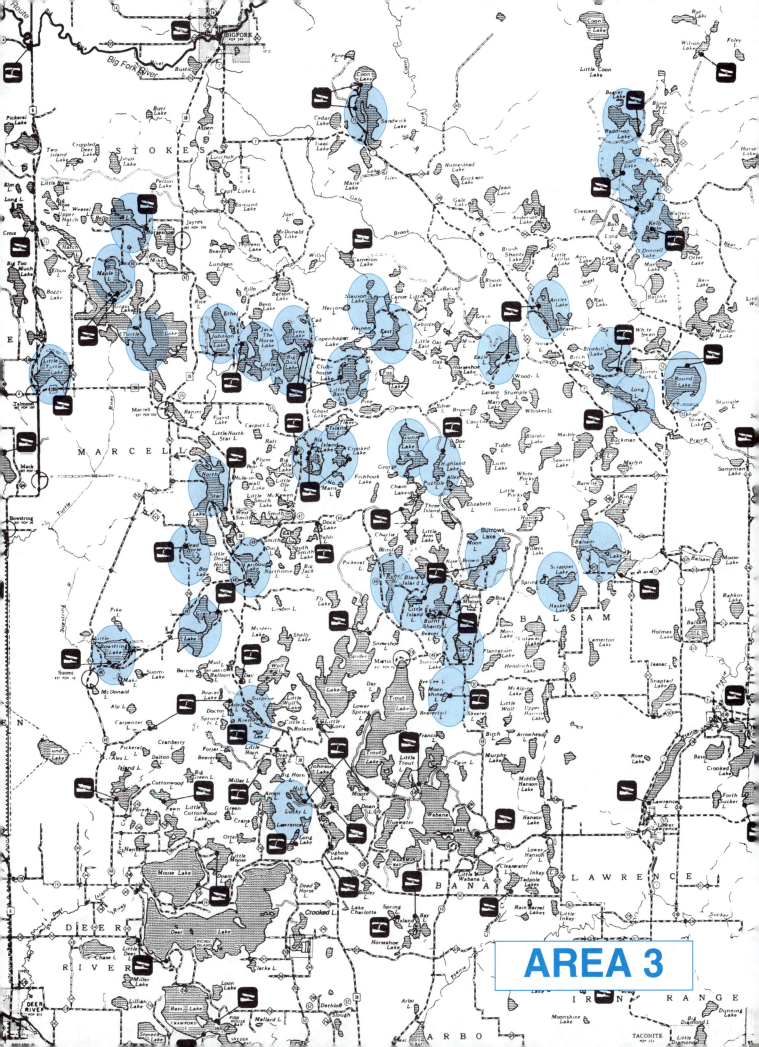

AREA 3

GRAVE LAKE   LITTLE BOWSTRING LAKE

Location: Township 58   Range 27
Watershed: Big Fork

Size of lake: 538 Acres
Shorelength: 7.5 Miles
Secchi disk (water clarity): 6.9 Ft.
Water color: Greenish-brown
Maximum depth: 39.0 Ft.
Median depth: 16.2 Ft.
Accessibility: USFS-owned public access on NE side
Boat Ramp: Concrete
Parking: Ample
Accommodations: None
Shoreland zoning classif.: Rec./Dev.
Dominant forest/soil type: Decid/Loam
Cause of water color: Algae
Management class: Walleye-Centrarchid
Ecological type: Centrarchid-Walleye

Size of lake: 314 Acres
Shorelength: 2.5 Miles
Secchi disk (water clarity): NA
Water color: Brownish
Maximum depth: 33.0 Ft.
Median depth: 20.0 Ft.
Accessibility: Access on S side, off County Road 48
Boat Ramp: Earth
Parking: Ample
Accommodations: Resort
Shoreland zoning classif.: Rec/Dev
Dominant forest/soil type: Decid/Loam
Cause of water color: Slight bog stain and algae bloom
Management class: Walleye
Ecological type: Hard-water Walleye

DNR COMMENTS:
Northern Pike numbers have increased from 1974 and are above medians but most Northerns are skinny. Yellow Perch population has been dropping dramatically but remains above medians. Walleye population is above medians and has been rising consistently from 1974. Other species appear to be in normal ranges for this lake.

FISH STOCKING DATA

year	species	size	# released
89	Walleye	Fingerling	3,814
91	Walleye	Fingerling	2,318

survey date: 8/17/88

NET CATCH DATA

species	Gill Nets # per net	Gill Nets avg fish wt. (lbs)	Trap Nets # per set	Trap Nets avg fish wt. (lbs)
Yellow Perch	17.4	0.31	1.0	0.29
White Sucker	0.4	1.33	-	-
Walleye	5.0	2.19	0.1	6.50
Tullibee (Cisco)	0.7	1.16	-	-
Rock Bass	2.7	0.84	0.3	0.95
Pumpkin. Sunfish	5.3	0.15	3.3	0.14
Northern Pike	12.4	1.50	1.6	1.77
Largemouth Bass	0.4	1.57	0.3	0.15
Brown Bullhead	0.7	0.82	-	-
Bowfin (Dogfish)	0.7	7.72	0.5	6.80
Bluegill	1.9	0.23	4.8	0.15
Black Crappie	0.1	0.70	-	-

LENGTH OF SELECTED SPECIES SAMPLED FROM ALL GEAR
Number of fish caught for the following length categories (inches):

species	0-5	6-8	9-11	12-14	15-19	20-24	25-29	>30	Total
Yellow Perch	2	52	16	8	-	-	-	-	78
Walleye	-	-	-	2	23	10	-	-	35
Tullibee (Cisco)	-	2	1	2	-	-	-	5
Rock Bass	-	4	15	-	-	-	-	-	19
Pumpkin. Sunfish	24	13	-	-	-	-	-	-	37
Northern Pike	-	-	-	8	48	29	1	-	86
Largemouth Bass	-	-	-	3	-	-	-	-	3
Brown Bullhead	-	1	2	2	-	-	-	-	5
Bluegill	3	7	3	-	-	-	-	-	13
Black Crappie	-	-	1	-	-	-	-	-	1

FISH STOCKING DATA

year	species	size	# released
89	Walleye	Fry	350,000
91	Walleye	Fry	960,000
93	Walleye	Fry	960,000

survey date: 8/30/89

NET CATCH DATA

species	Gill Nets # per net	Gill Nets avg fish wt. (lbs)	Trap Nets # per set	Trap Nets avg fish wt. (lbs)
Yellow Perch	95.4	0.15	2.8	0.14
White Sucker	1.2	1.50	-	-
Walleye	6.6	1.87	0.3	1.95
Tullibee (Cisco)	0.8	0.98	-	-
Pumpkin. Sunfish	0.6	0.13	0.7	0.20
Northern Pike	7.0	2.01	1.2	0.94
Bowfin (Dogfish)	0.2	3.30	0.5	4.63
Black Crappie	0.6	0.23	0.7	0.35
Rock Bass	-	-	1.2	0.51
Largemouth Bass	-	-	0.2	2.70
Brown Bullhead	-	-	0.8	1.34
Bluegill	-	-	1.0	0.25

LENGTH OF SELECTED SPECIES SAMPLED FROM ALL GEAR
Number of fish caught for the following length categories (inches):

species	0-5	6-8	9-11	12-14	15-19	20-24	25-29	>30	Total
Yellow Perch	1	133	6	-	-	-	-	-	140
Walleye	-	-	2	5	14	11	1	-	33
Tullibee (Cisco)	-	1	1	-	2	-	-	-	4
Pumpkin. Sunfish	-	3	-	-	-	-	-	-	3
Northern Pike	-	-	-	-	8	23	4	-	35
Black Crappie	-	3	-	-	-	-	-	-	3

DNR COMMENTS:
The Yellow Perch have increased in abundance since the first survey in 1971, from a gillnet CPUE of 29.0 to 15.5 in 1979, 14.2 in 1984 and 95.4 in this assessment. Walleye have trended downward in past surveys since the first survey in 1971 but increased to 6.6/gillnet during this assessment. Growth rates of Walleyes from this assessment compare favorably with other hardwater Walleye lakes in this area. Northern Pike abundance has remained fairly stable since the 1979 assessment but up since the first survey in 1971.

FISHING INFORMATION: Grave Lake (sometimes referred to as Graves Lake) is home of the two pound Bluegill, according to Don Wendt, owner of Rapids Tackle in Grand Rapids, with several pound-plus 'gills taking honors in the Fisherman's Blue Book every year. Walleye are also caught with some regularity with 1-1/2 to 2 pound averages being typical. Like most of the lakes in the area, Northern Pike and Largemouth Bass are also present, although the majority of those caught run on the small side. Little Bowstring doesn't receive much attention, but it also has some nice 'gills and Crappies. This is also a good lake to try for some lunker Largemouth Bass. Walleye fishing can be good, if not spectacular, with average sizes similar to those in Grave. Little Bowstring is somewhat bowl-shaped without a lot of structure, but there are some underwater islands and steep drops worth trying.

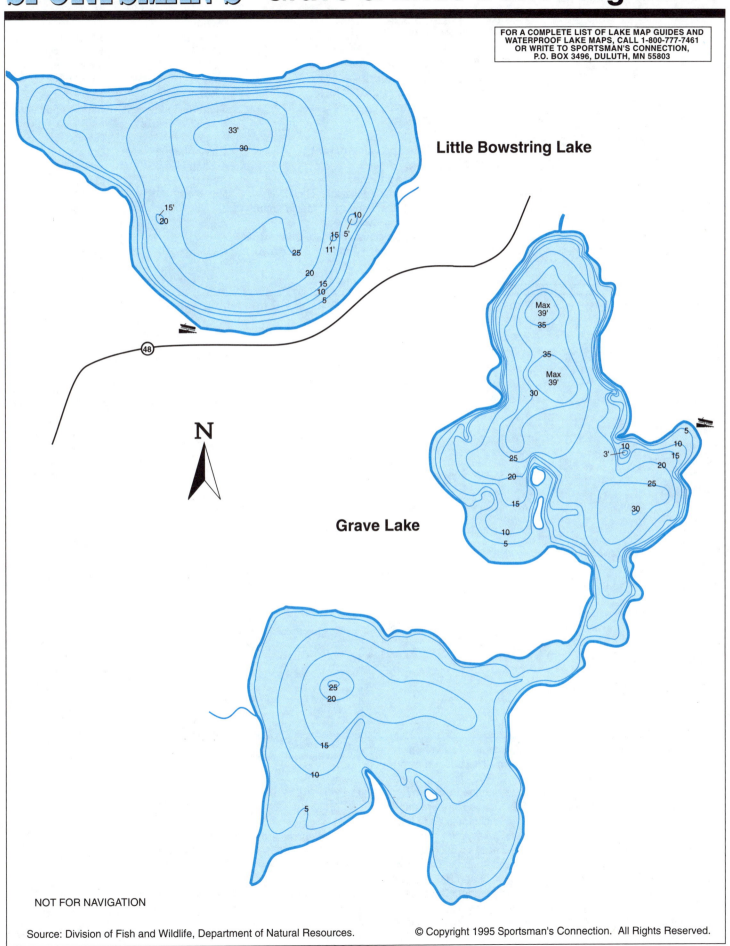

Little Bowstring Lake

Grave Lake

N

NOT FOR NAVIGATION

Source: Division of Fish and Wildlife, Department of Natural Resources.

Location: Township 58 Range 25
Watershed: Bigfork

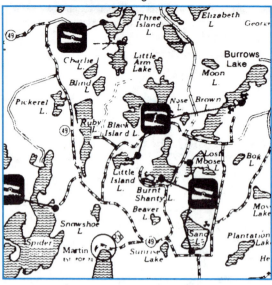

	RUBY LAKE	LITTLE ISLAND LAKE	BURNT SHANTY LAKE
Size of lake:	219 Acres	69 Acres	174 Acres
Shorelength:	3.8 Miles	1.9 Miles	3.3 Miles
Secchi disk (water clarity):	22.5 Ft.	NA	15.0 Ft.
Water color:	Clear	Blue-green	Light green
Maximum depth:	88.0 Ft.	35.0 Ft.	33.0 Ft.
Median depth:	25.0 Ft.	7.0 Ft.	15.0 Ft.
Accessibility:	Federally-owned access on SE side	State-owned access on E side of lake	State-owned access on S side, off Cty. Rd. 49
Boat Ramp:	Carry-down	Carry-down	Concrete
Parking:	Limited	Limited	Adequate
Accommodations:	None	Resort	Outhouses
Shoreland zoning classif.:	Rec. Dev.	Nat. Envt.	Rec. Dev.
Dominant forest/soil type:	Decid/Loam	NA	Decid/Loam
Cause of water color:	NA	Algae	Algae bloom
Management class:	Walleye-Centrarchid	Centrarchid	Centrarchid
Ecological type:	Centrarchid-Walleye	Centrarchid	Centrarchid

DNR COMMENTS:
Northern Pike very abundant, with gillnet catch of 7.4/set; growth good until age 5. Walleye pop. near 3rd quartile values; sample contains large number of Walleyes 20" or greater. Largemouth and Smallmouth Bass present. Bluegill pop. down sharply. Yellow Perch low. Tullibee pop. below lake class median.

Ruby Lake

FISH STOCKING DATA

year	species	size	# released
91	Walleye	Fingerling	17
91	Walleye	Adult	98
93	Walleye	Fingerling	900

NET CATCH DATA
survey date: 06/20/90

	Gill Nets		Trap Nets	
		avg fish		avg fish
species	# per net	wt. (lbs)	# per set	wt. (lbs)
Yellow Perch	1.8	0.13	1.3	0.20
White Sucker	3.8	3.65	-	-
Walleye	4.6	2.98	-	-
Tullibee (incl. Cisco)	1.8	0.21	-	-
Smallmouth Bass	0.2	1.50	-	-
Rock Bass	0.6	0.10	0.5	0.10
Northern Pike	7.4	2.64	1.3	0.50
Burbot	0.2	3.40	-	-
Bluegill	-	-	0.3	0.10
Black Crappie	-	-	0.5	0.95

LENGTH OF SELECTED SPECIES SAMPLED FROM ALL GEAR
Number of fish caught for the following length categories (inches):

species	0-5	6-8	9-11	12-14	15-19	20-24	25-29	>30	Total
Yellow Perch	-	-	1	-	-	-	-	-	1
Walleye	-	-	-	4	9	2	4	-	19
Tullibee (incl. Cisco)	-	1	5	-	-	-	-	-	6
Smallmouth Bass	-	-	-	1	-	-	-	-	1
Northern Pike	-	-	-	-	10	18	6	2	36

Little Island Lake

FISH STOCKING DATA NOT AVAILABLE

NET CATCH DATA
survey date: 06/25/79

	Gill Nets		Trap Nets	
		avg fish		avg fish
species	# per net	wt. (lbs)	# per set	wt. (lbs)
Yellow Perch	49.0	0.12	0.3	0.20
Yellow Bullhead	5.0	0.30	12.8	0.25
White Sucker	0.5	3.00	-	-
Pumpkin. Sunfish	3.0	0.13	46.0	0.11
Northern Pike	5.5	3.09	0.5	0.75
Bluegill	14.5	0.10	136.8	0.12
Black Crappie	3.5	0.46	12.5	0.18
Largemouth Bass	-	-	2.3	0.50

LENGTH OF SELECTED SPECIES SAMPLED FROM ALL GEAR
Number of fish caught for the following length categories (inches):

species	0-5	6-8	9-11	12-14	15-19	20-24	25-29	>30	Total
Black Crappie	-	29	14	1	-	-	-	-	44
Bluegill	1	53	-	-	-	-	-	-	54
Largemouth Bass	-	-	1	5	2	-	-	-	8
Northern Pike	-	-	-	-	3	7	3	1	14
Pumpkin. Sunfish	8	25	-	-	-	-	-	-	33
Yellow Bullhead	-	9	33	-	-	-	-	-	42
Yellow Perch	-	26	-	-	-	-	-	-	26

DNR COMMENTS:
Perch, Bluegill and Crappie populations are considerably higher than state and local medians. All other fish populations are within normal limits for this type of lake.

Burnt Shanty Lake

FISH STOCKING DATA NOT AVAILABLE

NET CATCH DATA
survey date: 08/30/89

	Gill Nets		Trap Nets	
		avg fish		avg fish
species	# per net	wt. (lbs)	# per set	wt. (lbs)
Yellow Perch	1.0	0.28	-	-
Yellow Bullhead	92.0	0.27	5.8	0.34
Pumpkin. Sunfish	6.5	0.18	1.5	0.17
Northern Pike	12.5	2.88	0.3	1.00
Largemouth Bass	1.0	0.90	-	-
Bluegill	60.3	0.21	17.3	0.19
Black Crappie	9.5	0.36	0.5	0.30

LENGTH OF SELECTED SPECIES SAMPLED FROM ALL GEAR
Number of fish caught for the following length categories (inches):

species	0-5	6-8	9-11	12-14	15-19	20-24	25-29	>30	Total
Yellow Perch	-	2	2	-	-	-	-	-	4
Yellow Bullhead	-	45	54	1	-	-	-	-	100
Pumpkin. Sunfish	8	17	1	-	-	-	-	-	26
Northern Pike	-	-	-	-	12	16	18	2	48
Largemouth Bass	-	-	3	1	-	-	-	-	4
Bluegill	5	140	3	-	-	-	-	-	148
Black Crappie	-	17	20	1	-	-	-	-	38

DNR COMMENTS:
Extremely high numbers of Yellow Bullheads. Black Crappie and Bluegill are abundant. Northern Pike size and abundance are very good. 200,000 Walleye fry were stocked in 1986, but no Walleyes were caught in the nets, or reported taken by fishermen.

FISHING INFORMATION: If you want a change of pace from some of the larger, more famous lakes along Scenic Hwy. 38, drop your canoe or small boat into one of these gems. Ruby 's deep, clear water makes for tough fishing which, along with the Perch and Tullibee forage base, contribute to the lake's large Northern and Walleye. Anglers can also find some nice Smallmouth and Large-mouth Bass in Ruby. Like most clear-water lakes, early morning and evening fishing with light line and small hooks work best. Burnt Shanty is a very good Largemouth Bass lake, according to Brian Krecklau of the Pole Bender Guide Service in Grand Rapids, with good numbers and some 5 pound-class fish present. Decent-size Northern Pike and a healthy Panfish population also provide good action. Little Island Lake is also a Bass, Northern, Panfish lake that yields a few decent Largemouth.

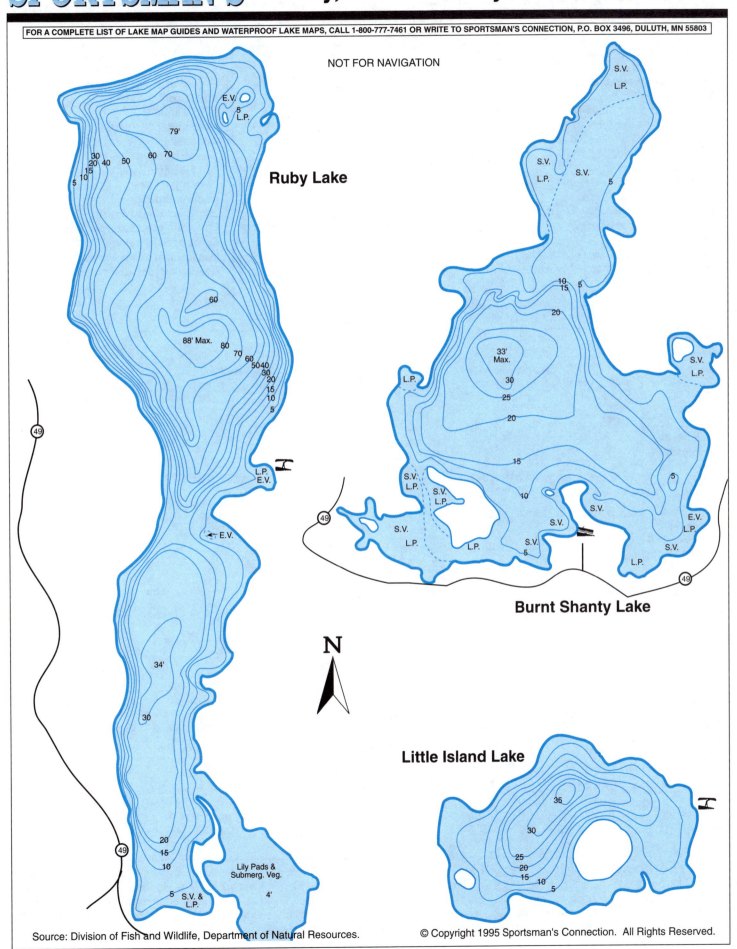

NOT FOR NAVIGATION

Ruby Lake

Burnt Shanty Lake

N

Little Island Lake

Source: Division of Fish and Wildlife, Department of Natural Resources.

BURROWS LAKE

SAND LAKE

Location: Township 58 Range 25
Watershed: Prairie-Willow

Size of lake: 272 Acres
Shorelength: 6.4 Miles
Secchi disk (water clarity): 6.6 Ft.
Water color: Clear
Maximum depth: 36.0 Ft.
Median depth: 15.0 Ft.
Accessibility: State-owned access on W. side, off Co. Rd. 53
Boat Ramp: Carry-down
Parking: Limited
Accommodations: None
Shoreland zoning classif.: Rec. Dev.
Dominant forest/soil type: NA
Cause of water color: NA
Management class: Walleye-Centrarchid
Ecological type: Centrarchid-Walleye

Size of lake: 172 Acres
Shorelength: 2.6 Miles
Secchi disk (water clarity): 15.8 Ft.
Water color: Clear
Maximum depth: 53.0 Ft.
Median depth: 20.0 Ft.
Accessibility: State-owned public access on S side
Boat Ramp: Earth
Parking: Limited
Accommodations: None
Shoreland zoning classif.: Rec. Dev.
Dominant forest/soil type: Decid/Loam
Cause of water color: NA
Management class: Centrarchid
Ecological type: Centrarchid

DNR COMMENTS:
Northern Pike slightly more numerous; sample consists mostly of ages 2,3 fish which have good growth rates. Walleye gillnet catch down, but normal for lake; sample dominated by age 3 fish with excellent growth rate; natural reproduction very limited. Largemouth Bass numerous; sample dominated by ages 1,2, with avg. growth. Bluegill and Black Crappies small in size; growth rates near avg. Yellow Perch pop. about normal for lake.

DNR COMMENTS:
Northern Pike population at very high levels and Perch numbers are low.

FISH STOCKING DATA

year	species	size	# released
90	Walleye	Fingerling	5,200

NET CATCH DATA

survey date: 07/19/89

	Gill Nets		Trap Nets	
species	# per net	avg fish wt. (lbs)	# per set	avg fish wt. (lbs)
Yellow Perch	5.4	0.11	0.5	0.10
White Sucker	1.8	2.64	-	-
Walleye	1.6	2.39	-	-
Northern Pike	5.8	2.43	0.5	3.10
Largemouth Bass	2.4	0.63	1.7	0.16
Golden Shiner	1.8	0.16	0.3	0.10
Bluegill	6.2	0.06	17.2	0.09
Black Crappie	1.6	0.31	2.7	0.18

LENGTH OF SELECTED SPECIES SAMPLED FROM ALL GEAR
Number of fish caught for the following length categories (inches):

species	0-5	6-8	9-11	12-14	15-19	20-24	25-29	>30	Total
Yellow Perch	-	27	-	-	-	-	-	-	27
Walleye	-	-	-	-	3	5	-	-	8
Northern Pike	-	-	-	1	26	2	-	-	29
Largemouth Bass	-	-	3	9	-	-	-	-	12
Bluegill	30	3	-	-	-	-	-	-	33
Black Crappie	1	6	-	1	-	-	-	-	8

FISH STOCKING DATA

year	species	size	# released
90	Walleye	Fry	175,000

NET CATCH DATA

survey date: 07/23/86

	Gill Nets		Trap Nets	
species	# per net	avg fish wt. (lbs)	# per set	avg fish wt. (lbs)
Yellow Perch	3.4	0.17	-	-
White Sucker	1.6	1.53	-	-
Walleye	2.2	2.32	-	-
Rock Bass	2.4	1.08	2.3	0.67
Pumpkin. Sunfish	0.8	0.35	-	-
Northern Pike	12.4	1.71	1.3	1.00
Largemouth Bass	0.2	1.10	0.3	0.20
Bluegill	2.6	0.32	11.3	0.18
Black Crappie	0.2	0.30	0.3	0.40

LENGTH OF SELECTED SPECIES SAMPLED FROM ALL GEAR
Number of fish caught for the following length categories (inches):

species	0-5	6-8	9-11	12-14	15-19	20-24	25-29	>30	Total
Black Crappie	-	2	-	-	-	-	-	-	2
Bluegill	26	30	3	-	-	-	-	-	59
Largemouth Bass	-	1	-	1	-	-	-	-	2
Northern Pike	-	-	2	11	30	24	1	1	69
Pumpkin. Sunfish	-	4	-	-	-	-	-	-	4
Rock Bass	1	4	12	5	-	-	-	-	22
Walleye	-	-	2	1	5	2	1	-	11
Yellow Perch	-	16	1	-	-	-	-	-	17

FISHING INFORMATION: Burrows Lake is off the beaten path and doesn't receive a lot of pressure. Some of the locals do pull some plump 2 to 3 pound Walleyes from the lake which has been receiving regular stocking in even years. The Northern Pike and Largemouth Bass fishing can be very good at times while Panfish tend to run on the small side. Sand Lake has also been receiving Walleye stocking efforts from the DNR which have provided anglers with some catches. Largemouth Bass fishing is pretty good and if you can get past the hammer handles, there are some good-sized Northern Pike in the lake. Panfish are plentiful, but small.

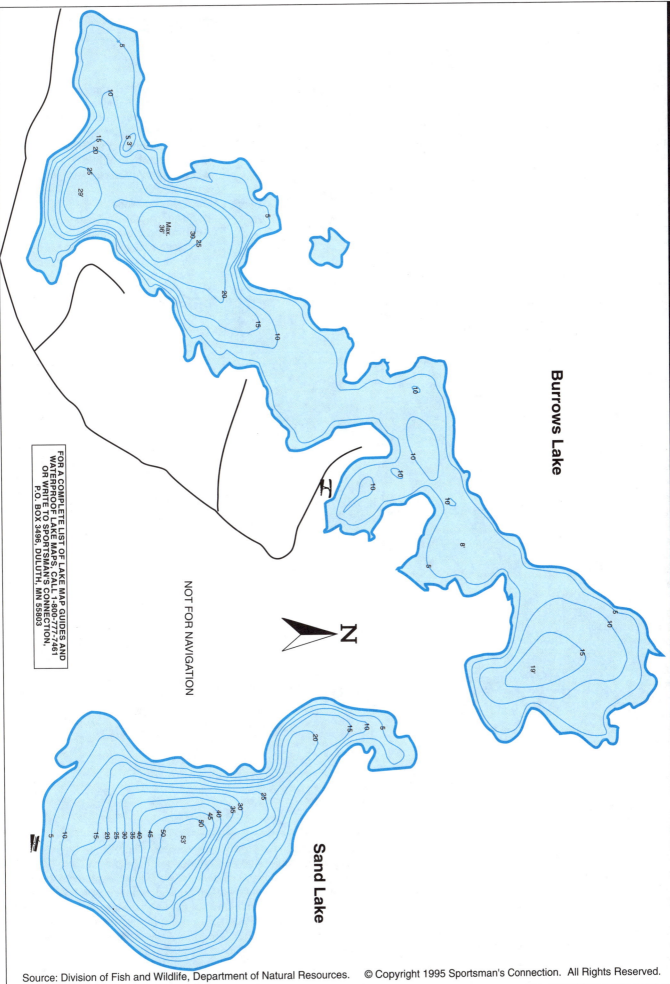

Burrows Lake

Sand Lake

N

NOT FOR NAVIGATION

Max. 36'

Burrows & Sand Lakes

SPORTSMAN'S Connection®

BALSAM LAKE   SCRAPPER LAKE

Location: Township 58, 59   Range 24, 25
Watershed: Prairie-Willow

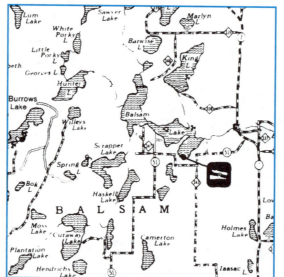

Size of lake: 651 Acres
Shorelength: 9.1 Miles
Secchi disk (water clarity): 9.8 Ft.
Water color: Light green
Maximum depth: 37.0 Ft.
Median depth: 16.0 Ft.
Accessibility: State-owned access 2 miles W of Hwy. 7 on Cty. Rd. 51
Boat Ramp: Earth
Parking: Ample
Accommodations: Resorts
Shoreland zoning classif.: Rec. Dev.
Dominant forest/soil type: Decid/Sand
Cause of water color: Light algae bloom
Management class: Walleye-Centrarchid
Ecological type: Centrarchid-Walleye

Size of lake: 156 Acres
Shorelength: 5.0 Miles
Secchi disk (water clarity): NA
Water color: Brown
Maximum depth: 28.0 Ft.
Median depth: 15.0 Ft.
Accessibility: Balsam and Brandon Lake Creeks
Boat Ramp: None
Parking: At Balsam Lake
Accommodations: None
Shoreland zoning classif.: Nat. Envt.
Dominant forest/soil type: Decid/Loam
Cause of water color: Swamp drainage
Management class: Centrarchid
Ecological type: Centrarchid

DNR COMMENTS:
Northern Pike present in about avg. numbers; growth avg., as well. Walleyes few; growth appears about avg., but sample numbers too small for reliable estimate. Largemouth Bass found during shoreline seining. Black Crappie pop. above 3rd quartile value; Yellow Perch few. Tullibees numerous at above 3rd quartile numbers.

FISH STOCKING DATA

year	species	size	# released
90	Walleye	Fingerling	2,153
92	Walleye	Fingerling	7,790
92	Walleye	Yearling	660

NET CATCH DATA
survey date: 06/29/92

	Gill Nets		Trap Nets	
species	# per net	avg fish wt. (lbs)	# per set	avg fish wt. (lbs)
Yellow Perch	0.8	0.09	0.7	0.09
White Sucker	1.5	2.67	-	-
Walleye	1.0	3.18	-	-
Tullibee (incl. Cisco)	9.1	0.73	-	-
Rock Bass	0.4	0.48	0.9	0.39
Pumpkin. Sunfish	0.2	0.10	2.8	0.18
Northern Pike	5.7	1.80	0.6	2.64
Largemouth Bass	0.1	2.50	0.2	1.65
Brown Bullhead	1.1	0.66	0.8	1.04
Bluegill	1.2	0.14	13.1	0.20
Black Crappie	7.9	0.28	1.6	0.25

LENGTH OF SELECTED SPECIES SAMPLED FROM ALL GEAR
Number of fish caught for the following length categories (inches):

species	0-5	6-8	9-11	12-14	15-19	20-24	25-29	>30	Total
Yellow Perch	-	9	-	-	-	-	-	-	9
Walleye	-	-	-	2	3	5	2	-	12
Tullibee (incl. Cisco)	-	25	25	25	34	-	-	-	109
Rock Bass	-	3	1	1	-	-	-	-	5
Pumpkin. Sunfish	1	1	-	-	-	-	-	-	2
Northern Pike	-	-	-	2	22	37	6	1	68
Largemouth Bass	-	-	-	-	1	-	-	-	1
Brown Bullhead	-	-	6	7	-	-	-	-	13
Bluegill	8	8	-	-	-	-	-	-	16
Black Crappie	5	45	43	1	-	-	-	-	94

FISH STOCKING DATA NOT AVAILABLE

NET CATCH DATA
survey date: 08/13/80

	Gill Nets		Trap Nets	
species	# per net	avg fish wt. (lbs)	# per set	avg fish wt. (lbs)
White Sucker	0.8	1.93	-	-
Tullibee (incl. Cisco)	0.6	1.50	-	-
Pumpkin. Sunfish	0.2	0.25	0.8	0.27
Northern Pike	10.4	1.45	1.3	1.50
Largemouth Bass	1.6	1.50	-	-
Brown Bullhead	7.2	0.58	6.0	0.52
Bluegill	3.6	0.15	6.0	0.15
Black Crappie	10.4	0.25	0.5	0.75
Rock Bass	-	-	0.3	0.30

LENGTH OF SELECTED SPECIES SAMPLED FROM ALL GEAR
Number of fish caught for the following length categories (inches):

species	0-5	6-8	9-11	12-14	15-19	20-24	25-29	>30	Total
Black Crappie	-	16	19	-	-	-	-	-	35
Bluegill	9	33	-	-	-	-	-	-	42
Brown Bullhead	-	-	38	14	-	-	-	-	52
Largemouth Bass	-	-	-	7	1	-	-	-	8
Northern Pike	-	-	-	7	29	15	6	-	57
Pumpkin. Sunfish	-	4	-	-	-	-	-	-	4
Rock Bass	-	1	-	-	-	-	-	-	1
Tullibee (incl. Cisco)	-	-	-	-	3	-	-	-	3

DNR COMMENTS:
Crappie and Northern Pike populations are quite high. Other fish populations are normal for this type of lake.

FISHING INFORMATION: Big Northern Pike and Largemouth Bass roam Balsam Lake's 9 miles of shoreline. Tony, at the Balsam Store along Scenic Highway 7, told us that the Crappie and Sunfish average about 1/2 pound and can be found throughout the lake. Walleye stocked by the DNR in recent years are starting to take hold with 1 to 1-1/2 pound fish being hooked more frequently. Reports of 3 pound-plus Walleye are also heard of at various times throughout the season. Balsam has some nice fish-holding structure with its numerous underwater points and sunken islands. The shallow water connecting the southeast bay with the rest of the lake provides excellent spawning habitat for the Bass, which reach 5 pounds, and the Balsam River and creek to Scrapper Lake are good Northern Pike spawning grounds. Scrapper Lake can be reached from the creek to Balsam and also has good numbers of Northerns, Bass and Panfish. The Northerns run smaller and some of the Crappie schools run a little larger than at Balsam. The Largemouth Bass are pretty nice with some scrappy 2 to 3 pounders.

Balsam & Scrapper Lakes

NOT FOR NAVIGATION

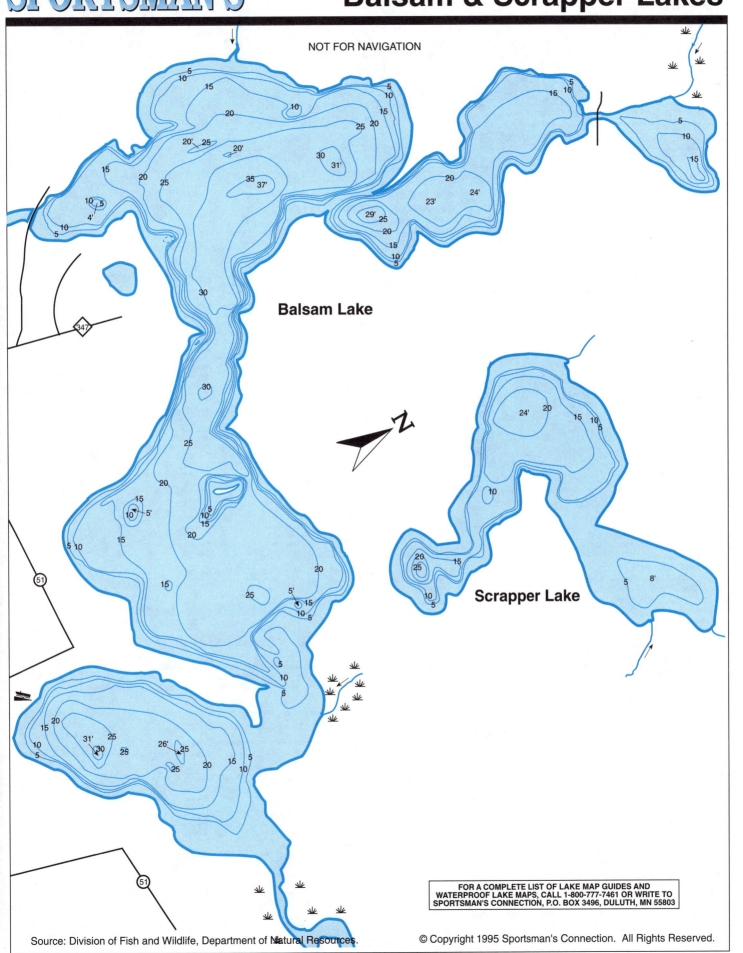

Balsam Lake

Scrapper Lake

Source: Division of Fish and Wildlife, Department of Natural Resources.

© Copyright 1995 Sportsman's Connection. All Rights Reserved.

Location: Township 57, 58 Range 25, 26
Watershed: Big Fork

	CARIBOU LAKE	**KREMER LAKE**	**LUCKY LAKE**	**MOONSHINE LAKE**
Size of lake:	222 Acres	64 Acres	13 Acres	24 Acres
Shorelength:	3.4 Miles	2.1 Miles	0.6 Miles	0.7 Miles
Secchi disk (water clarity):	26.5 Ft.	21.7 Ft.	NA	NA
Water color:	Clear	Clear	Clear	Green
Maximum depth:	152.0 Ft.	85.0 Ft.	44.0 Ft.	68.0 Ft.
Median depth:	47.0 Ft.	34.2 Ft.	10.0 Ft.	25.0 Ft.
Accessibility:	USFS-owned access off Hwy. 38 on SW corner of lake	Northeast end of lake	Federal-owned access trail off state Hwy. 38	East side, off Co. Rd. 49.
Boat Ramp:	Gravel	Carry-down	Carry-down	Carry-down
Parking:	Limited	None	None	None
Accommodations:	Resort, 3-4 campground sites	Campsite	None	None
Shoreland zoning classif.:	Rec. Dev.	Nat. Envt.	Nat. Envt.	Nat. Envt.
Dominant forest/soil type:	Conifer/Sand	NA	NA	NA
Cause of water color:	NA	NA	N	Algae bloom
Management class:	Lake Trout	Centrarchid	Stream Trout	Trout
Ecological type:	Trout	Centrarchid	Unclassified	Centrarchid

Caribou Lake

DNR COMMENTS:
Northern Pike pop. is well below statewide mean. Lake Trout pop. well above statewide mean; with 51% of sample between 12" and 18"; growth slow. Smallmouth Bass fairly numerous and small; growth slow. Bluegill pop. above statewide mean; growth slow.

FISHING INFO:
Caribou holds some nice Lake Trout, Splake and Rainbows. This "two story" lake also holds some nice Smallmouth and a few monster Northerns in its very clear, deep water. Terry, of the Frontier Sport in Marcell, said that the lake receives a fair amount of pressure, especially in the winter when fishermen catch some 3 to 4 pound Splake and some decent Lakers, through the ice.

FISH STOCKING DATA

year	species	size	# released
84	Rainbow Trout	Yearling	1,600
84	Lake Trout	Yearling	3,000
85	Lake Trout	Yearling	3,006
85	Rainbow Trout	Yearling	2,500
85	Splake Trout	Fingerling	7,688
86	Lake Trout	Yearling	3,018
87	Rainbow Trout	Yearling	3,250
87	Brook Trout	Fingerling	5,130
88	Rainbow Trout	Yearling	1,391
89	Lake Trout	Yearling	2,896
89	Rainbow Trout	Fingerling	6,256
89	Rainbow Trout	Yearling	1,200
90	Lake Trout	Yearling	3,000
91	Lake Trout	Yearling	3,000
93	Lake Trout	Yearling	1,200

NET CATCH DATA
survey date: 7/6/92

	Gill Nets		Trap Nets	
		avg fish		avg fish
species	# per net	wt. (lbs)	# per set	wt. (lbs)
Yellow Perch	6.8	0.12	-	-
White Sucker	0.7	2.75	-	-
Smallmouth Bass	7.3	0.23	0.2	0.35
Rock Bass	7.3	0.22	3.0	0.24
Northern Pike	0.2	12.00	-	-
Largemouth Bass	0.5	0.87	0.8	0.43
Lake Trout	0.2	3.80	-	-
Bluegill	2.0	0.09	7.3	0.18

LENGTH OF SELECTED SPECIES SAMPLED FROM ALL GEAR
Number of fish caught for the following length categories (inches):

species	0-5	6-8	9-11	12-14	15-19	20-24	25-29	>30	Total
Yellow Perch	-	42	22	3	-	-	-	-	67
Walleye	-	-	-	-	-	-	1	-	1
Smallmouth Bass	-	1	4	4	4	-	-	-	13
Rock Bass	6	43	11	-	-	-	-	-	60
Northern Pike	-	-	-	-	-	-	-	1	1
Largemouth Bass	-	-	2	1	1	-	-	-	4
Lake Trout	-	1	6	5	14	1	1	1	29
Bluegill	24	4	-	-	-	-	-	-	28

Kremer Lake

FISH STOCKING DATA

year	species	size	# released
84	Rainbow Trout	Yearling	2,000
84	Rainbow Trout	Fingerling	4,004
85	Rainbow Trout	Fingerling	3,990
85	Rainbow Trout	Yearling	2,000
86	Rainbow Trout	Fingerling	4,028
86	Rainbow Trout	Yearling	2,000
87	Rainbow Trout	Yearling	2,880
87	Rainbow Trout	Fingerling	4,000
87	Brook Trout	Fingerling	3,800
88	Brook Trout	Yearling	1,056
88	Rainbow Trout	Fingerling	2,714
88	Rainbow Trout	Yearling	4,101
89	Rainbow Trout	Fingerling	6,392
89	Rainbow Trout	Yearling	4,690
90	Rainbow Trout	Fingerling	6,392
90	Rainbow Trout	Yearling	3,200
91	Rainbow Trout	Fingerling	6,368
91	Rainbow Trout	Yearling	3,202
92	Rainbow Trout	Yearling	3,200
92	Rainbow Trout	Fingerling	6,400
93	Rainbow Trout	Yearling	3,200
93	Rainbow Trout	Fingerling	6,400
94	Rainbow Trout	Fingerling	5,500
94	Rainbow Trout	Yearling	2,600

NET CATCH DATA
survey date: 10/16/89

	Gill Nets		Trap Nets	
		avg fish		avg fish
species	# per net	wt. (lbs)	# per set	wt. (lbs)
Rainbow Trout	5.5	0.72	0.8	0.64
White Sucker	-	-	1.1	0.25
Golden Shiner	-	-	1.6	trace
Brook Trout	-	-	****.*	0.80

LENGTH OF SELECTED SPECIES SAMPLED FROM ALL GEAR
Number of fish caught for the following length categories (inches):

species	0-5	6-8	9-11	12-14	15-19	20-24	25-29	>30	Total
Rainbow Trout	-	-	-	9	2	-	-	-	11

DNR COMMENTS:
White Sucker have become established in Kremer Lake since the last reclamation in November, 1973. This assessment sampled a trapnet CPUE of 1.1 compared to 1.3 in 1981. No White Sucker were captured in the gillnets in this assessment. However, this was the first fall trapnetting conducted on this lake. Past studies on trout lakes in MN indicated a CPUE in heavily fished lakes of 1-5 trout in fall trapnetting. A trapnet CPUE of 0.8 was observed in this assessment. Growth rates of the Rainbow Trout are comparable to those in other trout lakes.

FISHING INFO:
Twelve inch Rainbows, with some larger ones, are taken. Moderately heavy fishing pressure.

Lucky Lake

DNR COMMENTS NOT AVAILABLE

FISHING INFO:
Lucky holds some nice Brown Trout for those willing to walk the mile or so to get into it. Darwin, of God's Country Outfitters on Hwy. 38, said that some 4 to 5 pound Browns are caught every year with good numbers of 1 to 2 pound fish.

FISH STOCKING DATA

year	species	size	# released
82	Brown Trout	Yearling	594
82	Brown Trout	Yearling	894
86	Brown Trout	Yearling	600
87	Brown Trout	Yearling	600
88	Brown Trout	Yearling	1,081
90	Brown Trout	Yearling	600
92	Brown Trout	Yearling	600
94	Brown Trout	Yearling	1,149

NET CATCH DATA
survey date: 10/18/88

	Gill Nets		Trap Nets	
		avg fish		avg fish
species	# per net	wt. (lbs)	# per set	wt. (lbs)
Brown Trout	-	-	2.2	1.17

LENGTH OF SELECTED SPECIES SAMPLED FROM ALL GEAR
Number of fish caught for the following length categories (inches):

species	0-5	6-8	9-11	12-14	15-19	20-24	25-29	>30	Total
Brown Trout	-	-	9	29	55	-	-	-	93

Moonshine Lake

FISH STOCKING DATA

year	species	size	# released
82	Rainbow Trout	Fingerling	999
84	Rainbow Trout	Fingerling	3,141
84	Rainbow Trout	Yearling	2,000
84	Rainbow Trout	Yearling	3,000
84	Brook Trout	Yearling	1,500
85	Rainbow Trout	Fingerling	1,995
85	Rainbow Trout	Yearling	2,052
86	Rainbow Trout	Fingerling	2,004
86	Rainbow Trout	Yearling	2,000
87	Rainbow Trout	Fingerling	3,200
88	Rainbow Trout	Fingerling	1,275
89	Rainbow Trout	Fingerling	2,516
90	Rainbow Trout	Fingerling	2,539
91	Rainbow Trout	Fingerling	2,500
92	Rainbow Trout	Fingerling	2,500
93	Rainbow Trout	Fingerling	2,653
94	Rainbow Trout	Fingerling	2,598

NET CATCH DATA NOT AVAILABLE

LENGTH OF SELECTED SPECIES NOT AVAILABLE

DNR COMMENTS NOT AVAILABLE

FISHING INFO:
Moonshine is another pothole that holds some nice Trout. Stocked Rainbows, reaching 5 to 6 pounds, are caught. Most of the fish run smaller in size and are fished fairly hard by area and visiting anglers due to accessibility.

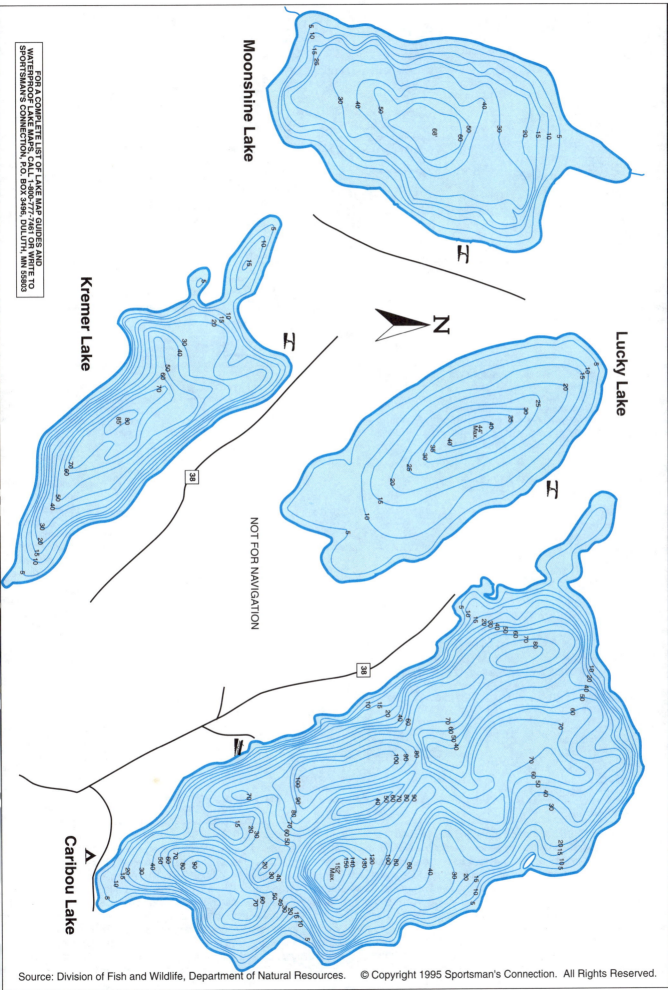

Source: Division of Fish and Wildlife, Department of Natural Resources.

NORTH STAR LAKE   DEAD HORSE LAKE

Location: Township 58, 59 Range 26
Watershed: Big Fork

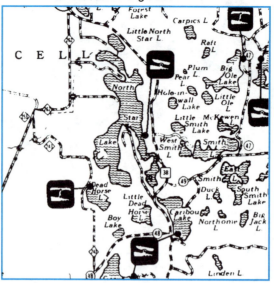

Size of lake: 907 Acres
Shorelength: 14.6 Miles
Secchi disk (water clarity): 7.7 Ft.
Water color: Green
Maximum depth: 80.0 Ft.
Median depth: 26.7 Ft.
Accessibility: Federal-owned access on S side, off Hwy. 38
Boat Ramp: Concrete
Parking: Ample
Accommodations: Resorts, Campground
Shoreland zoning classif.: Rec. Dev.
Dominant forest/soil type: Decid/Loam
Cause of water color: Algae
Management class: Walleye-Centrarchid
Ecological type: Centrarchid-Walleye

Size of lake: 96 Acres
Shorelength: 1.8 Miles
Secchi disk (water clarity): NA
Water color: Light green
Maximum depth: 36.0 Ft.
Median depth: 16.0 Ft.
Accessibility: USFS-owned public access on N side
Boat Ramp: Carry-down
Parking: Limited
Accommodations: None
Shoreland zoning classif.: Nat. Envt.
Dominant forest/soil type: NA
Cause of water color: Algae bloom
Management class: Walleye-Centrarchid
Ecological type: Centrarchid-Walleye

DNR COMMENTS:

Walleye, first introduced in the 1970's, have, in the past assessments, had a gill-net CPUE of 2.2 in 1979, 5.2 in 1984 and 3.7 in this assessment. Mean weight of the Walleye sampled was 2.2 pounds/fish. Northern Pike, in this assessment, were at gillnet CPUE of 3.1. This compares with a lake class median of 4.9. Growth rates for these fish were very good. Age 2 fish had a mean length of 17.9" (N=10) and age 3 fish were 22.6" (N=6). Yellow Perch abundance of 6.6/gillnet has dropped from 30.9/gillnet in the 1984 survey; however, it does compare with prior assessments.

FISH STOCKING DATA

year	species	size	# release
89	Muskellunge	Fingerling	314
89	Muskellunge	Fingerling	314
90	Walleye	Fingerling	346
90	Walleye	Yearling	1,798
91	Muskellunge	Fingerling	314
92	Walleye	Fingerling	20,535
94	Muskellunge	Fingerling	314

NET CATCH DATA
survey date: 08/20/90

species	Gill Nets # per net	Gill Nets avg fish wt. (lbs)	Trap Nets # per set	Trap Nets avg fish wt. (lbs)
Yellow Perch	6.6	0.11	0.3	0.10
Yellow Bullhead	0.1	0.70	-	-
White Sucker	0.4	2.48	-	-
Walleye	3.7	2.18	-	-
Tullibee (incl. Cisco)	2.6	0.28	-	-
Smallmouth Bass	0.5	0.50	0.1	0.10
Rock Bass	8.8	0.46	1.6	0.22
Pumpkin. Sunfish	1.7	0.11	0.6	0.18
Northern Pike	3.1	2.60	-	-
Largemouth Bass	0.5	0.70	-	-
Bowfin (Dogfish)	0.4	5.18	2.0	4.56
Bluegill	6.3	0.13	5.4	0.12
Black Crappie	1.0	0.25	0.3	0.10

LENGTH OF SELECTED SPECIES SAMPLED FROM ALL GEAR
Number of fish caught for the following length categories (inches):

species	0-5	6-8	9-11	12-14	15-19	20-24	25-29	>30	Total
Yellow Perch	-	67	3	1	-	-	-	-	71
Yellow Bullhead	-	-	-	1	-	-	-	-	1
Walleye	-	-	1	1	30	6	3	-	41
Tullibee (incl. Cisco)	-	14	10	2	1	-	-	-	27
Smallmouth Bass	-	-	4	2	-	-	-	-	6
Rock Bass	11	29	55	2	-	-	-	-	97
Pumpkin. Sunfish	9	10	-	-	-	-	-	-	19
Northern Pike	-	-	-	1	11	14	5	2	33
Largemouth Bass	-	1	1	2	-	-	-	-	4
Bluegill	25	39	-	-	-	-	-	-	64
Black Crappie	4	5	1	1	-	-	-	-	11

FISH STOCKING DATA

year	species	size	# released
89	Walleye	Fry	300,000
91	Walleye	Fry	100,000
93	Walleye	Fry	104,000

NET CATCH DATA
survey date: 08/15/88

species	Gill Nets # per net	Gill Nets avg fish wt. (lbs)	Trap Nets # per set	Trap Nets avg fish wt. (lbs)
Yellow Perch	1.3	0.20	2.3	0.19
White Sucker	3.3	2.59	-	-
Walleye	2.5	4.06	0.5	6.15
Rock Bass	0.8	1.07	0.3	0.10
Pumpkin. Sunfish	0.5	0.45	3.5	0.19
Northern Pike	10.0	3.99	1.0	3.15
Largemouth Bass	1.5	0.83	1.0	0.90
Golden Shiner	0.3	0.20	0.3	0.10
Bluegill	15.5	0.10	39.0	0.14

LENGTH OF SELECTED SPECIES SAMPLED FROM ALL GEAR
Number of fish caught for the following length categories (inches):

species	0-5	6-8	9-11	12-14	15-19	20-24	25-29	>30	Total
Yellow Perch	1	3	1	-	-	-	-	-	5
Walleye	-	-	-	-	2	8	-	-	10
Rock Bass	-	-	2	1	-	-	-	-	3
Pumpkin. Sunfish	-	2	-	-	-	-	-	-	2
Northern Pike	-	-	-	-	1	20	18	-	39
Largemouth Bass	-	-	-	6	-	-	-	-	6
Bluegill	48	11	3	-	-	-	-	-	62

DNR COMMENTS

Northern Pike populations are above state and local medians but quite low compared to those of past years. Panfish and Largemouth Bass are slightly above medians but none of these species was observed in 1975. Yellow Perch numbers are below medians and considerably lower than before even after the partial winterkill of 1977-78. Walleye populations are also below medians and decreasing from a high in 1975. Other species appear to be in a normal range for this lake.

FISHING INFORMATION: Terry, of Frontier Sport in Marcell, said that some huge Northerns roam North Star Lake and the Walleye are chunky, averaging 2 pounds or better. Northerns can be found near the weedbeds throughout the lake. Try the underwater islands, points and other shoreline structure for Walleye. North Star also provides some good Bass fishing, according to Terry, with Largemouth providing more action than the Smallmouth. Spinner baits, worms and other Bass baits produce results off the shallow reeds and cabbage patches. Along with regular Walleye stocking, the DNR has also been stocking Muskies and has designated North Star as a Muskie lake. The Muskies seem to be taking hold as anglers fishing for Northerns have reported hooking and releasing some small ones (check the current fishing regs for minimum length on Muskies). Bluegills run on the small side and the Crappies are average. North Star is fairly clear with some steep dropoffs. Fishing pressure is relatively heavy in the summer due to the many cabins and the resorts on the lake and its easy accessibility (good concrete ramp and ample parking). Little North Star is accessible through a channel from North Star and provides some 3/4 pound to one pound Crappies, Northerns, and an occasional Walleye. Dead Horse Lake has an abundance of Northerns, some Largemouth Bass and Walleyes. Weed growth is fairly heavy providing good cover for these species. Terry said that if you do find the Walleyes, you can count on some nice ones. Pressure is minimal due to the primitive access.

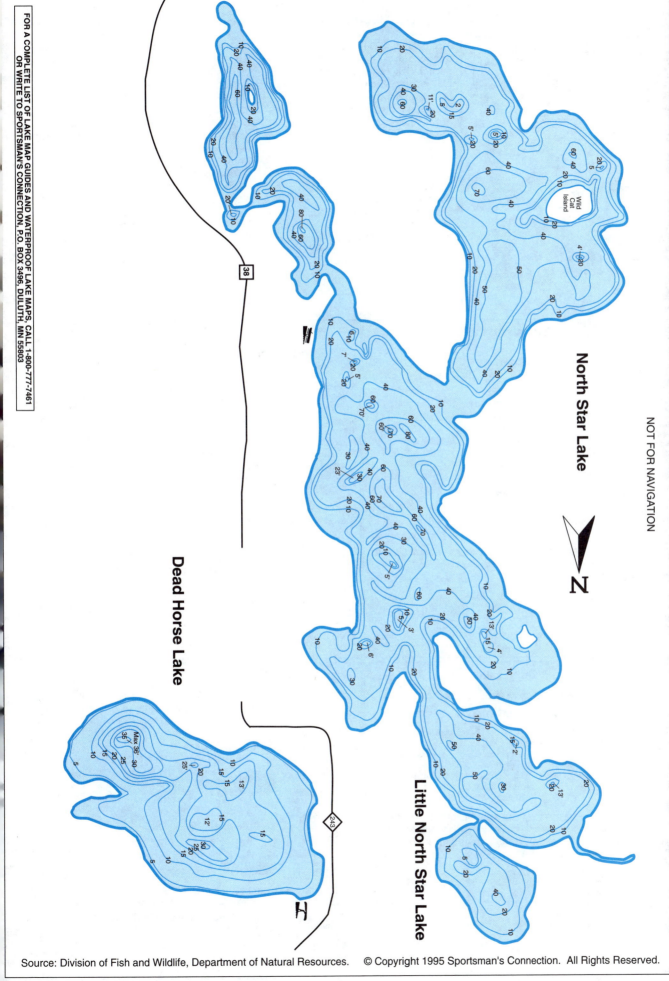

North Star & Dead Horse Lakes

NOT FOR NAVIGATION

N

North Star Lake

Wild Cat Island

Dead Horse Lake

Little North Star Lake

Max 36'

38

243

Source: Division of Fish and Wildlife, Department of Natural Resources. © Copyright 1995 Sportsman's Connection. All Rights Reserved.

Location: Township 59   Range 25, 26
Watershed: Big Fork

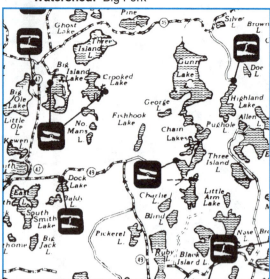

	BIG ISLAND LAKE	HIGHLAND LAKE	GUNN LAKE	CROOKED LAKE
Size of lake:	220 Acres	98 Acres	347 Acres	103 Acres
Shorelength:	4.1 Miles	2.8 Miles	5.1 Miles	3.7 Miles
Secchi disk (water clarity):	11.3 Ft.	10.8 Ft.	10.5 Ft.	NA
Water color:	Brown-green	Amber	Brown	Brown
Maximum depth:	44.0 Ft.	38.0 Ft.	39.0 Ft.	46.0 Ft.
Median depth:	6.5 Ft.	13.0 Ft.	10.1 Ft.	8.0 Ft.
Accessibility:	USFS-owned public access off Cty. Rd. #47	County-owned earthen access on N side, off Co. Rd. 45	Access by Lake #6 of the Gunn Lake Chain	Itasca Cty. Land Dept. access on SE side
Boat Ramp:	Earth	Carry-down	Concrete	Earth
Parking:	Ample	Limited	Ample	Ample
Accommodations:	None	None	Resort	None
Shoreland zoning classif.:	Rec. Dev.	Rec. Dev.	Rec. Dev.	Nat. Envt.
Dominant forest/soil type:	Decid/Loam	NA	Decid/Sand	NA
Cause of water color:	Bog stain, algae	Bog stain, algae	Bog stain	Swamp stain
Management class:	Centrarchid	Centrarchid	Centrarchid	Centrarchid
Ecological type:	Centrarchid	Centrarchid	Centrarchid	Centrarchid

DNR COMMENTS:
Northern Pike remain at relatively high levels with good growth. No Walleye were sampled in this assessment despite a 1986 fry stocking. Black Crappie have continued their downward trend although growth rates are very good. Only two Largemouth Bass were caught in the gill-nets and two in the shoreline seining. Anglers, however, report good fishing for Largemouth Bass.

FISHING INFO:
Big Island Lake holds some nice Largemouth Bass, many in the 3 to 4 pound range. Good numbers and sizes of Northern Pike also swim along the miles of shoreline and islands of this picturesque lake.

Big Island Lake

FISH STOCKING DATA NOT AVAILABLE

NET CATCH DATA

	Gill Nets		Trap Nets	
survey date: 7/22/90		avg fish		avg fish
species	# per net	wt. (lbs)	# per set	wt. (lbs)
Yellow Perch	3.0	0.13	-	-
White Sucker	0.2	3.20	-	-
Northern Pike	9.0	2.32	0.8	1.43
Largemouth Bass	0.4	1.05	-	-
Bluegill	9.6	0.19	9.0	0.25
Black Crappie	0.6	0.53	1.8	0.21

LENGTH OF SELECTED SPECIES SAMPLED FROM ALL GEAR
Number of fish caught for the following length categories (inches):

species	0-5	6-8	9-11	12-14	15-19	20-24	25-29	>30	Total
Yellow Perch	-	15	-	-	-	-	-	1	16
Northern Pike	-	-	-	1	13	25	5	-	44
Largemouth Bass	-	1	1	-	1	-	-	-	3
Bluegill	11	36	1	-	-	-	-	-	48
Black Crappie	-	-	2	-	-	-	-	-	2

Highland Lake

FISH STOCKING DATA NOT AVAILABLE

NET CATCH DATA

	Gill Nets		Trap Nets	
survey date: 6/20/88		avg fish		avg fish
species	# per net	wt. (lbs)	# per set	wt. (lbs)
Tullibee (Cisco)	4.5	0.66	-	-
Pumpkin. Sunfish	0.5	0.15	4.0	0.08
Northern Pike	9.5	2.98	1.0	1.48
Bluegill	0.5	0.20	39.0	0.17
Black Crappie	0.3	0.20	2.8	0.30
Rock Bass	-	-	1.5	0.30
Largemouth Bass	-	-	1.0	0.55
Hybrid Sunfish	-	-	1.3	0.32
Black Bullhead	-	-	0.3	0.20

LENGTH OF SELECTED SPECIES SAMPLED FROM ALL GEAR
Number of fish caught for the following length categories (inches):

species	0-5	6-8	9-11	12-14	15-19	20-24	25-29	>30	Total
Tullibee (Cisco)	-	2	3	13	-	-	-	-	18
Pumpkin. Sunfish	-	2	-	-	-	-	-	-	2
Northern Pike	-	-	-	-	10	19	6	3	38
Bluegill	-	2	-	-	-	-	-	-	2
Black Crappie	-	1	-	-	-	-	-	-	1

DNR COMMENTS:
Northern Pike abundant and good average size probably due to good Tullibee pop. Bluegill abundance is also higher than normal. No Yellow Perch were captured in gill-nets or trapnets but 36 young-of-year were caught in two shoreline seine hauls. All other species caught appear to be avg.

FISHING INFO:
Highland Lake has a primitive access classified as "carry-in" although it is possible to back a small boat into it. Bass are plentiful, but run small. Northerns are also plentiful and nice sized.

FISHING INFO:
Gunn Lake is the top lake of a chain of six lakes referred to as the Gunn Lake chain or Chain Lakes. You can reach the other lakes through a series of narrow channels deep enough to get a boat with motor through (watch the lily pads!). Each lake has good depth and healthy Largemouth Bass populations. Northern and Panfish are also abundant, but small. Scenery is spectacular along this chain.

Gunn Lake

FISH STOCKING DATA NOT AVAILABLE

NET CATCH DATA NOT AVAILABLE

DNR COMMENTS: Northern Pike pop. below local median and below 1st-3rd quartile values; sampled lengths range from 15-32", indicating a quality population structure. Largemouth Bass sampled in typically low numbers; however, local anglers report good success. Bluegills very numerous and above 3rd quartile range; most of sample in 5-6" range. Black Crappies sampled in near-avg. numbers and sizes. Tullibees present in moderate numbers.

LENGTH OF SELECTED SPECIES SAMPLED FROM ALL GEAR
Number of fish caught for the following length categories (inches):

species	0-5	6-8	9-11	12-14	15-19	20-24	25-29	>30	Total
Yellow Perch	-	2	-	-	-	-	-	-	2
Rock Bass	2	18	4	-	-	-	-	-	24
Pumpkin. Sunfish	6	86	-	-	-	-	-	-	92
Northern Pike	-	-	-	-	4	2	-	-	6
Largemouth Bass	-	8	8	-	2	-	-	-	18
Hybrid Sunfish	14	68	8	-	-	-	-	-	90
Bluegill	80	128	2	-	-	-	-	-	210
Black Crappie	-	18	10	2	-	-	-	-	30

Crooked Lake

FISH STOCKING DATA NOT AVAILABLE

NET CATCH DATA

	Gill Nets		Trap Nets	
survey date: 9/3/82		avg fish		avg fish
species	# per net	wt. (lbs)	# per set	wt. (lbs)
Yellow Perch	1.0	0.17	0.4	0.25
White Sucker	0.3	3.00	-	-
Northern Pike	5.3	2.11	-	-
Bluegill	23.0	0.20	7.4	0.17
Black Crappie	1.0	0.40	0.6	0.53

LENGTH OF SELECTED SPECIES SAMPLED FROM ALL GEAR
Number of fish caught for the following length categories (inches):

species	0-5	6-8	9-11	12-14	15-19	20-24	25-29	>30	Total
Black Crappie	-	2	4	-	-	-	-	-	6
Bluegill	29	77	-	-	-	-	-	-	106
Northern Pike	-	-	-	-	2	8	4	-	14
Yellow Perch	-	4	1	-	-	-	-	-	5

DNR COMMENTS:
Northern Pike and Bluegill populations are good. Perch and Crappie numbers are below catch medians. It does not appear that past stockings of Muskie were successful.

FISHING INFO:
A truck is recommended for accessing Crooked Lake which can be reached by a rocky, minimum maintenance road (see area map insert). The access has a steep dropoff. Bass and Northerns run small, but there are some nice ones mixed in.

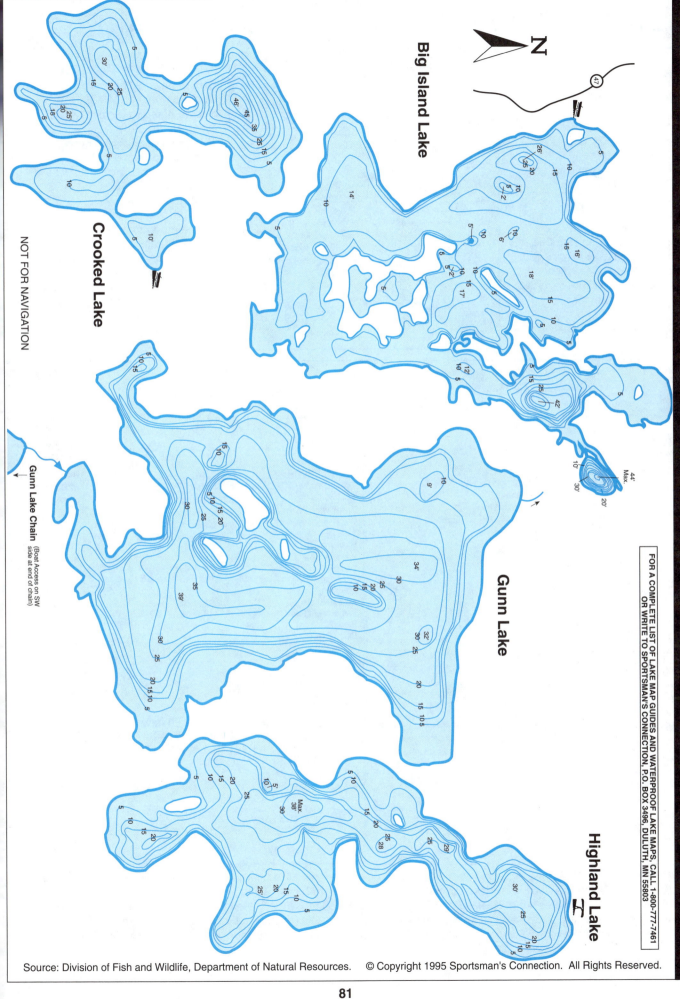

Gunn, Big Island, Crooked, & Highland Lakes

Big Island Lake

N

47

Crooked Lake

NOT FOR NAVIGATION

Gunn Lake

Gunn Lake Chain
(Boat Access on SW
side at end of chain)

Highland Lake

FOR A COMPLETE LIST OF LAKE MAP GUIDES AND WATERPROOF LAKE MAPS, CALL 1-800-777-7461 OR WRITE TO SPORTSMAN'S CONNECTION, P.O. BOX 3496, DULUTH, MN 55803

ANTLER LAKE   # EAGLE LAKE

Location: Township 59, 60   Range 24, 25
Watershed: Prairie-Willow

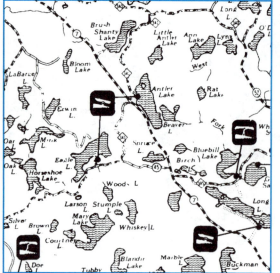

Size of lake: 232 Acres
Shorelength: 3.3 Miles
Secchi disk (water clarity): 16.1 Ft.
Water color: Green
Maximum depth: 90.0 Ft.
Median depth: 30.0 Ft.
Accessibility: State-owned access on NW side via Co. Rd. 341
Boat Ramp: Earth
Parking: Ample
Accommodations: Resort
Shoreland zoning classif.: Rec. Dev.
Dominant forest/soil type: Decid/Loam
Cause of water color: Algae bloom
Management class: Walleye-Centrarchid
Ecological type: Centrarchid

Size of lake: 261 Acres
Shorelength: 4.5 Miles
Secchi disk (water clarity): 7.5 Ft.
Water color: Brown
Maximum depth: 35.0 Ft.
Median depth: 18.0 Ft.
Accessibility: SE corner of lake off Cty. Rd. 45
Boat Ramp: Earth
Parking: Ample
Accommodations: None
Shoreland zoning classif.: Rec. Dev.
Dominant forest/soil type: Decid/Loam
Cause of water color: Bog stain
Management class: Walleye-centrarchid
Ecological type: Centrarchid

DNR COMMENTS: Northern Pike pop. low and typical for this lake at below 1st quartile values. Walleye pop. between 1st and 3rd quartiles; all from stocked age classes; growth normal for lake class. Largemouth Bass few. Bluegills slightly above avg. in numbers; growth good. Black Crappies avg. in number; growth good. Tullibee, White Sucker and Rock Bass near lake class median levels.

FISH STOCKING DATA

year	species	size	# released
90	Walleye	Yearling	223

NET CATCH DATA
survey date: 07/27/92

	Gill Nets		Trap Nets	
species	# per net	avg fish wt. (lbs)	# per set	avg fish wt. (lbs)
Yellow Perch	0.2	0.10	0.2	0.10
White Sucker	0.8	2.19	-	-
Walleye	1.3	2.10	0.1	1.70
Tullibee (incl. Cisco)	1.6	0.16	-	-
Rock Bass	0.6	0.26	-	-
Northern Pike	1.3	3.37	0.1	2.00
Largemouth Bass	0.2	1.25	0.04	0.28
Bluegill	0.2	0.10	25.3	0.09
Black Crappie	0.9	0.25	1.0	0.18
Yellow Bullhead	-	-	1.2	0.73
Pumpkin. Sunfish	-	-	1.1	0.19
Hybrid Sunfish	-	-	0.6	0.22
Brown Bullhead	-	-	0.3	0.73

LENGTH OF SELECTED SPECIES SAMPLED FROM ALL GEAR
Number of fish caught for the following length categories (inches):

species	0-5	6-8	9-11	12-14	15-19	20-24	25-29	>30	Total
Yellow Perch	-	3	-	-	-	-	-	-	3
Walleye	-	-	-	-	9	2	1	-	12
Tullibee (incl. Cisco)	-	7	7	-	-	-	-	-	14
Rock Bass	-	5	1	-	-	-	-	-	6
Northern Pike	-	-	-	-	2	5	3	-	10
Largemouth Bass	-	-	1	1	-	-	-	-	2
Bluegill	2	1	-	-	-	-	-	-	3
Black Crappie	-	4	3	-	-	-	-	-	7

FISH STOCKING DATA

year	species	size	# released
90	Walleye	Yearling	473
93	Walleye	Fingerling	2,940

NET CATCH DATA
survey date: 08/13/90

	Gill Nets		Trap Nets	
species	# per net	avg fish wt. (lbs)	# per set	avg fish wt. (lbs)
Yellow Perch	1.0	0.26	1.5	0.14
White Sucker	0.4	2.30	-	-
Walleye	1.4	1.86	0.3	2.85
Rock Bass	1.6	0.58	0.5	0.57
Pumpkin. Sunfish	0.8	0.25	3.2	0.20
Northern Pike	3.0	2.09	-	-
Largemouth Bass	0.2	0.10	0.3	0.40
Bluegill	7.4	0.25	17.0	0.10
Black Crappie	7.4	0.32	4.2	0.30
Brown Bullhead	-	-	0.2	1.70

LENGTH OF SELECTED SPECIES SAMPLED FROM ALL GEAR
Number of fish caught for the following length categories (inches):

species	0-5	6-8	9-11	12-14	15-19	20-24	25-29	>30	Total
Yellow Perch	-	4	1	-	-	-	-	-	5
Walleye	-	-	-	1	3	-	3	-	7
Rock Bass	-	3	5	-	-	-	-	-	8
Pumpkin. Sunfish	1	3	-	-	-	-	-	-	4
Northern Pike	-	-	-	-	6	8	-	1	15
Largemouth Bass	-	1	-	-	-	-	-	-	1
Bluegill	7	30	-	-	-	-	-	-	37
Black Crappie	9	15	12	1	-	-	-	-	37

DNR COMMENTS: Northern Pike population is low compared to lake class median. Yellow Perch gillnet catch per unit effort (CPUE) is very low. Walleye population is average compared to lake class median. Largemouth Bass CPUE is low for gillnet and trapnet. Black Crappie CPUE is high at 2-1/2 times lake class median. Everything else is within limits.

FISHING INFORMATION: Walleye averaging 1 to 1-1/2 pounds have taken hold in Antler Lake off Scenic Highway 7. The DNR also stocked some Lake Trout in this deep, clear lake several years ago, but there haven't been any reports of their showing up in anglers' creels or the DNR's nets. Northerns are good-sized with 5-pound average fish present and the Largemouth Bass fishing can be very good at times. Antler's access is very shallow with a loose gravel surface. Eagle Lake's Crappies are of the slab variety with some 2-to-3 pound fish caught occasionally. Walleye have been receiving a boost from DNR stocking and average 1-1/2 to 2 pounds. Most of the pressure on the lake comes from spring and winter Crappie fishermen.

FOR A COMPLETE LIST OF LAKE MAP GUIDES AND WATERPROOF LAKE MAPS, CALL 1-800-777-7461 OR WRITE TO SPORTSMAN'S CONNECTION, P.O. BOX 3496, DULUTH, MN 55803

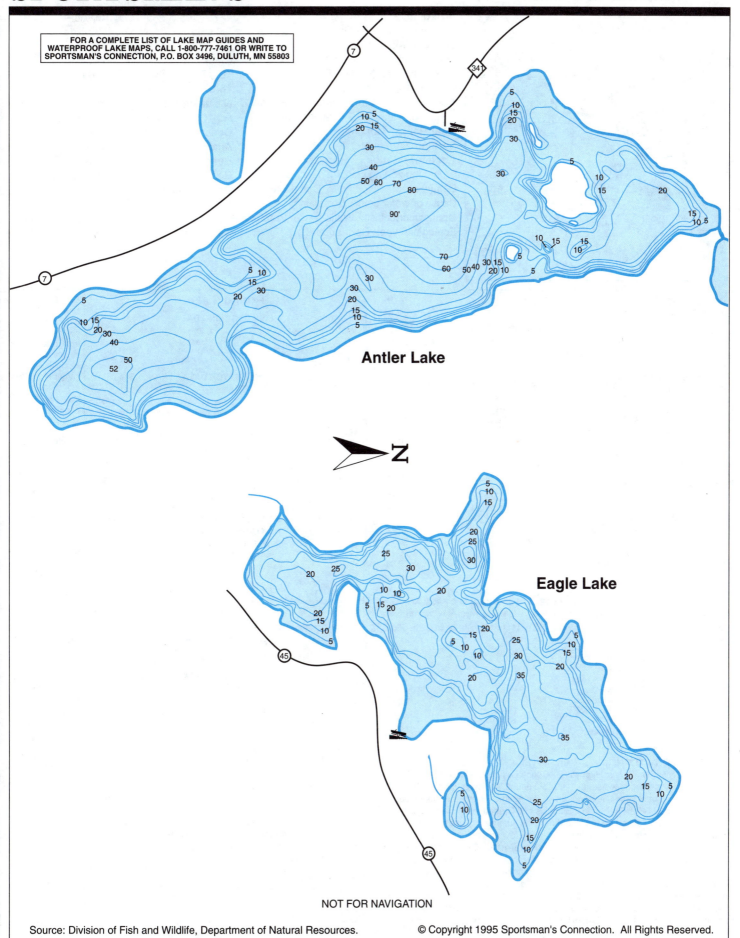

Antler Lake

Eagle Lake

NOT FOR NAVIGATION

Source: Division of Fish and Wildlife, Department of Natural Resources.

Location: Township 59 Range 24
Watershed: Prairie-Willow

	LONG LAKE	ROUND LAKE	BLUEBILL LAKE
Size of lake:	238 Acres	437 Acres	130 Acres
Shorelength:	9.0 Miles	5.0 Miles	2.8 Miles
Secchi disk (water clarity):	NA	NA	NA
Water color:	Brown	Clear	Brown
Maximum depth:	34.0 Ft.	40.0 Ft.	14.0 Ft.
Median depth:	17.0 Ft.	16.0 Ft.	NA
Accessibility:	State-owned access on S side, off Highway 7 (Section 16)	N side on Tabour Rd., County-owned	From feeder creek off Cty. Rd. 345
Boat Ramp:	Concrete	Concrete	Carry-down
Parking:	Adequate	Ample	Limited
Accommodations:	Resorts	Resorts	None
Shoreland zoning classif.:	Rec. Dev.	Rec. Devel.	Natural Environment
Dominant forest/soil type:	Decid/Sand	Decid/Sand	NA
Cause of water color:	Bog stain	NA	Bog Stain
Management class:	Walleye-Centrarchid	Walleye-Centrarchid	Walleye-Centrarchid
Ecological type:	Centrarchid	Centrarchid	Centrarchid-Walleye

Long Lake

DNR COMMENTS:
Although the present CPUE for Walleyes was low, local residents in attendance at a lake association meeting reported that Walleyes were being caught more frequently this last spring than during previous years. This raises some questions about the accuracy of the Walleye gillnet CPUE. Some local residents volunteered to collect scales and other pertinent information from individual Walleyes caught and creeled from the lake and return them to the fisheries section. Ageing these fish will help evaluate growth rates and to what extent stocked fish are providing to the angler creel. Data pertaining to Walleye fishing success and size of fish being caught can also be attained.

FISH STOCKING DATA

year	species	size	# released
91	Walleye	Fingerling	1,692

NET CATCH DATA
survey date: 7/5/89

	Gill Nets		Trap Nets	
		avg fish		avg fish
species	# per net	wt. (lbs)	# per set	wt. (lbs)
Yellow Perch	5.4	0.11	1.9	0.10
Yellow Bullhead	0.2	0.10	2.9	0.58
White Sucker	0.4	1.75	-	-
Walleye	0.6	2.80	-	-
Rock Bass	2.0	0.33	0.9	0.42
Pumpkin. Sunfish	0.6	0.17	9.6	0.12
Northern Pike	13.6	2.22	0.9	1.50
Largemouth Bass	0.4	1.35	-	-
Golden Shiner	0.2	0.10	-	-
Brown Bullhead	0.8	0.70	1.4	0.74
Bluegill	0.2	0.30	32.9	0.11
Black Crappie	4.2	0.16	5.0	0.19
Black Bullhead	-	-	0.1	0.60

LENGTH OF SELECTED SPECIES SAMPLED FROM ALL GEAR
Number of fish caught for the following length categories (inches):

species	0-5	6-8	9-11	12-14	15-19	20-24	25-29	>30	Total
Yellow Perch	-	27	-	-	-	-	-	-	27
Yellow Bullhead	-	1	-	-	-	-	-	-	1
Walleye	-	-	-	1	1	-	1	-	3
Rock Bass	-	8	2	-	-	-	-	-	10
Pumpkin. Sunfish	-	3	-	-	-	-	-	-	3
Northern Pike	-	-	-	2	27	24	14	1	68
Largemouth Bass	-	-	-	2	-	-	-	-	2
Brown Bullhead	-	-	1	3	-	-	-	-	4
Bluegill	-	1	-	-	-	-	-	-	1
Black Crappie	5	13	3	-	-	-	-	-	21

Round Lake

FISH STOCKING DATA

year	species	size	# released
89	Walleye	Fingerling	7,080
91	Walleye	Fingerling	3,841
94	Walleye	Fingerling	3,945

NET CATCH DATA
survey date: 6/29/88

	Gill Nets		Trap Nets	
		avg fish		avg fish
species	# per net	wt. (lbs)	# per set	wt. (lbs)
Yellow Perch	16.6	0.13	1.0	0.11
White Sucker	0.1	3.00	-	-
Walleye	2.4	2.40	-	-
Rock Bass	0.9	0.33	1.6	0.12
Pumpkin. Sunfish	0.1	0.20	0.1	0.30
Northern Pike	6.7	3.02	0.5	2.18
Largemouth Bass	1.4	0.85	1.4	0.26
Bluegill	11.6	0.20	75.4	0.18
Hybrid Sunfish	-	-	0.3	trace

LENGTH OF SELECTED SPECIES SAMPLED FROM ALL GEAR
Number of fish caught for the following length categories (inches):

species	0-5	6-8	9-11	12-14	15-19	20-24	25-29	>30	Total
Yellow Perch	-	115	1	-	-	-	-	-	116
Walleye	-	-	1	-	13	3	-	-	17
Rock Bass	3	1	2	-	-	-	-	-	6
Pumpkin. Sunfish	-	1	-	-	-	-	-	-	1
Northern Pike	-	-	-	3	4	30	8	1	46
Largemouth Bass	-	3	3	2	2	-	-	-	10
Bluegill	17	63	1	-	-	-	-	-	81

DNR COMMENTS:
Northern Pike and Bluegill populations are down slightly from 1982 but well above state and local medians. Largemouth Bass are down slightly from 1982 also but are above medians. No Black Crappie were caught, while Perch abundance is as high as ever and well above medians. Walleye populations are about even with state medians but well above local medians and historically at a high but all fish sampled run 16-20". All other species appear to be in a normal range for this lake.

Bluebill Lake

FISH STOCKING DATA NOT AVAILABLE

NET CATCH DATA
survey date: 7/11/83

	Gill Nets		Trap Nets	
		avg fish		avg fish
species	# per net	wt. (lbs)	# per set	wt. (lbs)
Yellow Perch	8.3	0.16	0.5	0.25
Yellow Bullhead	0.5	0.45	0.3	1.30
White Sucker	2.5	2.15	-	-
Walleye	3.3	0.93	-	-
Rock Bass	0.3	0.30	-	-
Northern Pike	5.5	0.79	0.5	0.60
Brown Bullhead	0.5	1.05	-	-
Black Crappie	5.8	0.32	-	-
Pumpkin. Sunfish	-	-	0.8	0.47
Bluegill	-	-	0.5	0.60

LENGTH OF SELECTED SPECIES SAMPLED FROM ALL GEAR
Number of fish caught for the following length categories (inches):

species	0-5	6-8	9-11	12-14	15-19	20-24	25-29	>30	Total
Black Crappie	-	18	4	1	-	-	-	-	23
Bluegill	-	1	1	-	-	-	-	-	2
Brown Bullhead	-	-	2	-	-	-	-	-	2
Northern Pike	-	-	2	3	13	6	-	-	24
Pumpkin. Sunfish	-	3	-	-	-	-	-	-	3
Rock Bass	-	1	-	-	-	-	-	-	1
Walleye	-	2	-	4	7	-	-	-	13
Yellow Bullhead	-	1	1	1	-	-	-	-	3
Yellow Perch	-	30	5	-	-	-	-	-	35

DNR COMMENTS:
Walleye are reproducing naturally and numbers are above the local median. Abundance of other species within limits for this type of lake.

FISHING INFORMATION: Long, Round and Bluebill (aka Rice) Lakes can be found by traveling up Scenic Highway 7. Round Lake is the largest of the three at 437 acres and it produces some 1-1/2 to 2 pound Walleyes, along with a few 9 to 10 pounders each year. Bev Truman, at the Scenic Pines Store near Round Lake, told us that Round's Sunnies, Bluegills and Crappies are average size and provide some good action for the kids during the summer. Some nice Northerns and Largemouth Bass also roam the lake. Tony, owner and operator at the Balsam Store on Scenic Hwy. 7, has weighed several 10 to 15 pound Northern from Long Lake. Walleye are also caught with a few chunky 3 to 4 pounders showing up now and then. Largemouth Bass fishermen have reported some good catches of 2 to 3 pound fish. Bluegill (or Rice) Lake doesn't get much pressure. Anglers can access the lake from the creek that adjoins Bluebill and Gunny Sack Lake (which has an access, but hasn't been mapped by the DNR). Bluebill has some nice Pumpkinseed and Bluegill Sunfish, decent Crappies and Walleyes.

SPORTSMAN'S Connection ®

FOR A COMPLETE LIST OF LAKE MAP GUIDES AND WATERPROOF LAKE MAPS, CALL 1-800-777-7461 OR WRITE TO SPORTSMAN'S CONNECTION, P.O. BOX 3496, DULUTH, MN 55803

Long, Round, & Bluebill Lakes

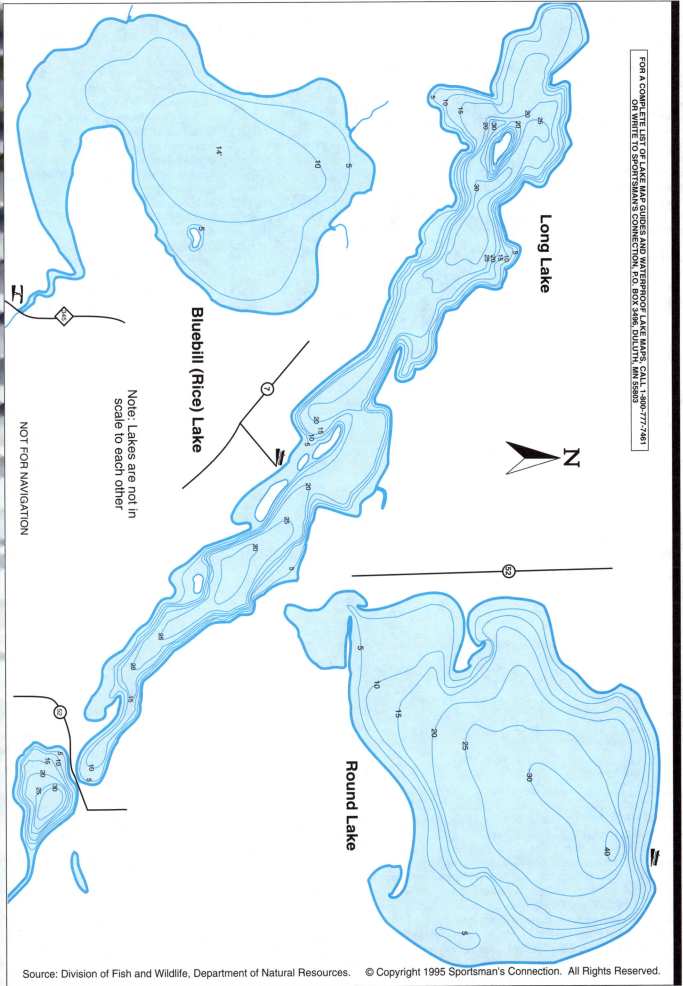

Long Lake

Bluebill (Rice) Lake

Round Lake

Note: Lakes are not in scale to each other

NOT FOR NAVIGATION

N

Source: Division of Fish and Wildlife, Department of Natural Resources.

TURTLE LAKE   LITTLE TURTLE LAKE

Location: Township 59, 60 Range 26, 27
Watershed: Big Fork

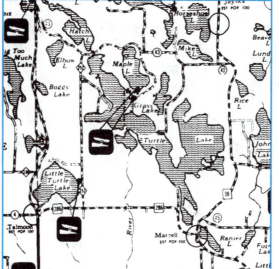

Size of lake: 2,066 Acres
Shorelength: 21.8 Miles
Secchi disk (water clarity): 12.8 Ft.
Water color: Light green
Maximum depth: 130.0 Ft.
Median depth: 33.9 Ft.
Accessibility: State-owned public access on NE side
Boat Ramp: Concrete
Parking: Ample
Accommodations: Resort
Shoreland zoning classif.: Rec. Dev.
Dominant forest/soil type: Decid/Loam
Cause of water color: Bicarbonates
Management class: Walleye-Centrarchid
Ecological type: Centrarchid-Walleye

Size of lake: 470 Acres
Shorelength: 3.8 Miles
Secchi disk (water clarity): NA
Water color: Green
Maximum depth: 30.0 Ft.
Median depth: 16.5 Ft.
Accessibility: County-owned public access off Co. Rd. 252
Boat Ramp: Earth
Parking: Adequate
Accommodations:
Shoreland zoning classif.: Rec. Dev.
Dominant forest/soil type: Decid/Wet
Cause of water color: Algae bloom
Management class: Walleye
Ecological type: Hard-water Walleye

DNR COMMENTS:

Walleye abundance, as indicated by gillnet catch, has increased substantially in this and the last assessment. The earlier assessments of 1950, 1969, 1975, and 1979 had Walleye CPUE's ranging from 0.3 to 1.1. Walleye fry and fingerlings were stocked periodically until 1978 apparently with little success. Fingerlings have been stocked since that time. Average size of the Walleyes is excellent and growth rates are considered good. Northern Pike abundance and size has remained stable over the past 39 years. Yellow Perch abundance has declined since the past assessment.

FISH STOCKING DATA

year	species	size	# released
89	Walleye	Fingerling	4,429
89	Walleye	Yearling	12
91	Walleye	Fingerling	27
91	Walleye	Yearling	190
91	Walleye	Adult	992

survey date: 8/7/89

NET CATCH DATA

	Gill Nets		Trap Nets	
species	# per net	avg fish wt. (lbs)	# per set	avg fish wt. (lbs)
Yellow Perch	2.1	0.16	0.4	0.10
Yellow Bullhead	0.2	1.57	0.1	0.60
White Sucker	0.8	1.89	-	-
Walleye	4.0	2.35	0.1	0.50
Tullibee (Cisco)	13.1	0.26	-	-
Smallmouth Bass	2.8	1.40	-	-
Rock Bass	8.8	0.41	0.6	0.41
Pumpkin. Sunfish	1.2	0.20	1.3	0.18
Northern Pike	3.2	3.25	0.1	1.80
Largemouth Bass	1.5	0.69	0.5	0.28
Lake Whitefish	0.5	1.62	-	-
Bluegill	0.3	0.20	7.4	0.16
Black Crappie	0.8	0.58	0.5	0.20

LENGTH OF SELECTED SPECIES SAMPLED FROM ALL GEAR
Number of fish caught for the following length categories (inches):

species	0-5	6-8	9-11	12-14	15-19	20-24	25-29	>30	Total
Yellow Perch	-	23	4	-	-	-	-	-	27
Yellow Bullhead	-	-	-	3	-	-	-	-	3
Walleye	-	-	-	4	25	19	3	1	52
Tullibee (Cisco)	-	42	44	22	-	-	-	-	108
Smallmouth Bass	-	1	5	14	16	-	-	-	36
Rock Bass	3	16	47	2	-	-	-	-	68
Pumpkin. Sunfish	4	11	-	-	-	-	-	-	15
Northern Pike	-	-	-	-	5	22	9	2	38
Largemouth Bass	-	-	10	8	1	-	-	-	19
Lake Whitefish	-	-	-	1	5	-	-	-	6
Bluegill	-	4	-	-	-	-	-	-	4
Black Crappie	3	1	3	3	-	-	-	-	10

FISH STOCKING DATA

year	species	size	# released
89	Walleye	Fry	500,000
91	Walleye	Fingerling	1,030
91	Walleye	Adult	49
93	Walleye	Fry	500,000
93	Walleye	Fry	100,000

survey date: 7/25/88

NET CATCH DATA

	Gill Nets		Trap Nets	
species	# per net	avg fish wt. (lbs)	# per set	avg fish wt. (lbs)
Yellow Perch	67.6	0.11	2.9	0.17
White Sucker	1.9	1.34	0.1	2.80
Walleye	2.1	1.77	-	-
Tullibee (Cisco)	2.6	0.53	-	-
Rock Bass	0.1	0.40	0.8	0.40
Pumpkin. Sunfish	0.4	0.27	3.1	0.20
Northern Pike	8.3	2.78	0.5	2.65
Largemouth Bass	0.1	2.00	0.3	1.55
Brown Bullhead	0.3	0.95	0.1	1.70
Bowfin (Dogfish)	0.1	7.20	0.6	7.08
Bluegill	1.3	0.38	1.6	0.22
Black Crappie	0.1	0.10	0.5	0.95
Yellow Bullhead	-	-	0.5	1.30
Black Bullhead	-	-	0.1	0.20

LENGTH OF SELECTED SPECIES SAMPLED FROM ALL GEAR
Number of fish caught for the following length categories (inches):

species	0-5	6-8	9-11	12-14	15-19	20-24	25-29	>30	Total
Yellow Perch	-	114	2	-	-	-	-	-	116
Walleye	-	-	5	1	5	3	1	-	15
Tullibee (Cisco)	-	3	9	6	-	-	-	-	18
Rock Bass	-	1	-	-	-	-	-	-	1
Pumpkin. Sunfish	1	2	-	-	-	-	-	-	3
Northern Pike	-	-	-	-	11	38	7	1	57
Largemouth Bass	-	-	-	-	1	-	-	-	1
Brown Bullhead	-	-	1	1	-	-	-	-	2
Bluegill	-	7	2	-	-	-	-	-	9
Black Crappie	-	1	-	-	-	-	-	-	1

DNR COMMENTS:

Northern Cisco numbers are holding close to normal but well below numbers of 1974. Northern Pike population is above state and local medians but down from the netting of 1982. The Yellow Perch population is well above medians and higher than any other net catches in the past, while Walleye numbers are below medians and the smallest number caught in any netting and well below catches of 1982. All other species appear to be in normal ranges for this lake.

FISHING INFORMATION: Turtle Lake, off of Highway 38, is a deep, relatively clear, pretty lake punctuated with numerous islands and bays. It has a reputation of giving up good sized Walleye, typically in the 2 to 4 pound range and some lunkers. According to Terry Schmitz, owner of Frontier Sport in Marcell, a half limit (3) of 3 pound average Walleyes is considered a good day on the lake. Turtle is a good choice for anglers seeking big Walleye and 5 pound-class Smallmouth Bass. It's rocky underwater points, and sunken islands are good holding areas for these species. Moose Bay on the west side of the lake holds some big Northerns in the 13 to 15 pound range. Panfish success seems to be confined to winter and early spring. Largemouth Bass, some in the 4 to 5 pound range, are also present. Little Turtle Lake is considerably smaller and more shallow than Turtle, making it easier to fish. Frontier Sport told us that fishing pressure had taken its toll on the Walleye in Little Turtle several years ago, but it has relaxed since and the Walleye fishing is picking up again with 1-1/2 to 2 pound sizes being the norm. Most of the Walleye are caught in 8 to 10 feet of water early in the season, moving out a little as summer progresses. Five to 6 pound Northerns are mixed in with some of the "snakes" that are inevitable. Largemouth Bass are fairly scarce, but some 3 to 5 pounders can be found. The Crappie and Bluegills are nice sized with the 'gills running up to a pound.

Turtle & L. Turtle Lakes

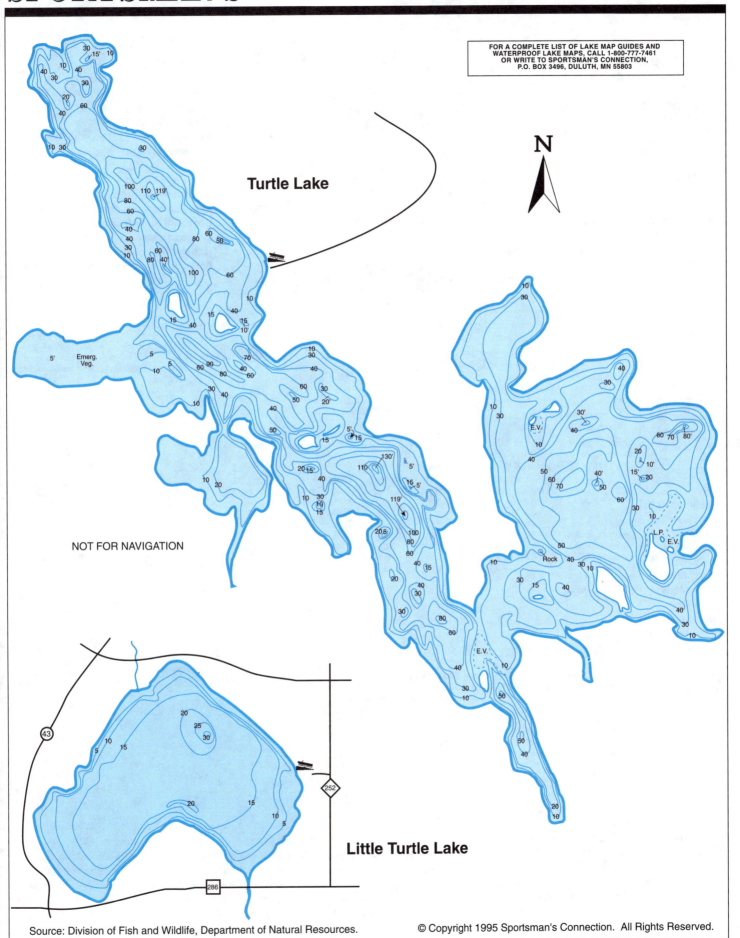

Turtle Lake

N

NOT FOR NAVIGATION

Little Turtle Lake

Source: Division of Fish and Wildlife, Department of Natural Resources.

BELLO LAKE

MAPLE LAKE

Location: Township 60   Range 26, 27
Watershed: Big Fork

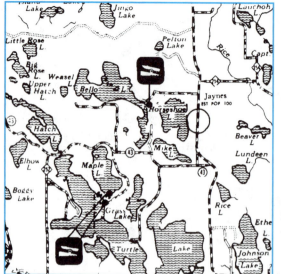

Size of lake: 492 Acres
Shorelength: 7.3 Miles
Secchi disk (water clarity): 10.5 Ft.
Water color: Brown
Maximum depth: 58.0 Ft.
Median depth: 30.0 Ft.
Accessibility: State-owned public access on SE side
Boat Ramp: Earth
Parking: Ample
Accommodations: Resort
Shoreland zoning classif.: Rec. /Dev.
Dominant forest/soil type: Decid/Loam
Cause of water color: Bog Stain
Management class: Walleye-Centrarchid
Ecological type: Centrarchid

Size of lake: 235 Acres
Shorelength: 3.2 Miles
Secchi disk (water clarity): NA
Water color: Green
Maximum depth: 35.0 Ft.
Median depth: 20.0 Ft.
Accessibility: State-owned public access on S side
Boat Ramp: Concrete
Parking: Ample
Accommodations: Resorts
Shoreland zoning classif.: Rec./Dev.
Dominant forest/soil type: Decid/Loam
Cause of water color: Slight algae bloom
Management class: Walleye
Ecological type: Hard-water Walleye

DNR COMMENTS:
Northern Pike pop. above normal; size small, with most fish in 16-19" range; growth good. Walleyes scarce, below 1st quartile values. Bowfin scarce as well. Largemouth Bass present in undetermined numbers. Many Black Crappies in 10-12" range reported caught by local anglers; pop. appears about normal for lake class. Bluegills very numerous; growth slower than normal.

FISH STOCKING DATA NOT AVAILABLE

NET CATCH DATA

survey date:
7/29/91

species	Gill Nets # per net	Gill Nets avg fish wt. (lbs)	Trap Nets # per set	Trap Nets avg fish wt. (lbs)
Yellow Perch	0.5	0.10	0.3	0.10
Walleye	0.8	2.76	-	-
Tullibee (Cisco)	4.8	1.42	-	-
Pumpkin. Sunfish	1.2	0.21	1.6	0.13
Northern Pike	10.7	1.32	0.4	1.10
Largemouth Bass	1.7	1.10	0.6	0.22
Bluegill	9.7	0.20	4.9	0.10
Black Crappie	1.2	0.46	0.8	0.15
Bowfin (Dogfish)	-	-	0.1	5.50

LENGTH OF SELECTED SPECIES SAMPLED FROM ALL GEAR
Number of fish caught for the following length categories (inches):

species	0-5	6-8	9-11	12-14	15-19	20-24	25-29	>30	Total
Walleye	-	-	-	-	2	3	-	-	5
Tullibee (Cisco)	-	7	-	3	19	-	-	-	29
Pumpkin. Sunfish	-	7	-	-	-	-	-	-	7
Northern Pike	-	-	-	-	47	10	5	2	64
Largemouth Bass	-	3	-	3	4	-	-	-	10
Bluegill	8	45	4	-	-	-	-	-	57
Black Crappie	-	3	1	2	-	-	-	-	6

FISH STOCKING DATA

year	species	size	# released
90	Walleye	Fingerling	693
92	Walleye	Fingerling	3,465

NET CATCH DATA

survey date:
8/20/90

species	Gill Nets # per net	Gill Nets avg fish wt. (lbs)	Trap Nets # per set	Trap Nets avg fish wt. (lbs)
Yellow Perch	6.0	0.11	0.5	0.10
White Sucker	1.6	2.90	-	-
Walleye	4.2	1.21	-	-
Tullibee (Cisco)	5.8	0.84	-	-
Rock Bass	1.6	1.14	0.5	0.20
Pumpkin. Sunfish	2.4	0.19	1.0	0.08
Northern Pike	7.6	1.83	0.8	0.70
Largemouth Bass	0.4	1.40	-	-
Bowfin (Dogfish)	0.2	2.40	0.3	3.70
Bluegill	3.2	0.26	6.3	0.07
Black Crappie	1.0	0.88	-	-

LENGTH OF SELECTED SPECIES SAMPLED FROM ALL GEAR
Number of fish caught for the following length categories (inches):

species	0-5	6-8	9-11	12-14	15-19	20-24	25-29	>30	Total
Yellow Perch	-	21	-	-	-	-	-	-	21
Walleye	-	-	-	9	10	2	-	-	21
Tullibee (Cisco)	-	3	16	3	7	-	-	-	29
Rock Bass	3	15	8	1	-	-	-	-	27
Pumpkin. Sunfish	4	8	-	-	-	-	-	-	12
Northern Pike	-	-	-	2	19	14	2	1	38
Largemouth Bass	-	-	-	2	-	-	-	-	2
Bluegill	7	6	3	-	-	-	-	-	16
Black Crappie	-	-	1	4	-	-	-	-	5

DNR COMMENTS:
Northern Pike populations have remained historically high with good numbers having normal growth rates. Yellow Perch abundance has fluctuated, increasing from a CPUE of 2.5/gillnet in 1973 to 13.6/gillnet in 1978. This population has now leveled off to 6.0/gillnet which compares more closely with lake class medians. The Walleye abundance has remained fairly constant over the years and has always been above the gill net third quartile figures for this lake classification in numbers and weight. Age class distribution shows 67% of the Walleyes sampled being of age class III's which was not a fingerling stocked year and suggests that natural reproduction could be having good success. All other species appear to be within normal ranges for this type of lake.

FISHING INFORMATION: Bello Lake is regarded as one of the better Panfish lakes in the area with good numbers of 1/2 to 3/4 pound Crappie and Bluegills. Terry Schmitz, of Frontier Sport in Marcell, told us that Bello has some excellent Largemouth Bass fishing including some 2 1/2 to 3 pound fish. Walleye caught are typically on the large side and the DNR has been stocking the lake in an attempt to increase the numbers. Northerns are abundant with some large ones taken occasionally. Maple Lake is much smaller than Bello and it produces some good Walleye. Bluegill fishing is good - especially around the sunken island on the west side of the lake. Bass fishermen also catch some nice Largemouth. You don't hear a lot about the Crappies, but when you do locate a school they're usually slabs in the pound-plus range.

FOR A COMPLETE LIST OF LAKE MAP GUIDES AND WATERPROOF LAKE MAPS, CALL 1-800-777-7461 OR WRITE TO SPORTSMAN'S CONNECTION, P.O. BOX 3496, DULUTH, MN 55803

Bello & Maple Lakes

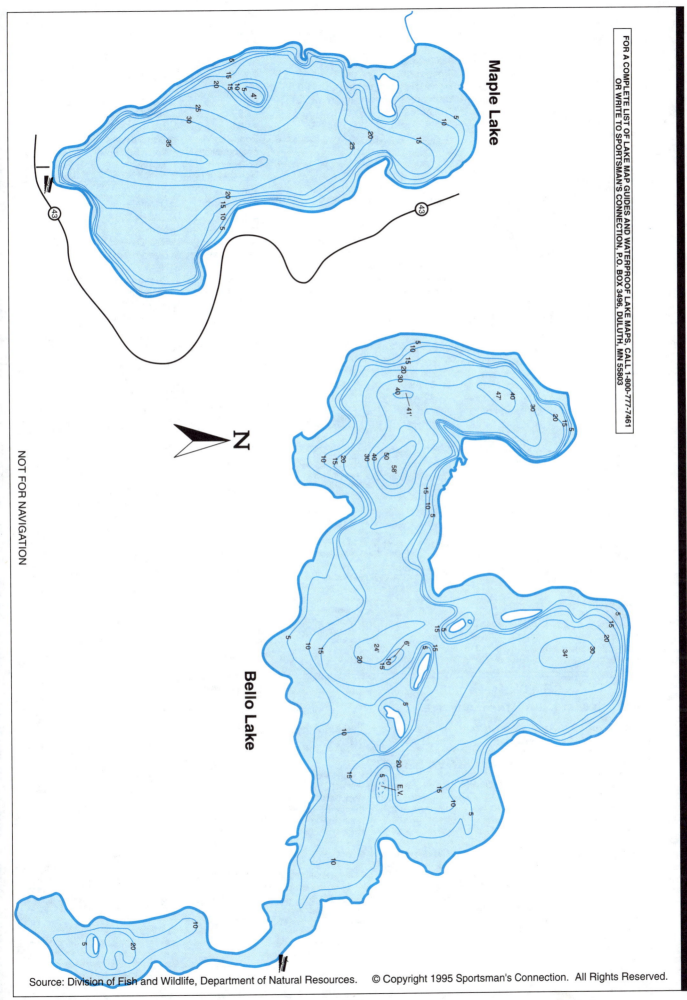

Maple Lake

Bello Lake

N

NOT FOR NAVIGATION

Source: Division of Fish and Wildlife, Department of Natural Resources.

Location: Township 59, 60   Range 26
Watershed: Big Fork

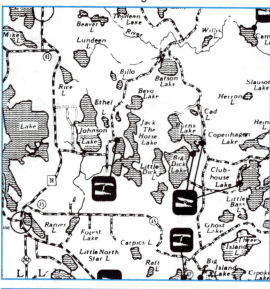

<table>
<tr><th></th><th>JOHNSON LAKE</th><th>JACK THE HORSE LAKE</th><th>BIG DICK LAKE</th><th>BURNS LAKE</th></tr>
<tr><td>Size of lake:</td><td>288 Acres</td><td>323 Acres</td><td>234 Acres</td><td>171 Acres</td></tr>
<tr><td>Shorelength:</td><td>3.7 Miles</td><td>7.7 Miles</td><td>2.6 Miles</td><td>3.6 Miles</td></tr>
<tr><td>Secchi disk (water clarity):</td><td>11.0 Ft.</td><td>NA</td><td>9.5 Ft.</td><td>20.3 Ft.</td></tr>
<tr><td>Water color:</td><td>Brown tint</td><td>NA</td><td>Clear</td><td>Clear</td></tr>
<tr><td>Maximum depth:</td><td>51.0 Ft.</td><td>45.0 Ft.</td><td>28.0 Ft.</td><td>100.0 Ft.</td></tr>
<tr><td>Median depth:</td><td>24.6 Ft.</td><td>11.0 Ft.</td><td>12.0 Ft.</td><td>14.0 Ft.</td></tr>
<tr><td>Accessibility:</td><td>Carry-down off Jack the Horse Road on S side</td><td>Poorly developed public access; off USFS road from state Hwy. #38</td><td>USFS-owned access on E side off USFS Rd. #2181</td><td>Federally-owned public access on SE bay off USFS Rd. 2181</td></tr>
<tr><td>Boat Ramp:</td><td>Carry-down</td><td>Carry-down</td><td>Concrete</td><td>Earth</td></tr>
<tr><td>Parking:</td><td>Limited; side of road</td><td>Limited</td><td>Limited</td><td>Ample</td></tr>
<tr><td>Accommodations:</td><td>Resort</td><td>Resort</td><td>None</td><td>None</td></tr>
<tr><td>Shoreland zoning classif.:</td><td>Rec. Dev.</td><td>Rec. Dev.</td><td>Rec. Dev.</td><td>Rec. Dev.</td></tr>
<tr><td>Dominant forest/soil type:</td><td>Decid/Loam</td><td>Decid/Loam</td><td>Decid/Loam</td><td>NA</td></tr>
<tr><td>Cause of water color:</td><td>NA</td><td>NA</td><td>NA</td><td>NA</td></tr>
<tr><td>Management class:</td><td>Walleye</td><td>Centrarchid</td><td>Centrarchid</td><td>Centrarchid</td></tr>
<tr><td>Ecological type:</td><td>Hard-water Walleye</td><td>Centrarchid</td><td>Centrarchid</td><td>Centrarchid</td></tr>
</table>

DNR COMMENTS:
High pop. of small Northern Cisco with a few big ones. High pop. of small Northern Pike; low pop. of Yellow Perch, Walleye and Bluegill. Every other species was about normal.

FISHING INFO:
Johnson's Walleye fishing has been picking up recently according to area reports. Some nice Crappies of the pound-plus variety are present, but they're tough to locate, especially in the summer. The north end of the lake, where the creek flows out to Rice Lake, is a good spot to try early. Some lunker Largemouth provide exciting action for those who take the time to learn their whereabouts. Northern Pike are easy to catch, but run on the small side.

Johnson Lake
FISH STOCKING DATA

year	species	size	# released
90	Walleye	Fry	300,000
92	Walleye	Fry	100,000

survey date: 7/5/88

NET CATCH DATA

	Gill Nets		Trap Nets	
		avg fish		avg fish
species	# per net	wt. (lbs)	# per set	wt. (lbs)
Yellow Perch	9.7	0.16	1.8	0.21
White Sucker	2.3	3.50	-	-
Walleye	3.3	1.22	0.5	0.40
Tullibee (Cisco)	2.2	2.78	-	-
Rock Bass	1.2	0.40	1.7	0.18
Northern Pike	6.3	2.04	1.5	1.58
Bluegill	0.2	0.10	1.3	0.19
Pumpkin. Sunfish	-	-	1.0	0.12
Largemouth Bass	-	-	0.2	4.30
Bowfin (Dogfish)	-	-	1.0	7.68
Black Crappie	-	-	0.2	1.30

LENGTH OF SELECTED SPECIES SAMPLED FROM ALL GEAR
Number of fish caught for the following length categories (inches):

species	0-5	6-8	9-11	12-14	15-19	20-24	25-29	>30	Total
Yellow Perch	1	47	10	-	-	-	-	-	58
Walleye	-	2	5	1	10	2	-	-	20
Tullibee (Cisco)	-	1	-	-	10	2	-	-	13
Rock Bass	-	5	2	-	-	-	-	-	7
Northern Pike	-	-	-	-	14	21	3	-	38
Bluegill	1	-	-	-	-	-	-	-	1

Jack the Horse Lake
FISH STOCKING DATA NOT AVAILABLE

survey date: 7/23/82

NET CATCH DATA

	Gill Nets		Trap Nets	
		avg fish		avg fish
species	# per net	wt. (lbs)	# per set	wt. (lbs)
Yellow Perch	3.0	0.11	1.4	0.09
White Sucker	0.3	1.50	-	-
Tullibee (Cisco)	12.7	0.28	-	-
Rock Bass	1.0	0.27	3.1	0.27
Pumpkin. Sunfish	0.7	0.18	6.0	0.15
Northern Pike	6.0	1.82	0.1	0.30
Largemouth Bass	0.2	0.50	0.1	0.30
Bowfin (Dogfish)	0.2	5.00	0.5	5.15
Bluegill	5.7	0.09	38.6	0.11
Black Crappie	0.5	0.23	1.8	0.40
Black Bullhead	0.5	0.13	0.1	1.10

LENGTH OF SELECTED SPECIES SAMPLED FROM ALL GEAR
Number of fish caught for the following length categories (inches):

species	0-5	6-8	9-11	12-14	15-19	20-24	25-29	>30	Total
Black Bullhead	-	3	-	1	-	-	-	-	4
Black Crappie	-	12	5	-	-	-	-	-	17
Bluegill	36	46	-	-	-	-	-	-	82
Largemouth Bass	-	1	-	1	-	-	-	-	2
Northern Pike	-	-	-	1	16	9	9	1	36
Pumpkin. Sunfish	26	38	1	-	-	-	-	-	65
Rock Bass	5	24	2	-	-	-	-	-	31
Tullibee (Cisco)	-	35	8	5	-	-	-	-	48
Yellow Perch	-	28	1	-	-	-	-	-	29

DNR COMMENTS:
High population of small Northern Cisco, Northern Pike and Bluegill. Very low population of Yellow Perch, Largemouth Bass, and Black Crappie.

FISHING INFO:
Jack the Horse's series of irregular bays are excellent habitat for Northern Pike and Largemouth Bass. Some of the Bass range in the 4 to 6 pound size. Plan on a good share of snaky Northerns for every keeper, but some 7 to 10 pounders can be found. Crappies aren't plentiful but the sizes are respectable.

DNR COMMENTS:
Big Dick has high populations of Northern Pike and Panfish.

FISHING INFO:
Hefty Northerns, some in the 10 to 13 pound range, roam the lake's weedbeds. Largemouth Bass are also nice-sized and numerous. The lake holds good numbers of Sunnies and Crappies, but most are on the small side. Big Dick Lake's primitive access and stuck-away location keep it fairly quiet.

Big Dick Lake
FISH STOCKING DATA NOT AVAILABLE

survey date: 7/17/85

NET CATCH DATA

	Gill Nets		Trap Nets	
		avg fish		avg fish
species	# per net	wt. (lbs)	# per set	wt. (lbs)
Yellow Perch	3.2	0.11	1.3	0.14
White Sucker	2.2	1.77	0.3	3.00
Rock Bass	0.2	0.20	-	-
Pumpkin. Sunfish	0.4	0.10	1.5	0.22
Northern Pike	6.2	3.98	0.3	7.00
Largemouth Bass	1.8	0.47	0.3	1.50
Golden Shiner	0.4	0.13	-	-
Bluegill	8.4	0.04	26.3	0.07
Black Crappie	4.8	0.28	3.3	0.08

LENGTH OF SELECTED SPECIES SAMPLED FROM ALL GEAR
Number of fish caught for the following length categories (inches):

species	0-5	6-8	9-11	12-14	15-19	20-24	25-29	>30	Total
Black Crappie	1	29	5	2	-	-	-	-	37
Bluegill	118	25	4	-	-	-	-	-	147
Largemouth Bass	-	1	8	-	1	-	-	-	10
Northern Pike	-	-	-	-	16	11	4	-	31
Pumpkin. Sunfish	2	5	1	-	-	-	-	-	8
Rock Bass	-	1	-	-	-	-	-	-	1
Yellow Perch	-	16	4	1	-	-	-	-	21

Burns Lake
FISH STOCKING DATA NOT AVAILABLE

survey date: 6/23/86

NET CATCH DATA

	Gill Nets		Trap Nets	
		avg fish		avg fish
species	# per net	wt. (lbs)	# per set	wt. (lbs)
Yellow Perch	6.2	0.15	0.8	0.10
Yellow Bullhead	0.2	0.40	-	-
Rock Bass	2.4	0.33	1.8	0.26
Pumpkin. Sunfish	2.0	0.30	6.8	0.23
Northern Pike	8.4	3.15	0.3	2.50
Largemouth Bass	1.4	1.26	0.3	0.10
Bluegill	4.8	0.18	46.3	0.14
Black Crappie	6.2	0.28	1.5	0.50

LENGTH OF SELECTED SPECIES SAMPLED FROM ALL GEAR
Number of fish caught for the following length categories (inches):

species	0-5	6-8	9-11	12-14	15-19	20-24	25-29	>30	Total
Black Crappie	1	19	17	-	-	-	-	-	37
Bluegill	71	70	-	-	-	-	-	-	141
Largemouth Bass	1	-	2	5	-	-	-	-	8
Northern Pike	-	-	-	1	17	22	2	-	42
Pumpkin. Sunfish	5	32	-	-	-	-	-	-	37
Rock Bass	1	13	5	-	-	-	-	-	19
Yellow Bullhead	-	1	-	-	-	-	-	-	1
Yellow Perch	-	34	-	-	-	-	-	-	34

DNR COMMENTS:
Bluegill population is very high and they are relatively small. Northern Pike population is a little above average, also other fish populations are near averages.

FISHING INFO:
Deep, clear waters hold some excellent Largemouth Bass and some good numbers of 5 to 6 pound Northern Pike. The underwater points and bars are most productive, especially in early morning and evening due to the clear water. Crappies are nice when you can find them.

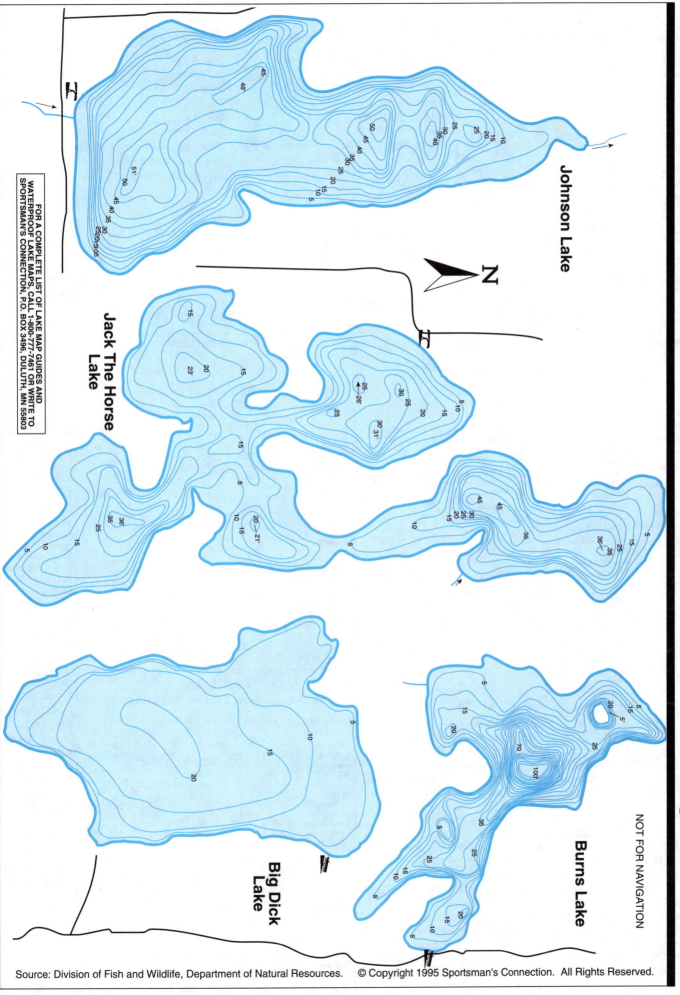

Johnson Lake

Jack The Horse Lake

Burns Lake

Big Dick Lake

N

NOT FOR NAVIGATION

FOR A COMPLETE LIST OF LAKE MAP GUIDES AND WATERPROOF LAKE MAPS, CALL 1-800-777-7461 OR WRITE TO SPORTSMAN'S CONNECTION, P.O. BOX 3496, DULUTH, MN 55803

Source: Division of Fish and Wildlife, Department of Natural Resources.

Location: Township 59, 60   Range 25, 26
Watershed: Mississippi Headwaters

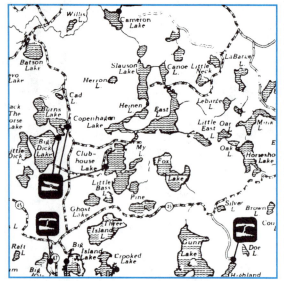

	SLAUSON LAKE	**CLUBHOUSE LAKE**	**EAST LAKE**
Size of lake:	110 Acres	244 Acres	179 Acres
Shorelength:	1.9 Miles	3.6 Miles	4.0 Miles
Secchi disk (water clarity):	NA	12.1 Ft.	NA
Water color:	Clear	Clear	Clear-brown
Maximum depth:	40.0 Ft.	103.0 Ft.	65.0 Ft.
Median depth:	NA	35.0 Ft.	19.0 Ft.
Accessibility:	From Clubhouse Lake	Federal-owned public access at campground, W-central side	From Clubhouse Lake
Boat Ramp:	None	Concrete	None
Parking:	None	Ample	None
Accommodations:	Resort	Campground	None
Shoreland zoning classif.:	Rec. Dev.	Rec. Dev.	Rec. Dev.
Dominant forest/soil type:	NA	Decid/Loam	Decid/Loam
Cause of water color:	NA	NA	Suspended silt
Management class:	Centrarchid	Centrarchid	Centrarchid
Ecological type:	Centrarchid	Centrarchid	Centrarchid

DNR COMMENTS:
The fish population looks similar to that found in the last lake survey. Northern Pike are more numerous than both the state and local medians. Perch rather low. Panfish population is close to state and local medians.

Slauson Lake

FISH STOCKING DATA NOT AVAILABLE

survey date: 9/4/84

NET CATCH DATA

	Gill Nets		Trap Nets	
		avg fish		avg fish
species	# per net	wt. (lbs)	# per set	wt. (lbs)
Yellow Perch	1.8	0.14	0.3	0.10
White Sucker	0.5	1.25	-	-
Tullibee (Cisco)	0.3	0.70	-	-
Silver Redhorse	0.3	2.00	-	-
Rock Bass	0.8	0.23	0.5	0.25
Pumpkin. Sunfish	3.0	0.21	0.3	0.30
Northern Pike	8.3	1.35	0.5	1.00
Largemouth Bass	0.8	0.67	-	-
Brown Bullhead	0.8	0.50	-	-
Bowfin (Dogfish)	0.5	4.00	0.8	3.67
Bluegill	21.3	0.06	1.3	0.14
Black Crappie	4.3	0.47	0.5	0.25
Silver Redhorse	-	-	0.3	4.00

LENGTH OF SELECTED SPECIES SAMPLED FROM ALL GEAR
Number of fish caught for the following length categories (inches):

species	0-5	6-8	9-11	12-14	15-19	20-24	25-29	>30	Total
Black Crappie	1	1	13	4	-	-	-	-	19
Bluegill	30	57	2	-	-	-	-	-	89
Brown Bullhead	-	-	2	1	-	-	-	-	3
Largemouth Bass	-	-	2	1	-	-	-	-	3
Northern Pike	-	-	-	3	27	3	1	1	35
Pumpkin. Sunfish	2	11	-	-	-	-	-	-	13
Rock Bass	1	4	-	-	-	-	-	-	5
Tullibee (Cisco)	-	-	-	1	-	-	-	-	1
Yellow Perch	-	7	-	-	-	-	-	-	7

Clubhouse Lake

FISH STOCKING DATA NOT AVAILABLE

survey date: 6/29/92

NET CATCH DATA

	Gill Nets		Trap Nets	
		avg fish		avg fish
species	# per net	wt. (lbs)	# per set	wt. (lbs)
Yellow Bullhead	1.8	0.56	2.4	0.50
White Sucker	0.8	2.90	0.1	2.60
Tullibee (Cisco)	2.8	0.36	-	-
Rock Bass	1.5	0.21	1.4	0.19
Pumpkin. Sunfish	1.2	0.23	3.0	0.15
Northern Pike	8.0	1.73	0.3	1.90
Bowfin (Dogfish)	0.2	3.50	0.4	5.40
Bluegill	1.3	0.10	10.2	0.11
Black Crappie	1.0	0.67	0.3	0.20
Yellow Perch	-	-	0.1	0.10
Silver Redhorse	-	-	0.1	6.10
Largemouth Bass	-	-	0.1	0.20
Hybrid Sunfish	-	-	1.4	0.14

LENGTH OF SELECTED SPECIES SAMPLED FROM ALL GEAR
Number of fish caught for the following length categories (inches):

species	0-5	6-8	9-11	12-14	15-19	20-24	25-29	>30	Total
Tullibee (Cisco)	-	2	12	2	1	-	-	-	17
Rock Bass	6	3	5	-	-	-	-	-	14
Pumpkin. Sunfish	1	7	-	-	-	-	-	-	8
Northern Pike	-	-	-	-	30	10	6	1	47
Bluegill	10	3	-	-	-	-	-	-	13
Black Crappie	-	2	4	-	-	-	-	-	6

DNR COMMENTS:
Northern Pike numerous and the dominant species in this lake; growth avg. for lake class; mean weight 1.73 lb., and about 1/3 of sample exceeds 21" in length. Black Crappie sample relatively small, but indications are the pop. is medium-size (7-9"), with avg. growth rates. Bluegills relatively numerous and small, with only 21% of pop. 6" or more. Yellow Perch pop. very low. Tullibees and Bowfin both fairly numerous. Yellow Bullhead fairly large.

East Lake

FISH STOCKING DATA NOT AVAILABLE

survey date: 7/14/82

NET CATCH DATA

	Gill Nets		Trap Nets	
		avg fish		avg fish
species	# per net	wt. (lbs)	# per set	wt. (lbs)
White Sucker	0.6	2.00	-	-
Warmouth	0.2	0.10	-	-
Tullibee (Cisco)	8.4	0.38	-	-
Rock Bass	1.0	0.30	-	-
Northern Pike	7.2	2.22	0.3	1.50
Bluegill	0.6	0.10	13.8	0.13
Black Crappie	0.2	0.30	1.0	0.23
Yellow Perch	-	-	1.5	0.12
Redhorse	-	-	0.3	7.50
Pumpkin. Sunfish	-	-	0.8	0.10
Bowfin (Dogfish)	-	-	0.5	3.75

LENGTH OF SELECTED SPECIES SAMPLED FROM ALL GEAR
Number of fish caught for the following length categories (inches):

species	0-5	6-8	9-11	12-14	15-19	20-24	25-29	>30	Total
Black Crappie	-	3	2	-	-	-	-	-	5
Bluegill	17	37	4	-	-	-	-	-	58
Northern Pike	-	-	-	1	12	17	5	2	37
Pumpkin. Sunfish	1	2	-	-	-	-	-	-	3
Rock Bass	1	2	2	-	-	-	-	-	5
Tullibee (Cisco)	-	-	8	24	-	-	-	-	32
Yellow Perch	-	4	2	-	-	-	-	-	6

DNR COMMENTS:
Cisco, Pumpkinseed and Crappie populations have declined since the 1974 survey. Northern Pike numbers have increased, while populations of other species have remained stable.

FISHING INFORMATION: Clubhouse, East and Slauson Lakes are part of the Rice River chain of lakes designated as the Rice River canoe route by the US Forest Service. Clubhouse Lake has a nice campground and concrete boat landing. East Lake and Slauson Lake can be reached by traveling north (downstream) from Clubhouse (see area insert map above). A beautiful stand of 200 year old pine trees exits on East Lake and the entire chain of lakes is very scenic. The Rice River area's virgin pine stands were logged from about 1890 to 1925 utilizing the Rice and Big Fork rivers to move the logs downstream to International Falls. For more information on the historical points of interest and other facts about this route, contact Chippewa National Forest, Marcell Ranger District, Box 155, Marcell, MN 56657, (218) 832-3161. Clubhouse Lake is a good Largemouth Bass lake that also holds some Smallmouth. Northerns and Panfish are abundant although not very large. The other lakes in the chain are all very similar to Clubhouse with good populations of Northern, Bass and Panfish. There are no motor restrictions on the chain, but a small boat or canoe is recommended for travel between the lakes.

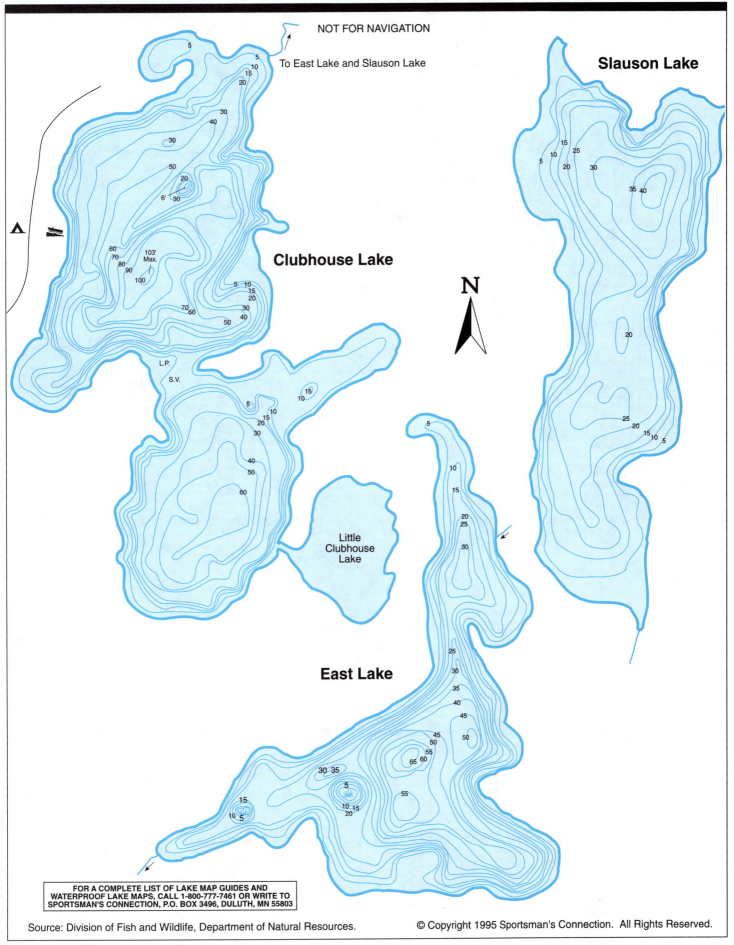

SPORTSMAN'S connection®

NOT FOR NAVIGATION

To East Lake and Slauson Lake

Slauson Lake

Clubhouse Lake

103' Max.

N

Little Clubhouse Lake

East Lake

Source: Division of Fish and Wildlife, Department of Natural Resources.

	OWEN LAKE	LOST LAKE	RADDISON LAKE	KELLY LAKE
Size of lake:	248 Acres	85 Acres	203 Acres	62 Acres
Shorelength:	10.0 Miles	1.6 Miles	3.6 Miles	2.2 Miles
Secchi disk (water clarity):	9.6 Ft.	15.1 Ft.	NA	NA
Water color:	Clear	Amber	NA	Brown
Maximum depth:	34.0 Ft.	27.0 Ft.	40.0 Ft.	40.0 Ft.
Median depth:	18.0 Ft.	14.6 Ft.	19.0 Ft.	15.9 Ft.
Accessibility:	USFS campground on N side; state-owned public access on W side	State-owned access on the SE side	County-owned public access on S side	Public access on N side
Boat Ramp:	Concrete	Concrete	Concrete	Carry down
Parking:	Ample	Ample	Limited	Limited
Accommodations:	Campground	Campground	None	None
Shoreland zoning classif.:	Rec. Dev.	Nat. Envt.	Rec. Dev.	Rec. Dev.
Dominant forest/soil type:	Decid/Sand	NA	Decid/Sand	NA
Cause of water color:	NA	Slight bog stain	NA	Swamp stain
Management class:	Walleye-Centrarchid	Centrarchid	Centrarchid	Unclassified
Ecological type:	Centrarchid	Centrarchid	Centrarchid	Unclassified

---

Owen Lake

DNR COMMENTS:
Northern Pike abundance is higher than state and local medians, but down slightly from 1982. Bullhead pop.s are rising, Yellow Perch pop.s are increasing slightly but still below state and local medians and Walleye abundance up from the 1982 netting. Other pop.s are normal for this lake.

FISHING INFO:
Owen Lake has some nice Walleyes and big Northerns according to the folks at Scenic Pines Store on Hwy. 52 near Round Lake. Largemouth Bass, Crappie and Sunfish are also plentiful.

FISH STOCKING DATA

year	species	size	# released
90	Walleye	Fingerling	4,675
93	Walleye	Fingerling	6,275

survey date: 6/27/88

NET CATCH DATA

	Gill Nets		Trap Nets	
		avg fish		avg fish
species	# per net	wt. (lbs)	# per set	wt. (lbs)
Yellow Perch	3.6	0.14	-	-
White Sucker	2.0	3.25	-	-
Walleye	1.8	1.30	-	-
Pumpkin. Sunfish	0.2	0.30	3.2	0.23
Northern Pike	5.8	1.93	0.7	1.30
Largemouth Bass	2.0	0.77	0.2	0.10
Brown Bullhead	6.0	0.94	-	-
Bluegill	2.2	0.23	39.3	0.24
Black Crappie	1.8	0.31	2.0	0.42
Black Bullhead	1.6	0.71	-	-
Hybrid Sunfish	-	-	0.5	0.30

LENGTH OF SELECTED SPECIES SAMPLED FROM ALL GEAR
Number of fish caught for the following length categories (inches):

species	0-5	6-8	9-11	12-14	15-19	20-24	25-29	>30	Total
Yellow Perch	-	18	-	-	-	-	-	-	18
Walleye	-	-	-	5	4	-	-	-	9
Pumpkin. Sunfish	-	1	-	-	-	-	-	-	1
Northern Pike	-	-	-	2	14	11	2	-	29
Largemouth Bass	-	-	5	5	-	-	-	-	10
Bluegill	2	9	-	-	-	-	-	-	11
Black Crappie	-	5	4	-	-	-	-	-	9

Lost Lake

DNR COMMENTS:
Northern Pike are very abundant at 19.3/gillnet, but growth is slow. Walleye abundance is low at only 1.5/gillnet. Five of the 6 Walleye samples were age 3, and coincide with fry stocking in 1986. Bluegill and Black Crappie indices, indicated by trapnets, are above state and local means. Both species exhibit good growth.

FISHING INFO:
Small and picturesque with a lot of hammer handle sized Northerns, small Panfish and some Walleye. Walleye are reaching a good size. Campground only has a few sites.

FISH STOCKING DATA

year	species	size	# released
90	Walleye	Fry	100,000

survey date: 6/21/89

NET CATCH DATA

	Gill Nets		Trap Nets	
		avg fish		avg fish
species	# per net	wt. (lbs)	# per set	wt. (lbs)
Yellow Perch	3.0	0.10	-	-
White Sucker	0.5	2.10	-	-
Walleye	1.5	1.32	-	-
Rock Bass	1.8	0.43	1.5	0.42
Northern Pike	19.3	1.52	1.0	1.15
Bluegill	2.0	0.06	20.3	0.13
Black Crappie	0.5	0.10	6.8	0.25
Pumpkin. Sunfish	-	-	7.0	0.10

LENGTH OF SELECTED SPECIES SAMPLED FROM ALL GEAR
Number of fish caught for the following length categories (inches):

species	0-5	6-8	9-11	12-14	15-19	20-24	25-29	>30	Total
Yellow Perch	-	12	-	-	-	-	-	-	12
Walleye	-	-	-	-	5	1	-	-	6
Rock Bass	3	1	3	-	-	-	-	-	7
Northern Pike	-	-	-	-	42	34	-	1	77
Bluegill	8	-	-	-	-	-	-	-	8
Black Crappie	-	2	-	-	-	-	-	-	2

Raddison Lake

DNR COMMENTS:
Suckers were not captured. Northern Pike abundance is high. Perch abundance has increased substantially while Smallmouth Bass have declined. Largemouth Bass are quite abundant. Both Pumpkinseed and Bluegill abundance has increased greatly. It appears natural reproduction is adequate for maintenance of fish pop.

FISHING INFO:
Raddison gives up some nice Crappie, some reaching 1 3/4 to 2 pounds. Late winter before ice out is a good time. Largemouth fishing is very good and some nice size Smallmouth can also be found. Northerns and Bluegills are plentiful and can be caught throughout the lake.

FISH STOCKING DATA NOT AVAILABLE

survey date: 7/2/82

NET CATCH DATA

	Gill Nets		Trap Nets	
		avg fish		avg fish
species	# per net	wt. (lbs)	# per set	wt. (lbs)
Yellow Perch	10.8	0.11	-	-
Smallmouth Bass	0.5	2.13	-	-
Pumpkin. Sunfish	2.0	0.09	12.8	0.18
Northern Pike	7.5	2.20	0.5	3.37
Largemouth Bass	0.3	0.20	2.5	0.69
Bluegill	2.8	0.11	73.2	0.19
Black Crappie	1.3	0.22	0.5	0.70

LENGTH OF SELECTED SPECIES SAMPLED FROM ALL GEAR
Number of fish caught for the following length categories (inches):

species	0-5	6-8	9-11	12-14	15-19	20-24	25-29	>30	Total
Black Crappie	1	2	4	1	-	-	-	-	8
Bluegill	9	106	3	-	-	-	-	-	118
Largemouth Bass	-	6	4	5	1	-	-	-	16
Northern Pike	-	-	-	1	7	15	9	-	32
Pumpkin. Sunfish	7	77	1	-	-	-	-	-	85
Smallmouth Bass	-	-	-	1	1	-	-	-	2
Yellow Perch	-	43	-	-	-	-	-	-	43

Kelly Lake

DNR COMMENTS:
Abundance of Perch and Northern Pike is slightly below local catch medians. Bluegill abundance is moderately higher than local medians while the numbers of other fish seem to be within normal limits for this lake. Natural reproduction for all fish except Northern Pike appears adequate for pop. maintenance.

FISHING INFO:
Bass, Panfish, Northern lake. Haven't heard if Walleye stocking has been successful.

FISH STOCKING DATA NOT AVAILABLE

survey date: 8/13/82

NET CATCH DATA

	Gill Nets		Trap Nets	
		avg fish		avg fish
species	# per net	wt. (lbs)	# per set	wt. (lbs)
Yellow Perch	5.3	0.09	3.0	0.11
White Sucker	0.7	2.15	-	-
Rock Bass	0.7	0.45	0.5	0.15
Pumpkin. Sunfish	4.0	0.08	3.0	0.09
Northern Pike	1.7	2.10	-	-
Bluegill	2.7	0.10	17.3	0.10
Black Crappie	6.3	0.14	0.8	0.27

LENGTH OF SELECTED SPECIES SAMPLED FROM ALL GEAR
Number of fish caught for the following length categories (inches):

species	0-5	6-8	9-11	12-14	15-19	20-24	25-29	>30	Total
Black Crappie	5	9	8	-	-	-	-	-	22
Bluegill	52	25	-	-	-	-	-	-	77
Northern Pike	-	-	-	-	-	2	3	-	5
Pumpkin. Sunfish	23	1	-	-	-	-	-	-	24
Rock Bas	1	2	1	-	-	-	-	-	4
Yellow Perch	-	27	-	-	-	-	-	-	27

FOR A COMPLETE LIST OF LAKE MAP GUIDES AND WATERPROOF LAKE MAPS, CALL 1-800-777-7461 OR WRITE TO SPORTSMAN'S CONNECTION, P.O. BOX 3496, DULUTH, MN 55803

Owen, Lost, Raddison, & Kelly Lakes

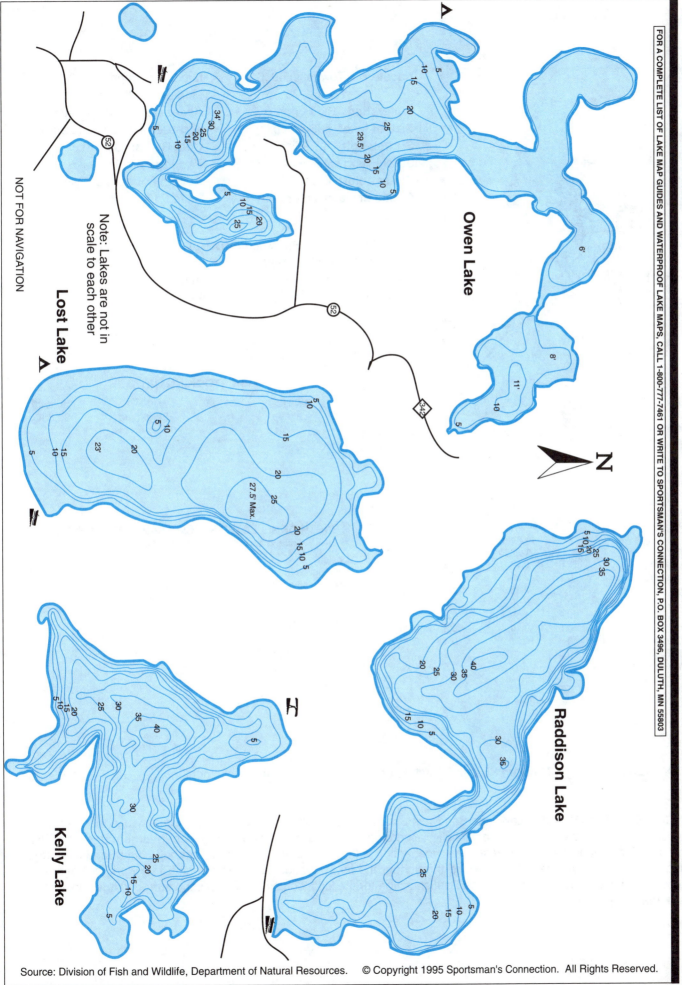

Owen Lake

Lost Lake

Raddison Lake

Kelly Lake

NOT FOR NAVIGATION

Note: Lakes are not in scale to each other

COON LAKE

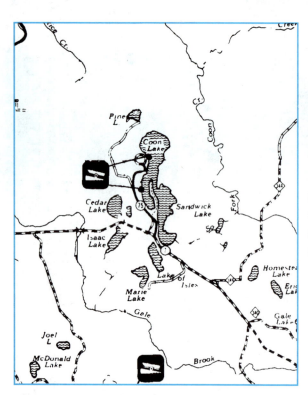

Location: Township 60, 61 Range 25
Watershed: Big Fork
Size of lake: 595 Acres
Shorelength: 8.9 Miles
Secchi disk (water clarity): 7.2 Ft.
Water color: Clear
Cause of water color: NA

Maximum depth: 36.0 Ft.
Median depth: NA
Accessibility: 2 State-owned accesses in Scenic State Park
Boat Ramp: Concrete
Parking: Ample
Accommodations: Campground, State Park

Shoreland zoning classification: Natural Environment
Dominant forest/soil type: NA
Management class: Walleye-Centrarchid
Ecological type: Centrarchid-Walleye

FISH STOCKING DATA

year	species	size	# released
90	Walleye	Fingerling	20,380

NET CATCH DATA

survey date: 7/9/84

	Gill Nets		Trap Nets	
species	# per net	avg fish wt. (lbs.)	# per set	avg fish wt. (lbs.)
Yellow Perch	16.6	0.14	0.9	0.21
White Sucker	0.1	2.50	-	-
Walleye	1.1	2.13	0.1	2.00
Pumpkin. Sunfish	3.1	0.09	9.5	0.13
Northern Pike	9.9	1.69	0.5	0.62
Bluegill	0.6	0.10	36.8	0.24
Black Crappie	0.3	0.37	0.4	0.33
Black Bullhead	0.3	0.10	-	-
Largemouth Bass	-	-	0.5	0.20
Brown Bullhead	-	-	0.1	1.50

LENGTH OF SELECTED SPECIES SAMPLED FROM ALL GEAR

Number of fish caught for the following length categories (inches):

species	0-5	6-8	9-11	12-14	15-19	20-24	25-29	>30	Total
Black Bullhead	-	3	-	-	-	-	-	-	3
Black Crappie	-	4	2	1	-	-	-	-	7
Bluegill	26	90	11	-	-	-	-	-	127
Brown Bullhead	-	-	-	1	-	-	-	-	1
Largemouth Bass	-	4	-	-	-	-	-	-	4
Northern Pike	-	-	4	15	52	15	3	5	94
Pumpkin. Sunfish	54	33	-	-	-	-	-	-	87
Walleye	-	-	-	-	7	4	-	-	11
Yellow Perch	-	100	20	3	-	-	-	-	123

DNR COMMENTS: Bluegill, Northern Pike and Perch abundance above state and local medians.

FISHING INFORMATION: Coon Lake and Sandwick Lake are essentially one body of water contained in the scenic state park. Walleye fishing has improved substantially, according to local fishermen, probably due in large part to the DNR's stocking program. Bluegill fishing provides the most action with good numbers of fish in the half-pound range. Northern Pike and Largemouth Bass can also be found throughout the lake's weedbeds. The Scenic State Park includes a nice campground and good boat launches. Good Panfish action for the kids, combined with pristine surroundings, make this an excellent area for a family vacation.

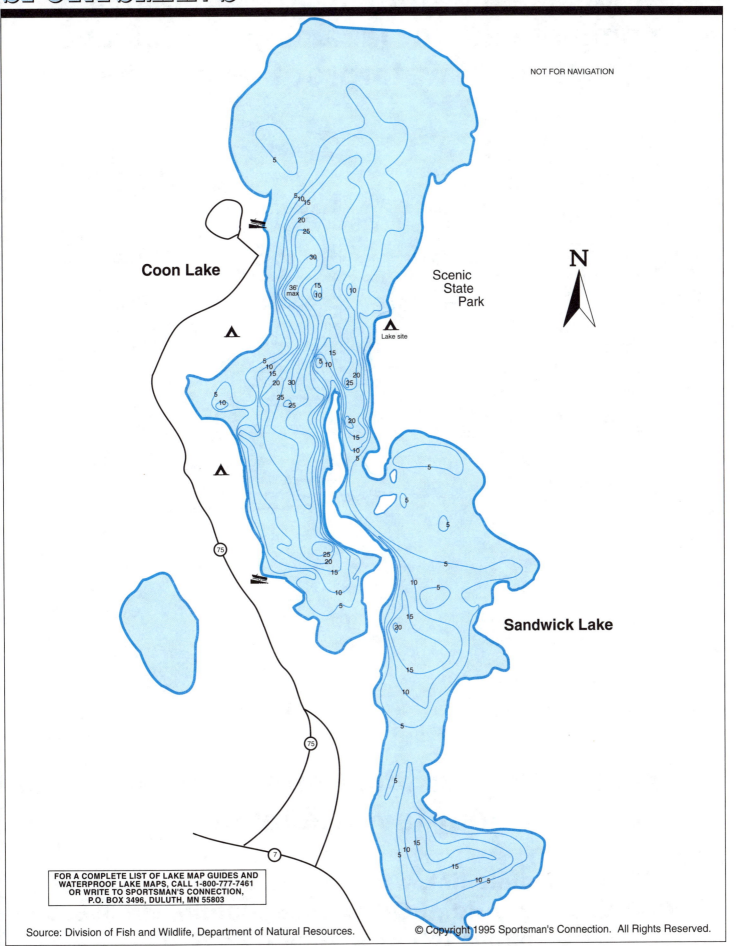

NOT FOR NAVIGATION

Coon Lake

Scenic
State
Park

Lake site

N

36'
max

Sandwick Lake

75

75

7

Source: Division of Fish and Wildlife, Department of Natural Resources.

Sportsman's Connection publishes a complete line of lake map guides and individual waterproof lake maps

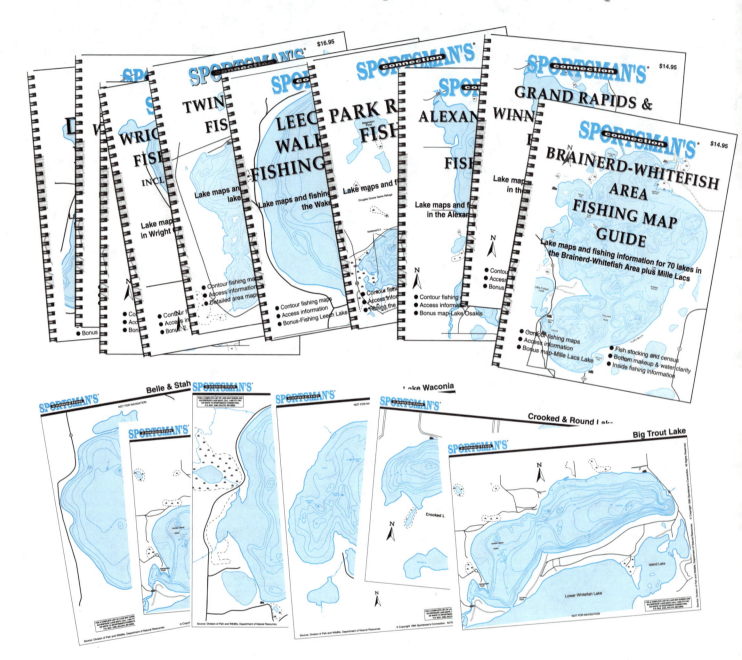

Check with your local retailer for maps of <u>your</u> favorite lakes.

For a complete list, write Sportsman's Connection, 3947 E. Calvary Rd., PO Box 3496, Duluth, MN 55803 or phone toll free: 1-800-777-7461